Conversations with Richard Ford

Literary Conversations Series

Peggy Whitman Prenshaw
General Editor

Conversations
with Richard Ford

Edited by
Huey Guagliardo

University Press of Mississippi
Jackson

Books by Richard Ford

A Piece of My Heart. New York: Harper & Row, 1976. Reprint, New York: Vintage, 1985.
The Ultimate Good Luck. Boston: Houghton Mifflin, 1981. Reprint, New York: Vintage, 1986.
The Sportswriter. New York: Knopf, 1986. Reprint, New York: Vintage, 1986.
Rock Springs. New York: Atlantic Monthly Press, 1987. Reprint, New York: Vintage, 1988.
Wildlife. New York: Atlantic Monthly Press, 1990. Reprint, New York: Vintage, 1991.
Independence Day. New York: Knopf, 1995. Reprint, New York: Vintage, 1996.
Women with Men. New York: Knopf, 1997. Reprint, New York: Vintage, 1998.

www.upress.state.ms.us

Copyright © 2001 by University Press of Mississippi
All rights reserved
Manufactured in the United States of America

09 08 07 06 05 04 03 02 01   4 3 2 1
⊗
Library of Congress Cataloging-in-Publication Data

Conversations with Richard Ford / edited by Huey Guagliardo.
        p. cm.—(Literary conversations series)
    Includes index.
    ISBN 1-57806-405-8 (cloth : alk. paper)—ISBN 1-57806-406-6 (pbk. : alk. paper)
    1. Ford, Richard, 1944——Interviews.   2. Novelists, American—20th century—
Interviews.   3. Fiction—Authorship.   I. Guagliardo, Huey.   II. Series.

PS3556.O713 Z63   2001
813'.54—dc21
[B]   2001026043

British Library Cataloging-in-Publication Data available

Contents

Introduction

Richard Ford's novels, stories, and essays exemplify a meticulous concern for the nuances of language, a poet's preoccupation not only with the meanings of words but also with their sounds, as well as with the rhythm of phrases and sentences. The interviews in this volume reveal that even in conversation Ford chooses his words and sentences with great care, aware as he is of their power and importance. As Gail Caldwell points out in a 1987 profile of the writer for *The Boston Globe,* "he talks the way he writes: in simple compound sentences as careful as they are reflective." In my interview with Ford a decade later, he discusses his desire to reinvent language and the revelation that came to him as a young man that language, beyond its denotative function in communication, is also, as he describes it, "a source of pleasure in and of itself—all of its corporeal qualities, its syncopations, moods, sounds, the way things look on the page." As I replayed the tape of our conversation while editing this collection, I noticed that Ford's slow and emphatic enunciation of the words *corporeal* and *syncopations* plainly displayed his own great pleasure in using language.

Over the years, the author's remarks to interviewers repeatedly have made clear his devotion to language. "When you talk to Ford," reports Michael Schumacher in a revealing 1991 profile in *Writer's Digest* that focuses on the creative process, "you are likely to hear plenty of discussion about language and writing good sentences. . . . Ford has dedicated his writing life to the composition of individual sentences, and everything else—theme, meaning, usefulness—rises from those sentences. It's a point Ford can't seem to emphasize enough." Certainly, the writer's abiding interest in language is a recurring topic in many of these interviews.

Ford's devotion to language is inextricably linked to another of his chief concerns, what he refers to in an interview as "the fabric of affection that holds people close enough together to survive." His fictional characters struggle to connect with others in an effort to overcome the inherent loneliness of the human condition. While acknowledging that language often fails to reverse feelings of alienation, Ford nevertheless believes that words have the potential "to narrow that space Emerson calls the infinite remoteness that separates people," for, as he says, "[y]ou get to participate in other lives through the agency of language." Again and again, Ford's art, constructed of language, testifies to his profound belief in the power of narrative to forge human connections. "If loneliness is the disease, the story is the cure," he says.

The very act of interviewing, of course, is an attempt to connect with another through the agency of language; and Ford has been an extremely generous interviewer throughout his writing career. A naturally gracious and affable man, Ford responds openly and eloquently to questions. Tall and lean with, in the words of one interviewer, "piercing pale blue eyes," Ford speaks with just a trace of the drawl that one associates with his native Mississippi. He is described in these pages as "straight-talking," "intensely engaging," and "self-effacing." Although he tends to be serious, especially when speaking about his work, it is not unusual for him to display a playful sense of humor during conversation.

At times the interviews provide the reader with a glimpse into the personal life of this intriguing contemporary writer. We learn about Ford's fondness for motorcycles, Brittany spaniels, bird hunting, fishing, and Bruce Springsteen. We also learn a good deal about his family history. In 1952, when Ford was eight years old, his traveling salesman father suffered a heart attack, and his family moved from its home in Jackson, Mississippi, into a hotel in Little Rock, Arkansas, run by Ford's maternal grandfather. This experience of growing up in a hotel no doubt shaped Ford's worldview and gave him a taste of the itinerant life. When Ford was only sixteen, his father suffered a fatal heart attack. The author talks about the years following his father's death and the close relationship that he and his mother developed after that traumatic event. He took a job working for the Missouri Pacific Railroad the summer before leaving for college, a job that he believes instilled in him the strong work ethic that he later applied to his writing. He started college at Michigan State University, enrolled in Hotel Management but soon switched to English. It was at Michigan State that Ford began writing fiction, and it was there that he met Kristina Hensley who would later become his wife. Ford talks openly in these interviews about those early years, his devotion to Kristina, and the trust that he has in her as his "first reader and listener." Not long before the couple married, Ford enrolled in law school, which he hated. He admits that he was actually relieved when his law books were stolen and he had an excuse to quit. He went on to graduate school to study literature and creative writing, and, after receiving his M.F.A., he taught at various universities. It was Kristina, he says, who encouraged him to quit teaching and to write full time. Her career as an urban planner enabled him to devote all of his time and energy to writing. In 1981, despondent about his mother's death and discouraged about his career, Ford gave up writing fiction to work at *Inside Sports* magazine. When the magazine ceased publication after only one year, Ford, at Kristina's urging that he write about a man seeking happiness, began work on *The Sportswriter* (1986), the critically acclaimed novel that would mark the birth of his reputation as a major American writer.

In these interviews Ford openly expresses his personal views on a wide variety of subjects. For example, he often describes his fascination with the West, especially Montana where he has lived, off and on, through the years. "It's your dream of what a place would be like. It's open. It's beautiful," he says, and admits to being "drawn to places where life is a little near the edge." He talks about his "tough guy" reputation, claiming that the label is undeserved while slyly acknowledging that there could be "a primitive" lurking inside of him. Ford is not reluctant to share his political views, and neither is he averse to expressing his opinion, in blunt language, about reviewers who have made unkind remarks about him or about his books.

Ford is equally forthcoming when the subject turns to his work. He describes in detail how he relies on his notebooks, which he has used from the beginning of his writing career, to create a framework for a story or novel. He describes his rigorous work habits. He discusses the intricacies of the writer's craft, how his preoccupation with "one isolated piece of language, word or a phrase," can be a source of inspiration and lead to the creation of an entire story or novel. Ford shares his view of writing as a "high calling," and he often talks about his desire to make his writing "useful" to others. "It is the fiction writer's duty," he says, "to put into words what people can't always express for themselves."

This collection contains "conversations" spanning the quarter of a century since the publication of *A Piece of My Heart* (1976), Ford's first novel. The volume begins with the *Arkansas Gazette's* brief 1976 profile based on a telephone interview with the author after the publication of that novel, and it concludes with the most recent interviews available. It is evident that interest in Ford and his work increased significantly following the publication of *The Sportswriter,* the story of suburbanite Frank Bascombe's struggle to survive loneliness and great loss, and that this interest intensified after the printing of a well-received volume of short stories, *Rock Springs* (1987). *Independence Day* (1995), a sequel to *The Sportswriter* and the first novel ever to win both the Pulitzer Prize and the PEN/Faulkner Award, solidified Ford's reputation as one of the best writers of the post-World War II generation. Critical studies of Ford's work began to appear, such as my collection of essays, *Perspectives on Richard Ford* (University Press of Mississippi 2000) and Elinor Ann Walker's study *Richard Ford* (Twayne 2000). Furthermore, a steady stream of new interviewers found their way to the writer's door. Over the past twenty-five years that door has opened in a variety of places that Ford has called home, including, but not limited to, the lush Mississippi Delta, the sparse, mountainous landscape of Montana, and the steamy French Quarter of New Orleans.

The various locations of the interviews reveal a great deal about Ford's so-called "restless" nature, and his nomadic existence is often a topic of discussion. "I get nervous with permanence," Ford (who has lived in no fewer than fourteen different states) tells an interviewer. In a *Publishers Weekly* interview, Ford explains his notoriously peripatetic lifestyle: "I need to be certain that I have new stimulus. New places give me something I can use." Ford's need to relocate can also be tied to his preoccupation with language. "I go because I can hear another idiom and can see a different landscape to which I can dedicate language," he says in *Writer's Digest.*

Ford, in fact, has dedicated language to many of the places where he has lived. Except for *A Piece of My Heart,* which is set primarily in Mississippi and Arkansas, the author, who was born in Jackson, Mississippi, and spent much of his childhood in Arkansas, has not written about his native south. His second novel, *The Ultimate Good Luck* (1981), takes place in Mexico. The Frank Bascombe novels, *The Sportswriter* and *Independence Day,* are set mostly in the suburbs of New Jersey, the *Rock Springs* stories and *Wildlife* (1990) in the Northwest, and two of the novellas in *Women with Men* (1997) take place primarily in Paris. In choosing such diverse settings for his fiction, Ford seems to reject any preoccupation with a particular place. Clearly, he has no interest whatsoever in being labeled as a "regional" writer, and in several of these conversations he vigorously resists all attempts to categorize him as such. "I suppose I've come to understand that term as a pejorative one," he remarks, explaining that he views regional writing as that which originates in "a small emotional and intellectual surround" and which is directed toward "people in an equally small emotional and intellectual surround." Not wishing to be confined by such narrow concerns, Ford serves notice that as a writer he is interested in exploring the entire country, that his goal is "to write a literature that is good enough for America."

Indeed, Ford is first and foremost an American writer whose works often offer penetrating explorations into American culture. In one interview he refers to his work as the reflection of "the American experience expressed in language." In my conversation with Ford he expresses his concern about the many factions which divide our culture and threaten the future of American democracy. In some respects, his fiction reflects this concern. "Primary to my understanding of what's going on in American life," Ford remarks to Richard Shea in reference to a discussion of *Independence Day* and that novel's suburban Everyman, Frank Bascombe, "is that there's a general sense that there's a wild world outside our perimeters. And the suburb is one response to it." According to Shea, the Frank Bascombe novels, "Like John Updike's 'Rabbit' books . . . are commentaries on the United States and, in particular, their middle-class suburban residents, with central New Jersey serving as microcosm."

Ford has often been compared to Updike, and also to William Faulkner, Ernest Hemingway, and Walker Percy. Reviewers so often compared *A Piece of My Heart* to Faulkner's work that Ford decided never again to write another novel set in the South. *The Ultimate Good Luck* is frequently compared to Hemingway and *The Sportswriter* to Percy's *The Moviegoer*. Ford resists all such comparisons as ultimately reductive and of little value, telling an interviewer, "You can't write a good story, you can't write a good novel, on the strength of influence. You can only write a good story or a good novel by yourself"; yet elsewhere he acknowledges having been influenced by the writers listed above, as well as by the French Existentialists, Jean-Paul Sartre and Albert Camus, and by more recent practitioners of the novel of alienation such as John Barth, Donald Bartheleme, Raymond Carver, John Cheever, and Frederick Exley. Ford, however, credits his fellow Mississippian with revealing to him the consoling power of language: "Faulkner—partly because I was a kid in Mississippi, and so was he, and he was writing in Mississippi when I was growing up—treated me with and to language which was about things that made the world more orderly to me." Faulkner's gift, he goes on to say, extended beyond language that gave meaning and order to the world: "There are all kinds of things in Faulkner the meaning of which you don't know, but you kind of luxuriate in the language, in almost an osmotic way. Feel what it's about . . . and when I didn't understand things, console myself into believing that it was all right just to feel the words, speak the words to myself, let the words live in my mind."

Ford displays a particular affinity for Existential philosophy by his fondness for quoting Sartre during interviews, but the breadth and complexity of Ford's intellect is shown by his numerous references to a diverse array of writers, poets, literary theoreticians, and philosophers. In addition to the figures mentioned above, the interviews are sprinkled with references to Walter Benjamin, John Berryman, R. P. Blackmur, Anton Chekhov, William Gass, Graham Greene, Thomas Hardy, Joseph Heller, Henry James, Randall Jarrell, Gabriel Garcia Marquez, Henry Miller, Octavio Paz, Percy Bysshe Shelley, Wallace Stevens, Henry David Thoreau, Eudora Welty, Virginia Woolf, and many others.

Certainly, these conversations testify to the depth of this intellectually complex writer. Sam Halpert, after interviewing Ford for *Raymond Carver: An Oral Biography* (University of Iowa Press 1995), an interview not included in this collection, reports that he "caught but a mere sighting of the exposed surface of Richard Ford" and that "the massive remainder is kept well submerged" (95). Perhaps this collection in its entirety will serve to reveal more of this somewhat elusive writer to readers and scholars alike. The interviews included here appear in their original form and are arranged, as best as I can determine, in the order in which they were conducted. Some repetition, of course, is inevitable in such a collection, particularly if the conversations selected for inclusion engage the author on those issues most dear to his heart. Scholars will find these unedited interviews of particular value. Not only do they offer insight into Ford's texts, but they also show that throughout his career (and these interviews represent various phases of that career) Ford has expressed with consistency his dedication to language and to the craft of writing, his views about the nature of literature, and his belief in the redeeming quality of human affection. As far as Ford's remarks are concerned, readers will find few contradictions of any substance in these conversations. Ford's many interviewers, on the other hand, coming as they do from diverse backgrounds in journalism or the academy, offer a wide range of approaches to their subject. The result is a rich exploration of one of the most powerful voices in contemporary American fiction.

I wish to express my sincere thanks to Richard Ford and Kristina Ford who opened their home to me and made their personal files available for this project. My thanks also go out to Seetha Srinivasan and the University Press of Mississippi for making this volume possible.

HG
December 2000

Chronology

1944 Richard Ford born on February 16 in Jackson, Mississippi.

1952 Ford's traveling salesman father, Parker Carrol Ford, suffers a heart attack. As a result, the Fords move into the Marion Hotel (managed by Richard's grandfather) in Little Rock, Arkansas.

1960 Ford's father dies of a heart attack on February 20, four days after Richard's sixteenth birthday.

1962 Enrolls at Michigan State University majoring in hotel management but changes major to English.

1966 Receives B.A. in English from Michigan State University. Teaches junior high school in Flint, Michigan. Enlists in United States Marine Corps, but receives discharge after contracting hepatitis.

1967 Attends Washington University Law School in St. Louis, Missouri, for one semester.

1968 Marries Kristina Hensley and decides to pursue a career as a writer.

1970 Receives M.F.A. degree in Creative Writing from the University of California at Irvine where he studied with Oakley Hall and E. L. Doctorow.

1975 Teaches for a year as assistant professor at the University of Michigan.

1976 *A Piece of My Heart* is published.

1979 Teaches for a year as assistant professor at Williams College.

1980 Teaches for a year as lecturer and George Perkins Fellow in the Humanities at Princeton University.

1981 *The Ultimate Good Luck* is published. Ford, discouraged by his inability to find a significant readership, quits writing fiction to work for *Inside Sports* magazine. Ford's mother, Edna, dies.

1982 *Inside Sports* ceases publication. Ford begins work on *The Sportswriter.*

1986 *The Sportswriter* is published.

1987 *Rock Springs* is published.

1989 Receives the American Academy of Arts and Letters Award in Literature.

1990 *Wildlife* is published, as well as *The Best American Short Stories* (edited by Ford).

1991   The film *Bright Angel,* based on Ford's screenplay, is released.
1992   *The Granta Book of the American Short Story,* edited by Ford, is published.
1994   Teaches for a year as a lecturer at Harvard University.
1995   *Independence Day* is published. Ford wins the Rea Award for the Short Story.
1996   Wins Pulitzer Prize and PEN/Faulkner Award for *Independence Day.*
1997   *Women with Men* is published. Ford accepts appointment as visiting professor at Northwestern University, Evanston, Illinois, where he teaches for two years.
1998   Elected to the American Academy of Arts and Letters. *The Essential Tales of Chekhov,* edited by Ford, *Eudora Welty: The Complete Novels,* co-edited by Ford and Michael Kreyling, and *Eudora Welty: Stories, Essays, and Memoir,* co-edited by Ford and Michael Kreyling, are published.
1999   *The Best American Sportswriting 1999,* edited by Ford, is published.

Conversations with Richard Ford

Ex-Arkansan's First Novel Set in State, Sold for Film

Arkansas Gazette / 1976

From the *Arkansas Gazette* 30 November 1976: 7A. Used by permission.

Richard Ford, thirty-two, of Princeton, N.J., a native of Jackson, Miss., who was reared at Little Rock, has written a first novel called *A Piece of My Heart,* which has been published by Harper and Row. The publisher said in a news release that Paramount has acquired film rights and has asked Ford to write the script.

Ford taught English at the University of Michigan and received a master of fine arts degree from the University of California at Irvine, where he also taught before he turned to full-time writing. Ford is a graduate of Michigan State University and was a junior fellow in the University of Michigan Society of Fellows, which awarded a three-year Ford Foundation grant to him to write a novel.

The publisher said the book, set in Arkansas, is ambitious and that Ford "is a born writer, a major literary talent also blessed with humor, warmth and an unusual blend of charm." It said the book has "lots going on at once—a headlong suspense, heavy sexual undercurrents, the salty humor of the [Arkansas River] island sequences."

In a review published recently in the *New York Times Book Review,* Larry McMurtry, a Texas novelist, said Ford's minor characters "are vividly drawn, and his ear is first-rate." It added, "If he can weed his garden of some of the weeds and cockleburrs of his tradition, it might prove very fertile." Excerpts from the novel appeared in August's issue of *Esquire* magazine.

Ford said in a telephone interview that it had "gotten some good reviews, and some bad ones."

Ford, who unsuccessfully sought work as a *Gazette* sports writer in 1967, said his parents moved from Little Rock to Jackson the year he was born, but that he spent his time away from school at Little Rock with his grandparents. His mother, Mrs. Edna Ford, lives at the Lakewood House at North Little Rock.

Ford said he "practically grew up at" the old Marion Hotel, which his grandfather, Ben Shelley, "operated more years than I can remember."

Ford said his father, who died when he was sixteen, became extremely ill when Ford was eight years old and that he practically moved back to Little Rock then to allow his mother more freedom in caring for her husband. He returns to Arkansas regularly, although he says its easier now to fly his mother to Princeton for visits. He and an aunt own a soybean farm in Pope County, and he has relatives at Atkins, Russellville and in other parts of West and Northwest Arkansas. His wife, the former Kristina Hensley of Virginia, is a research professor at Rutgers University.

Author Returns to Native State

Glynda Duncan / 1984

From the *Clarksdale Press Register* 29 March 1984: 1B. Used by permission.

After some twenty years away, a Mississippi native son has come back home.

If one didn't know Richard Ford was birthed and reared in Mississippi, nothing in his manner or voice would give him away, perhaps because he has spent as many years in northern states as in Mississippi.

He is the author of two novels and an impending third, several short stories and essays and also a screenplay bought by Paramount Studios, but never produced.

Ford was born in Jackson, Mississippi, the son of two transplanted Arkansans. His father was a traveling salesman from Atkins, Ark., "where they make pickles," grins Ford from across his kitchen table. His mother, Edna, hailed from Little Rock, the daughter of Ben Shelley, owner of the well known Arkansas dwelling, the Marion Hotel, now leveled and a modern construction filling its void.

Ford graduated from high school in Jackson in 1962. It was then he decided to embark on another world and way of life—the north—mainly because he didn't want the turbulent times of the south to make any demands or interruptions upon his education.

He attended Michigan State for four years, went to Law School at the Washington University in Saint Louis for one year and then left for the University of California at Irvine.

With a Masters of Fine Arts degree, Ford has taught creative writing and literature at the University of Michigan, Williams College, Princeton University and Goddard College in Vermont.

Writing is Richard's first career choice, teaching is just an alternative. His roustabout existence as a teacher is only tolerated in order to supply him with the financial support needed to continue his writing.

"I've always been flattered for people to ask me to teach," but added, "if I am to be a servant, I would rather serve myself than serve some students."

After his father's death, Richard's mother returned to her family in Arkan-

3

sas. When she died in 1981, Richard gave new thought to being a Mississippian.

At the coaxing of his classmates at his twenty-year high school reunion, he returned to his native state to claim his southern heritage.

"I think of myself as a Mississippian," said the thirty-nine-year old author of *A Piece of My Heart* and *The Ultimate Good Luck.* "This was my chance to live here. To see if I could live here and work," he added.

Now that he has a home here, Ford will be alternating his time between Mississippi and Missoula, Montana, his home for the past several years.

Richard's wife of sixteen years, Kristina, is the Director of Planning for the City and County of Missoula, and is currently on leave as Professor of Graduate Studies of Public Administration at New York University.

"Our intention was to share our time between here and Montana. Kristina's job is interesting to her, much more so than we first thought, so she is sticking with her job as long as it is interesting," Ford said matter of factly.

Living in Michigan, Illinois, California, Vermont, Pennsylvania and New York has not made the Fords impatient to reside in Mississippi full time. On the contrary, the author says he thinks he'll never live here year round, just part of the year.

Richard and Kristina searched for the perfect house in the perfect setting in a Delta town.

"A year and a half ago I described this house (to the real estate agent) out of a dream," notes Richard. The search ended when Richard bought their Jonestown home in September.

He is currently working on his third novel, *The Sportswriter.* The book, set in Detroit and New Jersey, concerns the life of a divorced sportswriter with two children, living through the aftermath of a failed marriage, rearing children and the like. "It's a sweet tempered book," quipped Ford as he sat at the kitchen table peeling turnips which he was to cook for himself and weekly dinner guest, Mr. Campbell. "The book is meant to be funny, earnest and honest."

Ford's first book—*A Piece of My Heart* set in Helena, Arkansas—was made possible by a Ford Foundation Scholarship and took three years to write (1972–75), much too long he thinks. He has been working on *The Sportswriter* for some time now and hopes to finish it for publishing by Simon and Schuster by 1985. *The Ultimate Good Luck* is set in a southern Mexico town called Oaxaca.

Ford likes working in the mornings and unplugs his phones in order to work uninterrupted. "I have the best chance not to be fatigued. I am most alert in the morning."

Sometimes he works throughout the entire day in the study, where he is now sitting cracking his very own pecans from his very own pecan orchard and digesting them as he ponders the best atmosphere for his best work.

"Usually I do my best writing when I am alone," but noted that this particular time his work has taken second place to getting the house in order.

The Mississippi author considers the Delta an ideal place to carry on his work—a quiet place where people will leave you alone to write, Ford acknowledges. "People don't treat me like an outsider," Ford claims, as sometimes is the usual treatment of migrants from the north.

Ford actually doesn't like comparisons, but obliges the curious by saying "southerners are more decorous and friendly on the outside," but Montana people for instance, "are outwardly not interested in you. They are really a self-propelled and self-motivated people."

When away from Kristina on one of his writing jaunts, Ford is never without his faithful companions—a motorcycle and a trusty Brittany Spaniel. The dog, Dixie, seconds as his bird dog for hunting—a pastime that Ford's southerner counterparts readily understand.

This particularly damp, cold Delta day, Ford unleashes Dixie for an exuberant run through the pecan orchard surrounding the house then to the small creek running parallel to the back yard. Dixie takes a dip in the cold water to show off her retriever skills. Coming ashore and shaking off the water, she returns to her previous excursion.

Back in the kitchen, Ford adds more spices to his still cooking dishes on the electric stove and tastes for approval. Ever puttering around the kitchen, Ford says he cooks, not as a hobby, but because he likes to eat.

Turning his attention back to his writing Ford says, "I don't ever feel like I work hard enough," but modestly adds "but I don't feel like I'm qualified to do anything else."

Fiction Author Revels in His Introspective Craft

Patti Dale / 1985

From *The Gateway* [University of Nebraska / Omaha] 26 April 1985: 8–9. Used by permission.

"I thought, then, how I never planned things well enough. There was always a gap between my plan and what happened, and I only responded to things as they came along and hoped I wouldn't get in trouble. I was an offender in the law's eyes. But I always thought differently, as if I weren't an offender and had no intention of being one, which was the truth. But as I read on a napkin once, between the idea and the act a whole kingdom lies. And I had a hard time with my acts, which were oftentimes offender's acts, and my ideas, which were as good as the gold they mined there where the bright lights were blazing."

—from "Rock Springs" by Richard Ford

"If I could, I would have three months a year in which I worked and nine months a year I hunted and fished," said Richard Ford during his visit to UNO last week. He met with students in the Writer's Workshop and gave a reading of his short story, "Communist."

Introducing his story "Fireworks" in the October 1984 issue of *Esquire,* the editors said Ford "is one of a group of writers—including Joyce Williams, Ann Beattie, Tobias Wolfe, Raymond Carver—who have established the forms and concerns of realism in fiction today. Coming out of the confusion and literary entropy of the 1970s and early 1980s, Ford's work is remarkable for its rich moral tone."

Richard Duggin, chairman of the Writer's Workshop, said Ford writes about the "other side" of American life, the counterpart to the traditional notions about secure employment and commitment to family in which the illusion of some sort of permanence and contentment exists. Ford's characters are the dispossessed: out of work, out of love, out of luck—and yet, never totally out of hope, each of them knowing somehow that all things have their seasons, that what goes around comes around, and affairs of fortune and the heart have their cycles.

"Lives are frustrating and sometimes bitter with despair," Ford said, "but what makes them continue is they find some way or something in them to redeem them—something as fragile as a good moment."

Ford said he always tries to find a little bit of goodness because that is what makes people go on with life.

"I'm not talking about any high-dollar ascendance," he said, "though I guess that would be conceivable too. It just doesn't happen very much. Something that does happen a lot, though, is on a bad day realizing how much you love someone, or what your resources are."

Ford said because he is interested in how people like him, in the middle of their lives, are engaged in the struggle for life, that is what he writes about.

Although he was born in Jackson, Miss., and grew up in Mississippi and Arkansas, Ford does not consider himself a Southern writer. "Start scratching the surface of things in the South and you get back real fast to the Civil War—that's sadness, disappointment, and destruction," he said.

Ford is fascinated by the West, not only because it has such a recent history but also a remarkable, changing current history.

Ford and his wife live in Princeton, N.J. Kristina Ford teaches urban and regional planning at the graduate school of public administration at New York City University. Ford said they would like to be able to arrange their affairs so they could move to Montana.

Until he went to Montana and "hit it hard the first time," Ford said he never felt he was doing anything but responding to a culturally determined selective experience. "When you're a writer," he explained, "you write about a specific place. Even if you don't say now I'm going to write my New Jersey novel, over a period of time that is what accrues."

Ford said everything in the West seems familiar to him; there is not the awful built-in defeat of the South where it's all sour grapes.

"I'm drawn to places where life is a little near the edge," Ford said. He has lived in Mexico, North Africa and throughout the United States but has never been interested in places that are highly civilized.

Ford is going to England next month to give a reading at Oxford. He said he probably never would have gone to Europe if he had not been invited to read his work. "Western European culture is advanced," he admitted, "but it's too institutionalized. I want to be some place that's not dead yet."

Ford's novel, *A Piece of My Heart,* is being republished next month by Vintage Contemporaries. A new novel, *The Sportswriter,* is being published next spring by Random House. *The Ultimate Good Luck* was published in 1981 and is scheduled to be reprinted in about a year and a half.

Yet Ford is best known for his short stories. Eight short stories have been published, but they have been reprinted in such collections as *Fifty Who Made the Difference, Matters of Life and Death, Last Night's Stranger, Fifty Great Years of Esquire Fiction, Graywolf Anthology, Editors' Choice Stories, Esquire Reader: 1984, Tri-Quarterly 20th Anniversary Anthology, Mississippi Writers,* and *Writers of the Purple Sage.*

Duggin said Ford is a careful, deliberate and artful writer for whom the quality of work takes precedence over the quantity.

Ford said he didn't want to be a writer, he wanted to be a wonderful athlete and wanted all the girls to love him. He never really thought of being a writer until he realized how much he hated law school.

"The only thing I'd ever done in my life that gave me any pleasure and that I was any good at and could still do was write," Ford said.

Ford left Washington University in Saint Louis law school and went to graduate school at the University of California, where he got his MFA in 1970.

Kristina Ford encouraged her husband to write rather than become entrenched teaching writing. Ford said he wanted to see if he was intelligent enough to teach at a university. "I was, but that didn't mean much about how smart I was."

He has taught for brief periods at Princeton, Williams, and Michigan Universities, but said he enjoys it too much. "If I taught, I wouldn't get any work done," Ford said. "I don't want to blame anything else for my own negligence."

Ford said the satisfactions of writing are rather impecunious compared to teaching. "My days aren't rich days. Nobody's telling me I did a good thing that day, admiring me, telling me I sounded smart."

However, Ford said his wife is very encouraging and his greatest supporter. "She gives me a pat on the back just by not calling me to account. If I spend four years writing a book," he said, "that's all right with her."

Ford has a very tedious and painstaking way of writing a story. He keeps extensive journals, writing down at the end of each day things that made an impression on him. When he wants to write a story Ford goes through his notebooks for the last five or six years and transcribes passages from them that apply to the idea floating around in his head. Ford studies the notes he's compiled to see what they add up to, what interests him the most. Then he tries to spin a first line.

"I kind of have a notion where the story will end and where I want it to begin, but I really don't know what's going on in that story 'til I write it," Ford said. To him one of the most pleasurable things about writing is taking a shapeless story and giving it substance.

Ford said how one gets the work done is really subordinate to its excellence, and if it is excellent, that's all that matters.

In a workshop at UNO, Ford discussed how the elements of a story—point of view, character, dramatic structure and imagery—all come together to form the meaning. "You can extract some little sentence that will give you a synthetic notion of what the story is about, but only with all of its parts will the story give you the experience," Ford said.

Without the story, Ford said, the sentiments seem mawkish and silly, like a greeting card. "Through the complications of a story the texture achieves the conditions of life, the illusions of life," Ford said. "What is like a greeting card is then like life."

Ford said in anything he's ever written that was any good there was always a play of light and dark. His work used to be much bleaker, he said, but is more hopeful now.

"I'm kind of a hopeful person," Ford said. "People have loved me in my life. When I talk about love I mean affection. Affection can sometimes make your life worth bearing."

Since there is no writing profession, no community of writers to help one another, Ford said all writers' expectations are, at heart, unrealistic.

When a person enters law school, Ford said, he can reasonably think in three years he'll be educated in law. Very few writers, however, will ever see their work in print.

Ford said in 1969 he read a newspaper article that said *Playboy* magazine received 16,000 manuscripts a year. How can you hope to beat those odds, Ford said he asked himself, and answered you can't, so you might as well quit worrying about it. "If nothing is possible," Ford said, "then everything is possible. I quit thinking about 16,000 manuscripts a year and started thinking about one—mine, which had nothing to do with all the others."

According to Ford, writing is basically non-competitive, absolutely solitary and self-motivated. "Other people's successes do not diminish you, your failures don't help others," he said.

"Wonderful writing is wonderful writing. Do the best you can," Ford advised. "Jump for joy at the success of others. If you can't say my brother's success is my success, you must say my brother's success is not my failure."

A Novelist with Many Voices

Jane A. Mullen / 1986

From *The Christian Science Monitor* 30 July 1986: 19. Used by permission.

Richard Ford is one southern writer who doesn't believe in southern writing.

"Regionalism is the bane of writing in the South," Mr. Ford said during a recent interview in his nineteenth-century planter's home in the Mississippi Delta, "and not only in literature, but in every other aspect of life."

Asked what it means to be a southern writer, Ford, whose widely received third novel, *The Sportswriter,* is set in New Jersey and the Midwest, replied that it doesn't mean anything at all. "What it used to mean was that you wrote like Faulkner. That's mostly all it has ever meant, because before Faulkner there was no such thing as an important, isolable tradition of southern literature. And there is none now. There are just good writers, and not-so-good writers."

Such opinions cast Ford as something of an iconoclast, since there are, as he himself says, a great number of critics, scholars, and publishers who trade profitably on the supposed uniqueness of southern writing. But Ford suspects something akin to cultural slumming here.

"It's been the case that southerners are sometimes perceived as not very adept, not very smart," he says. "So that in every way in which the rest of the world reveres southern writing, there is in that chemistry suspicion of narrowness and lack of respect. I have a hard time wanting to preserve that."

Ford, who grew up in Jackson, Miss., left the South in 1962, partly because of increasing racial tensions and partly because his grandfather, who was in the hotel business, encouraged him to enroll in the Kellogg School of Hotel Management at Michigan State University. Ford did enroll, and waited five weeks before changing his major to English.

Although he subsequently lived for long periods in California, New York, Vermont, Montana, and Princeton, N.J.—where he taught writing for seven years—Ford, like Frank Bascombe, the narrator of *The Sportswriter,* retains an abiding affection for Michigan and the Midwest, a fondness shared by his wife Kristina, whom he met while both were students at Michigan State. It was in part Kristina's work in land planning that brought the Fords to the

Mississippi Delta three years ago, and it is her work that will take them back to Montana this fall.

Ford was living in Michigan when he wrote his first novel, *A Piece of My Heart,* recently reissued by Vintage Contemporaries. The book was nominated for the Ernest Hemingway Award for the best first novel of the year in 1976. Set in Mississippi, where the paths of two displaced, self-destructive men converge, the novel was lauded for its eloquence and power, and Ford himself was greeted as a new, distinctly southern voice in the tradition of Faulkner and Flannery O'Connor.

"Obviously, I hadn't left Mississippi so completely that I didn't have it to write about," Ford says. "But when I wrote that book, I used up all the things I cared about, and all the things I had to say about it."

There is nothing remotely southern about Ford's second novel, *The Ultimate Good Luck,* set in Oaxaca, Mexico, where a tight-lipped Vietnam veteran arrives to rescue his girlfriend's brother, who has been jailed on drug charges. And it is yet another voice, radically different from the economic and efficient one employed in *The Ultimate Good Luck,* that speaks in *The Sportswriter.*

The voice, eminently appealing, is that of Frank Bascombe, about to turn thirty-nine, who has given up a promising career as a fiction writer for that of a sportswriter, despite the rave reviews and financial rewards garnered by his one book of short stories. His wife, an equally appealing character, has left him, taking with her their two surviving children, after enduring for two years the period of emotional drifting that engulfed Frank following the death of their oldest child at age nine. A far-from-gloomy book, *The Sportswriter* is a celebration of middle age and middle America.

"I have read that, with enough time, American civilization will make the Midwest of any place—New York included," Frank muses upon revisiting Detroit, where he had spent a lot of time as a college student. "And from here that seems not at all bad. Here is a great place to be in love; to get a land-grant education; to own a mortgage; to see a game under the lights as the old dusky daylight fails to blue-black, a backdrop of stars and stony buildings."

The Sportswriter is a spoken book ("What else is literature," Frank asks, "but someone telling us what someone else is thinking?"), with the bulk of the action taking place in Frank's mind. As such, it is—in both form and content—a novel that seemingly goes against the grain of contemporary American fiction, where the keynote is disaffection with everyday life as lived, and where the preoccupation of most writers is with the surface of life, rather than with the introspection and retrospection that characterizes *The Sportswriter.*

But this is not where Ford sees his work as going against the current trend in American fiction. There is a form to accommodate almost every kind of intellectual voice, he says, and so he writes one story one way and another story another.

"Now that may go against some kind of localizable grain in American letters or criticism. It's easier for the reviewers if all of your work sounds the same, if it's about the same thing, if it is all of a piece, even superficially. But while I was writing *The Sportswriter,* I also wrote a book of stories, set in Montana, which are nothing like it. I'm probably never going to write out of one voice and don't wish that I could. But it's also true that reviewers often ignore diversity and change in a writer's work over time, in behalf of easier generalizations."

Although in *The Sportswriter* Ford deliberately set out to write a book that says everything it is about, rather than leaving it to the reader to find its meaning, he hastens to add that he does not think that form is necessarily superior to novels or stories that say less.

"I think about Ray's (Raymond Carver) and Ann's (Ann Beattie) work, and in fact those works are not as silent as they seem. I don't think that the kind of elliptical qualities that they have are at all mute. And as for *The Sportswriter* being wordy, I don't think it ends up being necessarily more articulate. I have found Ray's and Ann's work to be immensely eloquent about the things they mean to be about. It's just the different kinds of dramatic situations they choose which makes fewer words more appropriate."

Ultimately, Ford believes in literature as a moral force or instrument, something that can change not only individual lives, but the world. "I believe that literature—art in general—is a curative. That's at least one of the things it is. It's a way for people of the world to see themselves, in a wider and more complex way," he says.

"It presumes that if people can see and understand the world better, they will make it better. It doesn't mean that you yourself have to be an optimist. In the very least sense, if you give somebody something, it means that they will have something more to do, to look forward to. I give you a book."

Ford Is in Season

David Beard / 1986

From *The Clarkesdale Press Register* 26 July 1986: 8A. Reprinted with permission of The Associated Press.

Like the cotton that rises outside his rural Mississippi home, author Richard Ford is in season.

In the past few months, the forty-two-year-old author has enjoyed his greatest literary success and come to terms with his home state after nearly a quarter-century away.

His third novel, *The Sportswriter,* has received widespread critical acclaim and sold a robust 42,000 copies since its release three months ago. The success has enabled Ford to get his second novel reissued and negotiate a "comfortable" contract for his next book, his first published collection of short stories.

His personal life has also settled.

In December 1984, after a lifetime of wandering, Ford and his wife Kristina bought a restored planter's home in Mississippi's Delta (living there part-time. The house is currently on the market.)

"I got tired of everybody telling me, 'oh, you can't know about that because you're not from here,' " said Ford, a thin, tanned man dressed in a worn khaki shirt, chinos, and dock shoes.

The couple grows vegetables in a garden out back, where shade trees surround the white, high-ceilinged home that former Mississippi governor James Alcorn built for his sister in 1867. His neighbors are now cotton and soybean farmers, not fellow instructors at Princeton or Williams or former colleagues at *Inside Sports* magazine in New York.

"The move is an experiment, but then, life is kind of an experiment," he said. Since he left, "Mississippi has changed and I have changed, and I suppose we've come to terms."

In 1963, Ford graduated from Jackson's Murrah High School and moved away from the state's racial conflicts to Michigan State University in Lansing. He joined a fraternity, the subject of his essay in June's *Esquire* magazine, and discovered that he fit between two stereotypes.

"In those days, being from the South was a mixed issue," Ford said. "In the North, everybody assumed that I was a racist. As soon as I got back to Mississippi, after one semester, I was a Yankee, a freedom rider in disguise."

He graduated and briefly attended law school at Washington University in St. Louis, then moved in with family at Little Rock, Ark. He became a substitute teacher and applied for jobs at banks, newspapers, and the Arkansas State Police.

Ford credits his wife with his decision to become a writer. He moved to New York where she worked, took an editing job on a magazine, got married, and moved to graduate school in California. He later taught at Michigan, Princeton, and Williams, but his wife's career allowed him to devote more time to writing.

"We decided that writing was a thing worth doing," he said. "If it ever came to the point where it made money for us, that would be fine. We never got highly practical about it."

He spends much of his time scribbling daily events and ideas in notebooks, or raiding them for raw material for fiction or essays.

"The whole thrust of my writing has been to try to get the most important things in my life in my work, and also for the work itself to reflect life, the way it really is, which is really random. And the order that we make of it is our lives."

Ford's writing, usually in the first person, is often compared with that of Raymond Carver, Tom McGuane, or Frederick Exley. He says it hinges on the strength of his characters and his ability to reflect real life.

Ford's settings range from Montana, where he lived with Kristina while she worked as a city planner, to the cities in the Northeast and Midwest. In both *The Sportswriter* and the short story "Rock Springs," he portrays rootless characters moving on interstates and through the hotel rooms of America.

He does not consider himself a "Southern" writer and does not use Southern settings for his stories. Even as he sits in the study of his home, writing short stories for the coming collection, his fiction returns to Montana.

His topics range from Bruce Springsteen to baseball and his reviews and essays have no geographic or categorical limits, which is the way he wants it.

Although he seemed content as he sat on his front porch one recent afternoon, he did not romanticize the move to Mississippi.

"I did not come down here seeking an advantage," Ford said. "I was not trying to rekindle anything. I'm just living here the way I would live anywhere."

Richard Ford: Author Ventures Home with Love in His Heart

Mitchell Diggs / 1986

From the *Daily Journal's View Magazine* [Tupelo, Mississippi] 16 August 1986: 4–5. Used by permission.

Richard Ford is particularly pleased with the view from his armchair. Having spent two days cleaning windows, he can sit here in his living room and observe the outside world without the annoying brown haze that recently hung between his chair and the giant oaks in the front yard.

Gazing through the hot August afternoon past the columned front porch and the shaded front yard, Ford can see cars snaking their way along Mississippi 316 between Jonestown and Coahoma. Beyond that, the cotton and soybean fields of the Mississippi Delta stretch for miles in nearly every direction.

Ford is a writer. His stories have been published in *Harper's, Playboy, Paris Review,* and *TriQuarterly.* Three of his essays and excerpts from his new novel have run in *Esquire* during the past year. His recently-published third novel, *The Sportswriter,* received critical acclaim, so some might be surprised that Ford lives in this rural setting rather than New York City, Chicago, or California. He has lived in all those places but moved away from them.

His stately white house sits in a five-acre oasis of decades-old magnolias and oaks beside the narrow highway. He and his wife of eighteen years, Kristina, share their home with Lulu, an Airedale, and Dixie, a playful Brittany spaniel.

The walls are decorated with contemporary art and photographs of the couple and friends. A framed black-and-white photo of President Harry Truman hangs just to the right of the front door.

"That is there so that all these farmer Republicans who come into my house can't leave without realizing and remembering that they are in the house of a lifelong Democrat," Ford explained with a grin.

Both of his parents also were Democrats. His father, a traveling salesman for the Faultless Starch Co., was a native of Atkins, Ark., and his mother hailed from rural Benton County, Ark.

A Jackson native, Ford left Mississippi when he was eighteen. His parents wanted him to study business so he could join the family's hotel business in Little Rock.

"I went, for one reason because of that and also because I just wanted to get out of Mississippi," he recalled. "I don't know why. I could say it was because of the increasing tension of the racial business, but I'm not sure if that's right.

"I was quite aware at the time that race relations were reaching a bad pass, and that I—although not particularly a visionary—wasn't always on the side of my race, if my race had a side. That's hindsight, though. I guess it just felt at the time, 1962, like a good time for me to get out of Mississippi."

He moved to Michigan and earned a bachelor's degree from Michigan State University with plans of becoming a lawyer. He enrolled in law school at Washington University in St. Louis, but dropped out after one year.

"I was twenty-three years old and I wanted to get on with my life. I didn't grow up with a lot of money, and it just never did seem to be the way I wanted to calibrate my life. I realized that I probably wasn't going to be a brilliant jurist, and money would be the next most likely object. And the law practiced just for money has nothing to do with the reasons that I wanted to study the law."

Shortly afterward, Ford got married and moved to New York, where the couple lived for a year. He decided to try his hand at writing and moved to California, where he earned a master's degree in literature from the University of California.

"I thought when I got out of school and was looking around that I had only done one thing in my life that interested me, and that I was any good at, and that was to write stories. I didn't feel gifted. I just felt that I had done that, and it was pleasurable and I liked it. I had a high regard for literature because I had studied literature in college. There seemed to me to be at least a kind of hope that if you like literature and you like writing, you can bring those two things together. It didn't seem crazy in 1968."

The couple moved to Chicago, and his wife went to work. Ford devoted his time to writing, although he admits that his first stories were not very good. After a year, he received a grant from the Ford Foundation to work on a novel. He and his wife moved to Ann Arbor, Mich., where he taught at the University of Michigan and penned *A Piece of My Heart.*

Hailed by critics, that first novel was runner-up for the Ernest Hemingway Award in 1976. Ford began writing short stories, publishing them in magazines, and taught at Williams College and Princeton University. Another novel, *The Ultimate Good Luck,* followed in 1981.

He resigned from teaching in 1981, at his wife's urging, to devote himself fully to writing. His mother's death that year prompted him to return to his home state.

"After she was gone, I had no close family left, and I just realized that if I left Mississippi at that point, I probably would never come back," he said. "I was interested in seeing if I could live here comfortably and happy as the kind of fellow I'd become in the twenty years I had been away. I can. That's one of the wonderful things about living here; it's perfectly comfortable living here as a writer, as a guy who's lived away for a long time. I wanted to live in Mississippi as though it were just like anyplace else, and I'm convinced it is."

He and his wife also own a house in western Montana, where they plan to move at the end of the month. They want to isolate themselves there for several months so they can write without interruption.

Ford is working on a book of short stories, which is scheduled for publication next summer. Mrs. Ford is finishing a book on land use. She is a former director of planning for the city and county of Missoula, Mont., and also has worked as a professor in the graduate school of public administration at New York University.

When both complete their projects, they will move back to Mississippi, he said.

Ford dismisses the romantic image many people hold of the South. Mississippi, he observes, has many of the same problems as other parts of the country, both rural and urban.

"If you live in the Mississippi Delta, for instance, you would have a very hard time romanticizing life. This is an economy in real trouble, a whole life in real trouble. I mean, there may be Spanish moss on those cyprus trees out there, but a lot of people don't have enough to eat. And a lot of farmers who have worked hard all of their lives are going out of business."

Ford's observations about life and ideas for stories are recorded in several black-and-white softbound composition books. From those notebooks comes the "stuff" that provide frameworks for his stories.

"My notebooks keep me constantly reminded of what it is that I'm here on the earth to do, and they remind me that I'm supposed to be paying attention. If I go for a long period of time without writing anything in my notebook, the notebook's presence reminds me of that.

"Probably most importantly, it is a surrogate for memory. If you don't write things down, you forget them and when you've forgotten them, many times they're lost. I can't afford to lose those things; they become sometimes very quickly what something I want to write is all about."

After deciding to build a story around an idea, Ford reads through his notebooks and transcribes passages that seem appropriate for the story. Working in pencil, he arranges the material into groups, searching for ideas to form the beginning, middle, and end of a story.

"I try to keep it in that pencil form as long as I can because when I type it up, then it tends to harden a little bit. I try to be careful with my first draft; I just try to write the story as close to what it is going to be as I can. There are some writers who write stories by kind of throwing words on a page, and later they organize them. I don't do things that way. I like to have things as close to the form of the story as can be."

Once he is satisfied with the pencil draft of the story, Ford types it and starts refining the structure further. Part of the revision process involves reading the story aloud to his wife, sometimes several times, Ford said.

"I just don't think I can hear a story well enough until I've heard them in my own voice, and until she's heard them. She can judge certain strategies and certain choices of words, and judge the end. Kristina is more than just a mute listener; she has her own opinions about these things, which I pay great attention to. We've been married a long time—eighteen years—so she knows what I think about and I know what she thinks about. I trust her."

Ford pays particular attention to his stories' endings, which he terms his "last whack at the reader." An ending must have impact to close a story satisfactorily, he said.

Describing his method of writing as "rather workmanlike," Ford noted that other authors probably have entirely different approaches to building stories. Ford prefers to continue working on a story—sometimes five-to-eight hours a day—until it is completed.

He is interested in the starting and completion dates of his stories. *The Sportswriter* took more than three years, including periods when Ford did not work on the manuscript, to complete—from April 1982 to September 1985. He recently finished a forty-five page story called "Empire," which took little more than a month—from May 5 to June 11.

"Every book goes along at a different pace and asks of you different kinds of addiction," he said. "I always wished that I could write books more swiftly than I do, and maybe the next book I write, I will write more swiftly."

Commercial success or a spot on the best seller chart is not the primary motivation for a writer, though, he said. The driving force for a writer, he explained, is the persistent belief that what he does is right.

"You can't as a writer think to yourself, 'I'm not publishing a book every two years, so I'm not keeping up.' There's no 'up' to keep. Somebody said to me the other day, 'Well, you've made it as a writer.' There's no 'it' to make. You write a book, and that is what consumes you and takes everything you have. When you finish that book, maybe you write another one.

"Basically, if you're a writer, what you want to do is write. If a book succeeds, that's wonderful. If it doesn't succeed or has less than complete success, you've still got to write it."

Although he enjoys writing, he dismissed the notion that writing is a "fun" thing to do.

"It's hard work and it's not fun, but I like it. It seems like a worthwhile thing to dedicate your life to.

"I don't know where Americans came by the notion that anything should be fun. Things are interesting, things are hard, and things are rewarding. Fun is what kids have; what adults do is different. Even when I go out and ride my motorcycle, I don't think I'm having fun. When I go out and spend the day hunting, I don't think I'm having fun. I'm doing something else, something better than fun."

When he is not working on a story, Ford most enjoys spending time with his wife. During the autumn months, both are avid hunters and fishermen. The couple also enjoys working out at a local health club.

Ford enjoys reading magazines and books by his contemporaries. American fiction is flourishing, he said.

"I really like for novels to tell me things I don't know about a subject. I have the old-fashioned notion of wanting to be enlightened by a book. There is the old admonition that a book should please and enlighten, and I put enlighten first.

"I also would like them to be funny, but only in the way that Shakespeare is funny. Shakespeare could always turn a sometimes even gruesome subject, a terrifying subject, to make you laugh a little bit. I don't mean comedy. I mean something at its most serious can also be funny. I like that."

Several of Ford's stories deal with memories of childhood, trying to focus and understand them. Many childhood memories cannot be understood fully because they involve one's parents, and those events were part of their lives, he said.

Being unable to explain those happenings does not, though, make them any less important to an individual's memory, he said. Although a part of one's life, many memories are random and disconnected.

"Through the agency of writing about them, I can point to their randomness and say that randomness is alright. The fact that I didn't know a lot about my parents, for instance, but I knew some things, makes as much a fabric of life as a fully-remembered life would.

"It's my predilection as an adult to want to find life to be okay, to have it be liveable rather than to wring my hands about it or, on the other hand, to glorify it in some unconvincing way."

An Interview with Richard Ford

Kay Bonetti / 1986

From *The Missouri Review* 10.2 (1987): 71–96. Used by permission. This is a print version of an audio recording available from the American Audio Prose Library, Inc. Copyright © 1986. All rights reserved. For more information call 800/447-2275.

Richard Ford is the author of several books, including *A Piece of My Heart, The Ultimate Good Luck,* and *The Sportswriter.* This interview was conducted by Kay Bonetti, Director of the American Audio Prose Library Series. The Prose Library offers tapes of American authors reading and discussing their work. For information, contact AAPL, PO Box 842, Columbia, MO 65205.

Interviewer: Why do you live where you live?

Ford: When I left Mississippi in 1962, it was kind of an awful place, for me, and I was curious to know if I could come back and be the kind of fellow I had become. It's kind of an experiment of the heart, in a way.

Interviewer: This is the place of *A Piece of My Heart,* isn't it.

Ford: Just about ten miles away. Quite by coincidence, when I grew up in Mississippi, I lived down in Jackson. I was always fond of the Delta, but I never thought about living here until after my mother died. I came back to Mississippi thinking that if I didn't find some way to attach myself here, I would go away and lose Mississippi forever. I would have to make some willful act to continue my associations with Mississippians. So I came to the Delta because it seemed like the prettiest place in the state to live.

Interviewer: You have said that place is wherever we can gain dominion over our subject and make it convincing.

Ford: That's right, that's right. I think that you have to be imaginative in your relationship with place. You have to be sensitive to the fact that it makes a claim on you and then try to make up what that claim is. Otherwise, you're left reliant upon the conventional wisdom, which is where, of course, literature falls apart, where imaginative writing is defeated.

Interviewer: How does a piece set itself for you?

Ford: Oh—that's actually a very hard question. It guess it sets itself for me without ever becoming conceptualized; you can't abstract a sense of place. Someone else can do it; the critic can do it. But for me, a place makes itself felt entirely through particulars. I don't ever think about, say, writing stories about Montana in terms of writing stories about Montana. I just am in Montana and the things that appeal to me go into stories.

Interviewer: You mean you are in Montana in your mind, or—

Ford: When I want to write a story about Montana I can do that, yeah. I can be in Mississippi and write about Montana. I wrote "Communist," as a matter of fact, sitting in this very house.

Interviewer: *The Sportswriter,* too, I imagine.

Ford: I started it in New Jersey, and wrote most of it in Montana, then I finished it down here in Mississippi. I've got in my notebook a whole lot of details, and that's really where that sense of place comes from. As I get older, I think it's true, too, that I hang out in fewer and fewer places that I don't like. I try to go to the places where I am willing to be attentive, where I am willing to participate in the life there and to notice what is going on; a writer's obligation is to pay attention. I don't pay a great deal of attention in Mississippi anymore. I figure, by and large, that I've written the one piece about Mississippi that I'm happy ever to write.

Interviewer: And that's *A Piece of My Heart*?

Ford: That's *A Piece of My Heart.* "Shooting the Rest Area," which was in *The Paris Review* twelve or so years ago, was really just a kind of a precis piece for *A Piece of My Heart.* I'm not in Mississippi to write about it.

Interviewer: You said you keep a notebook.

Ford: I always have, in the most conventional writerly way. As I have told students of mine, it reminds me every day when I see it what my days are about, and when I want to sit down and write a story I can just go back through my notebook page by page by page and write out of it, transcribe out of it, make outlines, make lists, make the beginnings of what will be a story, which I think has a consequence in the kinds of stories that I write and a consequence in what my stories are about. I end up writing in my notebook only those things that seem like the most important things to me, and then when I go back through it and winnow out again what seems of interest, then an even higher demand gets made on things. So when I sit down and commit a story it may be a failure of a story for any number of reasons, but it won't be a failure because it's not about something consequential. I've often been criticized for writing stories which are gloomy or overserious.

Interviewer: But you certainly have a lot of comedy, too, or humor—

Ford: I think that's one of the few great pleasures in getting to write. A lot of funny things happened to me and I was raised around humorous, mirthful people. But I have rarely tried to write stories that were simply funny.

Interviewer: Is the process of keeping a notebook a daily discipline, a craft routine, or is it spontaneous?

Ford: It is a discipline, but it isn't a daily discipline. There will be times when I write in my notebook every day. And then months will go by—for instance, last summer, while I was working on *The Sportswriter*—when I didn't write in my notebook at *all*. I'm always sorry when I don't write in my notebook, but not too sorry. I write in it whenever I can. I write on backs of people's matchbook covers and the backs of people's business cards and on napkins and then I stick them into my notebook and at some point or other I open that notebook and try to transcribe them all. I don't know if all writers do it or not. I don't think it really is too consequential, except for the very beginning writer who, because I don't teach, I'm not that interested in anymore. That's one of the reasons I quit teaching; I was giving all my time away to somebody whom I would never see again. If young writers want to keep journals, that's great. If they don't, great.

Interviewer: You mentioned looking through your notebook for a story. Do you find stories in your notebooks?

Ford: Well, you get a story in different ways. Sometimes you have an ending for a story, and sometimes you have a beginning. Sometimes you have a first line. I just go through my notebook looking, with the notion that I can make it all jam in together to make a story because it interests me, and it will occupy me enough to make me able to fit it in.

Interviewer: So you do find a story in your notebook? You use it that way?

Ford: Yeah, but when I say a story I don't mean I find a note in my notebook which says, "Story idea: start at A; go to B; end at C." I find lines of dialogue, random, out of the blue, completely isolated. I find descriptions. I find people's names. I just work at it and work at it and work at it until there's a story. But I believe that's the way literature gets made, because it's certainly the way life gets made sense of. We remember things about life that seem to be consequential, things that, for one reason or another, pop out of the dust of experience.

Interviewer: Is there a discernible germ from which a story will start for you?

Ford: No, not that I know of. It's always different. The one thing that seems for me consistent—but it really doesn't have anything to do with any individual story—is that my life, or my time, anyway, in my life, is dedicated to writing a story, to writing a novel. When I finish something, I'll go back and start another one. That's the only consistent part, and I'll do it again, if I can, if I'm able. Sometimes I start them and they don't go anywhere, and that really is pretty vexing to me; I try not to let that happen very much. I don't want stories not to work. Same with novels. I don't have unfininshed novels stuck in drawers. Life has never seemed long enough for unfinished novels.

Interviewer: You worked in a short form for quite a few years before you wrote *A Piece of My Heart.*

Ford: I started writing in 1968, seriously, and I started writing *A Piece of My Heart* in 1972. But from 1968 to 1970 I was in graduate school, and then from 1970 to right at the beginning of 1972, Kristina and I were living in Chicago and I was flopping around like a fish trying to figure out what to do, writing—I guess I wrote about three or four stories, all of which are awful. So I hesitate to say that I worked in a short form. *A Piece of My Heart* was really the first sort of muscled up piece of work I started to do. When people ask me why I started writing novels, I say I did because I got so frustrated with writing bad stories. But in truth, I didn't write bad stories very long. I got pretty sick of sending them off and getting them back in a short amount of time, and I thought, well, I'll write a novel, and then, at the end of the time it takes me to write it, I'll send it off. Instead of getting a story back every couple of weeks and having that day ruined, I would dedicate myself to something that would keep me from having those bad days.

Interviewer: You mentioned getting "muscled up" for a novel. Is that the primary difference between the long and the short form for you?

Ford: Well, I do it the same way with short stories, and to a more massive extent with novels; I get myself fairly well organized before I ever start. I collect and collect and collect and I make a lot of notes, and I think as much as I can without actually starting about what the trajectory of this story or this novel is going to be. I don't overplan because I do like the notion that you get to places where the story goes in surprising ways, but I just want to feel like when I get embarked on this thing, a year into it, that I won't turn around and find I don't have anything else to write about. That, to me, would be a bad pass. So I muscle up in that way, get my mind, for a novel, set to the fact that I'm going to be here awhile.

Interviewer: It's more workmanlike.

Ford: In that way it is. I don't like the idea of "workmanlike" because it seems plodding and uninteresting. It, to me, is just a writer's life, and it doesn't have any actual parallels. But people say to me—businessmen, carpenters—you and I really do a lot of things the same. I think well, yes—and no. And I don't mean that in an elitist sense. I just think that what I do is what I do, and the way in which it bears upon what other people in other disciplines do is of only minor interest to me. The similarities are somewhat trivializing of the thing that I do, and perhaps trivializing of the things that they do.

Interviewer: Is there a typical length of time it takes you to finish a short story?

Ford: Well, Kristina still would say I usually spend about ten days writing a first draft, and if that's what she says, then she's right. I try to write first drafts that are as close to the bone as I can. I'm not one of the people who rips it off, you know, in a torrid dash from dawn till dusk. I will try to work as long in the day as I can, but I really think that the writing of the first draft of the short story may take a few days. Ten days, seven days. I know other people do it differently. But I just like to do it that way. It's one of the few pleasures of being a writer; I can do it the way I can best do it, and how other people do it—at my age, anyway—is of not much interest. My friends and I rarely talk about that kind of thing. Sometimes, if I'll see a story that is so wonderful and so of a piece, a story like "Cathedral," say—

Interviewer: By Raymond Carver?

Ford: Yeah—I may have asked Ray how long it took him to write this story. Though, of course, there is no reason to think that he would ever tell me the truth.

Interviewer: Raymond Carver had something to do with the making of "Going to the Dogs." Would you care to tell that story for us?

Ford: I wrote that while living in a barn up in Bennington, Vermont. Ray was visiting, and we had been going to the dog track. Ray had just come from

New York—he, like anybody who is in New York not that much, was sort of not at ease—and he told a story about coming out of a subway kiosk into the bright light, and was standing there sort of looking around—he was blinking, and his eyes were spotty—but he was sort of looking around, and a whore said to him, "Hey, Curly, wanna have a good time?" And after that I always called Ray Curly. When I wrote "Going to the Dogs" I had in mind a fellow a little bit, I suppose, like Ray, essentially being accosted and outdone by two rather forceful women, which is what that story is about.

Interviewer: Do you enjoy writing?

Ford: I would never use that word, no. Writing's what I felt early in my life I might be best suited to do, and I didn't mind doing it. Even as a sort of untaught fellow in Mississippi, I always thought writers were people who had a high calling. My mother used to take me over to Jackson and she would say to me, "That's Eudora Welty." I didnt' know who Eudora Welty was, and I would say, "Who's she?" And my mother would say, "She's a writer." I could tell in her voice that that was something other than the ordinary.

Interviewer: Many writers will say outright that it's painful to write.

Ford: Well, that sounds too much like a complaint to me, and I don't like complaining in public. A lot of things you like might be painful. It just doesn't seem to be an adequate way of talking about that thing that you do all your life. To say that it was painful would be really perverse. Being a novelist, being a story writer, being an essayist, there's nothing perverse about it at all. Most of the time it's really quite interesting. And sometimes quite exhilarating. I think if one is a writer and has made a little bit of a go at it, he's lucky.

Interviewer: Robert Stone says, "I judge my work by whether or not what I'm doing entertains me; I write to entertain myself."

Ford: I think that makes perfect sense. You're always looking at something you've written and say to yourself, "Is that interesting?" And I think Robert Stone's work meets the test—all the way. It's always interesting; it's always engaging; it's always smart.

Interviewer: And would you apply that to Richard Ford?

Ford: That's Bob's word. I write to see if I can say something that I think is surprising and smart, to see if I can add to what I know, and maybe add to what my reader would know about something that they may already know a lot about. Love and affection, for instance. As Frank says in *The Sportswriter,*

he believes in the possibilities of passion and romance, and I would like to
be able to say something about passion and romance that would surprise and
educate me.

Interviewer: You wrote about the gifts to you of Faulkner, Hemingway,
and Fitzgerald, the efficacy of telling, recommending language for its powers
of consolation against whatever ails you.

Ford: Faulkner was very consoling to me in that way. Fitzgerald and Hemingway did it in their ways, also. To me, Faulkner—partly because I was a
kid in Mississippi, and so was he, and he was writing in Mississippi when I
was growing up—treated me with and to language which was about things
that made the world more orderly to me. There are all kinds of things in
Faulkner the meaning of which you don't know, but you kind of luxuriate in
the language, in almost an osmotic way. Feel what it's about. So I was able
to read others and now know what everything meant, and when I didn't
understand things, console myself into believing that it was all right just to
feel the words, speak the words to myself, let the words live in my mind.

Interviewer: Does that same principle apply to the act of writing for you?

Ford: To some extent it does. I'll have a sentence in my mind which has
got a hole in it—I want a word that's got three syllables, and it ought to have
an *a* at the beginning, and it ought to have, you know a long vowel sound at
the end. Maybe I'm really thinking about a word that I know and I just can't
remember. But sometimes I'll start thinking about words and look for words
in the places I customarily look for words, and I'll come up with something
really unexpected which fits perfectly, and actually makes the sentence mean
something a little bit more than it might have meant if I had found the word
I thought I was looking for.

Interviewer: You've also spoken of writing as something that has deeply
and intimately to do with reconciling the irreconcilable and making accommodation. Can you elaborate on that?

Ford: Maybe I can. Literature is really useful to us for many reasons, but
one way in which it's useful to us is to try to find a way to say those things
which haven't been said. And a lot of times, one's inability to say those
things is what keeps problems problems, is what makes things stick in your
mind and not go forward. Now I want to be very clear about this, that I don't
mean that literature is therapeutic. It *can* be consoling. It *can* say the thing
not before said. But that's about all I really mean. We think we know what

love is; we think we know what passion is; we think we know what hatred is. We know, in fact, a lot about those things. And literature's opportunity is to say about those concepts what hasn't been said yet, so that we know more about them, so that we'll find a way to take some solace in them.

Interviewer: It seems to me that your stories are love stories.

Ford: I hope so. I don't know if *A Piece of My Heart* is so much about love as it is about errant passion. But *The Ultimate Good Luck* tries to be a love story. I guess I find the most challenging passion arise in my own life from that relationship between men and women. I read something the other day that a fellow in England wrote about me—he said what I always was writing about was men trying to deal with their own sensitivity. I think that's selling me a little short . . . maybe that's true of some things I write, but usually I try to write about men and women together.

Interviewer: You once wrote that the thing missing in Thoreau was the sense of a lived life.

Ford: *Walden* is a laboratory piece, as wonderful as it is—and I don't mean to take anything away from it, but if you were to ask Thoreau if this wasn't his real life, he would tell you yes, it is his real life. But it doesn't have the feel, to me, of life; it has the feel of life lived for literary purposes.

Interviewer: It seems to me that you're trying to get the sense of a lived life.

Ford: That's exactly right—because lived life comes first for me. I write afterwards. I'm not there writing down all the things my friends say in conversations or standing around with my notebook in my hand at baseball games. I'm really just out there with the people I care about and doing the things I want to do. It may later seem to me that that's worth writing about, but that will always be after the fact. I'm not going out into the world trying to show the world that I'm a writer, day to day. I'm just out there working in my garden. Whatever that garden is.

Interviewer: One of the places where most of us live it is in relationships and your characters often have to deal with important losses, especially of parents. Where does this come from?

Ford: Lately, in the last four or five years, I think probably fairly directly from my mother, whom I love very much and miss now that she's gone. She died in 1981, and I think it probably is natural for a writer to end up writing about that thing that was so important in his life. And she was important in my life. My father died when I was young, and we accommodated each other pretty much as adults in the time he was gone. That was a great gift to me from her, and we stayed friends, close friends, for the next twenty or so years until she died. I don't write about those things because they have archetypal value. I just write about them because she was my mother and I loved her.

It was always interesting to me that other people got along so poorly with their mothers and I got along so well with mine. And, as I say, my father was absent before he died because he was a traveling salesman. Even though I'm sorry my father wasn't around, for his sake and for mine, we did okay, the two of us. We did fine. I can't think of one bad thing, one bad moment. She threw things at me, yelled at me and hit me, but that's just—you know—that's just being somebody's mother.

Interviewer: Tell us about Frank Bascombe. It strikes me as a real challenge that you've written a novel that you say is not in your voice, and moreover it is a first person narrative—by a man who has stopped being a writer.
Ford: And is divorced.

Interviewer: Is divorced.
Ford: And has children.

Interviewer: Uh-huh.
Ford: None of those things that I do.

Interviewer: Was this the reason for it coming to be?
Ford: No. I don't know why it came to be. I wanted to write about a certain stratum of life that I knew, which was life in the suburbs. I also wanted to write a novel about a decent man. Frank is very definitely just a man who was trying his best to make his life happy. Against some odds— though not extraordinary odds, just some odds. I found that pretty challenging, really. Drama, if you have a dramatic situation, just gives forth a lot of language, at times. A less markedly dramatic situation gives forth language in different ways. That he is a sportswriter was really the reason for that. I was trying to find the language for this fellow, and sports is so much the language of modern America. Sports metaphors, sports preoccupations. And that he would have been a writer, an imaginative writer, I thought—I'm saying this as if I plotted it out—kind of gave me the opportunity to move from a sort of quotidian language to the language of introspection and speculation. That's what all writers are always trying to do, is find language which will

let them say as much about the subject as they can figure out, from low to high.

Interviewer: One of the things that readers are going to have a ball with in this book is Frank's description of what he was like as a writer.

Ford: Everybody who is a writer, I think, comes up against the kinds of problems that Frank comes up against in *The Sportswriter,* which is to say, the limits of his imagination. When you're a young writer, especially, you're constantly being brought up against what you can't do, how smart you aren't, how good everything else is that you read and how inadequate you are. And being the kind of fellow that he is—I speak about him as if he existed; he doesn't exist; I made him up—Frank tried to make the best of that that he could. He quit. He put his burden down, and went to doing something that he felt he might be better suited for, in an entirely unselfconscious way. There are worse things in the world than not being a writer.

To a literary audience, I think, for a writer to stop being a writer seems a kind of world-class defeat, and for him to say, "Well, it's no big deal" is kind of ironic. Except that just isn't the way I mean it to be. I mean it to be all right. I mean it to be fine. Because he goes ahead and lives the happiest life he can live, full of mirth and tragedy and affection.

Interviewer: And he quit writing, but you still do.

Ford: Today I do. I do think though, that if next year I decided I didn't want to write another book, or if I couldn't write another book, it wouldn't be the worst thing in the world to happen to the world or to literature or to me; it would just be something else that happened. That's the way Frank looks at things. I don't mean that he's a foolish optimist; I just mean that he's a guy who sees that there is always an option. As he says in the book, "What we all need is choices all the time. Choices." And even if you don't take them, you need to think that nothing is banging away at you, making your life miserable. I think people are going to tell me this is perhaps a sad book. It has its sad moments, as everyone's life does, but it's a book about—I don't want to say surviving, because that sounds pretentious—but it's a book about getting on.

Interviewer: At what point did you decide to set that book on Easter weekend?

Ford: It was always meant to be a book that went from the Thursday before Good Friday to Easter night, because that was when I started writing the book. I was trying to imbue the book with the feeling of those days when I began it, sunny, crisp, warm Sunday days. I came around to being *about* Easter later. But I will say that the Easter myth—whatever it is—is a fairly compelling myth. When I realized I was harnessing my book up to some provocative Judeo-Christian myths, I really tried to pull back. But it suddenly started connecting up in ways that I didn't like and I just took out, out. Out, out, out. Near the end of the book Frank goes into his would-be, future in-laws' room to make a phone call. They're Catholics, and the copy editor said, "Any modern-day Catholics would have a crucifix hanging in their room." I gave serious thought to that because I thought it was right. Then I thought, that's just nothing I care about. So I didn't put it in. There is a big crucifix hanging on the outside of the Arcenault's house. I didn't make that up. Kristina and I were riding down in southern New Jersey one time—just whiling away a Sunday afternoon—and we went through a little subdivision where, in fact, on this nice, split-level house was hanging this enormous crucifix. I don't remember if it was Easter day or not; I think, probably, it wasn't. That's where that came from. I don't want to sound like Mr. Faulkner used to: "Well, I don't know what this means; I just put it in here." You can't put this into your novel and not have some sense of what it's about. But I was shocked at the number of things that began to give way to that particular way of reading that book. And I certainly would hate for the book to be read as a book just about Christian redemption, because it's not a Christian book. The kind of redeeming that goes on in that book is entirely unreligious; it's really Frank figuring out ways to redeem his life based on nothing but the stuff of his life.

Interviewer: It's about the death of the family.

Ford: Yes. It's about the sustaining of the modern family apart. The family doesn't go away because its members don't live together. There's a line in the book to that very point, that sometimes you can love someone and not be where they are, but you still love them.

Interviewer: Why is the ex-wife X?

Ford: Well, the best of all reasons, in one way. I couldn't find a name that I liked. I decided quite early on that I would put X on the page because I didn't have a name for her and I thought, eventually I'll come to the name. So all along as I was writing the book, I would write X. And finally X is who she became. Looked at in other ways, Frank can't bear to say her name; he can't—it's an intimacy he doesn't have anymore. I don't think in any way that her being called X depersonalizes her. I think she is as personable as she would be if her name had been Mary or Nancy or Jenny, but any of those names hurt my ears. I couldn't make myself say them, and Frank can't make himself say them, through my agency.

Interviewer: Names are very important, then.

Ford: Very important to me. Frank had another last name all through the writing of that book. But that name turned out not to be a usable name. And to find another name for Frank was a real pill, a real pill. Kristina and I went through a lot of names. The names in my books are hardly contemplated; that is, I contemplate them hard.

Interviewer: What's involved?

Ford: Probably too much in my estimation. Somebody else could go along and find names for my characters that would work. But I've got to feel *kin* to them. I've got to be able to have with that name the intimacy that I would have with that character were he or she to exist. So I get very picky about those things. And language is a concern—how language feels in your mouth, how it sounds in your ear, what it looks like on the page, how many syllables it's got, how many stresses it has—almost poetic concerns. I knew, for instance, that Bascombe—which is Frank's name in my book—was always going to be a two-syllable word and that the first syllable would be a short vowel and that the second syllable would be an *um* sound.

Interviewer: What we're coming up with here is your aesthetic view, that literature is language, but it also has to have some intimate link with life.

Ford: Life of a purely literary kind. It exists through language and on the page and isn't like life in any way but that one referential way. I don't want to say that literature *must* be this way. Literature can and should be any way it can be made, in the widest, most variegated sense. But, for me, if a guy's good at building round houses, he should try to build the best round houses he can build. Writing stories the way I've been writing stories and novels is the best way I can do it. So it's only an imperative for *me* at this point. Maybe in ten years I'll do it differently.

Interviewer: I'm always fascinated by first person narratives; here is a book about a man who chose to stop writing, but he's telling us his story.

Ford: Odd, isn't it, how literature has that double reflex? I would have to be a fool not to be aware of it, but you start looking in those double reflecting mirrors and you can look forever.

Interviewer: The illusion—

Ford: "I can tell you this—my name is Frank Bascombe. I am a sports writer." That's what he can tell you—in his own voice, not in his sportswriter's voice, necessarily, or in his story writer's voice, but in his own voice. That, in fact, is the measure of the book's urgency. "I can only tell you this."

Interviewer: Do you think of writing as telling?

Ford: Yes, I do. And telling that as it gets better verges closer and closer to a completely believable telling, completely persuasive telling. I used to think about that subject a great deal more than I am able to think about it now because I'm too busy *doing* it. When I was young I *did* it less, and I thought about it more. Now I think about it a lot less and I do it a lot more.

Interviewer: Is there someone to whom you are telling your stories when you write?

Ford: No, no. No. I read everything to Kristina; she's a good reader but she's not the ideal reader for me. I don't have an ideal reader. I want everybody to look at this novel, this story, *exactly* as I do. And maybe, exactly as I would if I were just a little smarter.

Interviewer: One of the most devastatingly successful things about *The Sportswriter* was the issue of parenting and the loss of a child. And you are childless. Did you want to think at some point, what it would be like to lose a child?

Ford: No, I don't think I ever got to that speculative point. It seems that for a parent to lose a child is an unqualified thing in a parent's life. It's just one of those big sources of drama. And if you're living a relatively observant life around people who live and die, young and old, it shouldn't be a subject that's particularly foreign to you. I'm willing to believe that somebody would know more about it than I do. But it is part of the public domain; that's what living teaches you. The people you love die; they go away. And sometimes they die too soon, and that's something one can know without having to have it happen to you.

Interviewer: You have written about the act of reading; are you a reader of other people's fiction?

Ford: As I have admitted widely, I'm a slow reader. I never read for pleasure when I was a kid. I always read in a kind of an aggressive, studious way, wanting to get something back. That's why I can't read light-hearted books very much; I can't read thrillers; I can't read best-sellers. I want to learn something. So I try to keep my reading limited to those things that I think are going to be important to me. And when I review, I try to read books that I think will evoke an interesting response from myself. For better or worse, literature is an important issue to me. That's what I've dedicated my life to, and I want to accord other people's work the same amount of seriousness as I do my own. It doesn't have to be always sober; it doesn't have to be always gloomy. It can be perfectly happy and light-hearted and funny but I want something from it, something that I can't get out of the rest of the world.

Interviewer: You have several friends who are also very, very fine writers. Has somebody like Raymond Carver been an influence on you?

Ford: He's a wonderful writer, and I would be happy to think that I have learned from reading his stories. He was a friend of mine when I started trying to write stories seriously for the first time. Ray suggested to me, by indirection, that it was possible for one to write a story. I mean, you can't read his stories without thinking "Gee, that's wonderful." And for a writer, that's the first step towards saying to yourself, "Gee, I'd like to write something wonderful." He and I had similar backgrounds and we found that we understood what was written between the lines of our own lives a little bit the same. I don't think I write about the same kinds of people Ray does and I don't think I have the same temperament, but there are things that he and I appreciate the same. I think that's true of other writers, too, but they don't happen to be close friends of mine.

Interviewer: Do you think of yourself as a New Realist?

Ford: Inevitably, people are going to understand any story in terms of whatever categories exist in their minds. I had to find out that what I was writing was Realist by other people telling me. It hasn't made much difference to me at all. It just seemed like the way I could write stories and novels. And there are plenty of other people who don't get looped into that group who might very well fit into it. So wide is that net that all the people who get caught in it finally bear as much relationship to it as any other group of people do in any other part of the world. Our dissimilarities are as interesting, I think, as our similarities.

Interviewer: Some people say we're beyond purely experimental, avant-garde writing, like Sukenick's and Barthelme's, that it's been a grace note.

Ford: We'll be to it again. Not that I believe life to be cyclical. In the '60s the kind of stories that I wrote seemed to be in disfavor and decline. People

were yawning about them and not liking them very much. These people
whom you mentioned were writing successfully. I recently asked a friend of
mine, "When is that kind of cycle going to happen again? When is whatever
kind of work that we do going to fall from favor, and *then* what's going to
happen?" I don't know. Something will, something will happen. And I don't
look forward to it with any trepidation because if I live, I'll be out there
trying to write the best I can. It doesn't bother me—unless it were to be a
literature which I felt was dangerous.

Interviewer: What would that be?

Ford: Well, literature curtailed by the small minds of this country. Republican literature, basically. Church-sponsored literature. Literature not of the
imagination. Literature by precept. That would worry me. That would be, I
think, an abomination. But anything that owes its source to the imagination
and to lived life, however it comes out, I think that's good and useful and can
delight. If people stopped reading stories like mine, I'd be sorry; I don't want
that to happen, but I certainly don't dread the fact that somebody in the years
to come would write differently from how I do. I just don't know how it'll
be. So I don't think about that period of the '60s and '70s—that which is
now called postmodernism—as being a bad time, nor am I particularly relieved that it seems to be for the moment in subsidence. It's literature trying
to cope with the world it sees, and I think that's fine, that's fine. I have an
open mind to it.

Interviewer: Does it ever annoy you that anybody would imply that fiction
has to be, if it's good, experimental? Isn't every story you write in some
sense an experiment?

Ford: Absolutely. Absolutely. You sit down at the page and there's nothing there, and it's quite an experiment to see if you can fill it up with something that makes sense. I don't use the term experimental in part for that
reason. Experimental can also be used in a pejorative sense; as though it has
a quality of the tentative to it.

Interviewer: I've also heard it used as the opposite of traditional fiction.

Ford: The people who work in colleges talk that way, and that's fine for
them. But, you know, I can sit down with a *New Yorker* and read a Barthelme
story—since we seem to seize upon Barthelme—with huge pleasure, with
huge pleasure. He sees the world differently from how I see it and he thinks
about language differently from how I think about it, but there's more that's

alike between him and me than there is that's different, just as probably
between Toby and Ray and me, there's more that's different than what seems
alike. We're all trying to be good writers. That's all that matters.

Interviewer: You mentioned earlier that you used to teach. How do you
feel about that?

Ford: I certainly don't have any bad feelings about it. I did it until I no
longer had any curiosities about it, and then I quit. I did it also until I felt
like my work should be occupying more of my time than teaching was allow-
ing it to occupy. Kristina believed that—and she, you know, in a way was
setting a hard task for me—if you're going to be a good writer, you'd better
write, and not teach and sit around talking about it. That was true for me.

Interviewer: So you quit because you found it a hindrance to your work.

Ford: A hindrance in the sense it took up too much of my time. And there
certainly wasn't the financial imperative to do it, if what I was being paid
was what I was supposed to be living on. I make about as much money now
as I made when I taught, and I don't have to read essays. But that's just me.
For somebody else, it might be entirely different. I was not particularly well
educated, and I was always curious to see if I could thrive in a place where
people were very well educated. And when I found out that I could do reasonably well in those circumstances, then my curiosity was, I think, satisfied.

Interviewer: When did you actually start writing?

Ford: I started writing in college, I think, probably in the fraternity house
at Michigan State.

Interviewer: A very unlikely place!

Ford: It was actually very good—more unlikely than it even seems. I
guess the notion of taking a creative writing class interested me, because I
had fiddled around with that when I was younger. But when I got out of
college and went to law school at Washington University in St. Louis, I got
sort of interested in Stanley Elkin, who was over there. Reading his stories, I
began to realize how much I liked the idea of writing stories. One day, I just
said to myself, "Well, I'm making a terrible mistake here. I'm about to embark on a life which I don't even like; I know I don't want to do this, to be a
lawyer. What have I ever done that I thought I could do reasonably well that
might turn into a life?" And I had to ask that question of someone else,
frankly. That someone else was Carl Hartman. He said, "Well, you know,
you used to write stories pretty well in college. Why don't you go to the

University of California at Irvine and stay there two years and write some stories and see if you can make any progress; see if you can get somebody to read them and don't worry about getting things published. Just write for awhile." That was in 1968. And then one thing really did lead to another. After I got out of graduate school in 1970, Kristina and I forsook the job I was offered at the University of New Orleans and went to live in Chicago because we thought it was a nice place to live. And it was. But while we were there, I toyed with the idea of going back to the University of Chicago, back to graduate school, and was at the same time writing all those terrible stories I told you about before. Then somebody from the University of Michigan wrote me a letter, and said I'd been nominated for one of the fellowships that they were giving there to bring people who were involved in work not normally sheltered by a university to the University of Michigan. They knew I was writing fiction; did I have anything ongoing that they might consider? I said oh yes, I have a novel, which I that very day sat down and started to begin.

Interviewer: *A Piece of My Heart.*

Ford: *A Piece of My Heart,* which didn't have any shape or idea in my mind at that point. But I thought, something's calling you here; you'd better respond seriously to this. So I did. I sat down and I wrote a few pages and I sent it off to them, and Donald Hall, who was integral in my life, read those pages and thought this seemed to be pretty good. Then they asked me to come to the University of Michigan and I went over there. At Ann Arbor I wrote *A Piece of My Heart,* from 1972 to 1975. Then after that it was just kind of leaping out of one fire into another vat and going to jobs and quitting them, and Kristina always saying to me, "Don't teach. Write." So I did that. That's kind of how it's been, trying to make a living here, make a living there. Without kids you can live a somewhat more feckless life. We have. Sold a book to the movies, that kind of thing.

Interviewer: Which one was that?

Ford: *A Piece of My Heart.* Sold it to the movies and made some money and bought a house in New Jersey. We've just kind of been—I don't want to say hand-to-mouth—but just kind of living transiently.

Interviewer: You have been praised for having a moral vision. Is this something that rings any bells to you as a writer?

Ford: No. I can't make myself responsible for what other people take to like about my stories, and on that particularly tricky subject I'm not smart enough to talk about anything. I know what John Gardner meant about moral literature, and I thought at the time, and I think now, that he was dead wrong. Dead wrong. But about anything else that has to do with my own work, I don't really have an opinion. I'm just lucky to get to do the work, to write stories. If someone likes them for one reason, then I'm really pleased.

Interviewer: You've spoken of the voice in "Rock Springs" as being your voice. Now, you are obviously not Earl in that story. What do you mean when you say that?

Ford: I don't mean anything arcane or artsy in the way that sometimes poets can talk about voice. I just mean that I find that the choice of words, the cadence of the sentences, are familiar to me, the language of my own day-to-day life. I didn't have to rise to a new voice to speak what I thought was good writing, which was what I was doing, trying to speak good writing.

Interviewer: Can you trace what interested you in those characters?

Ford: I think it's people on the edge; things could really get worse, or things could get a little better. That, I think, is where the two lines of dramatic action take place in all these stories. In "Fireworks," it's people who are kind of down on their luck, and things seem really to be in kind of a downward spiral. And what seems to redeem them is affection. Without that affection, without making that little crucial contact, that day passes and the next day starts and then things may go from bad to worse. I believe, in my heart of hearts, that it's just those little moments of time, those little, almost invisible, certainly omittable, connections between people which save your life or don't, and that if your life has a habit of seizing those little moments, then, I think, life can go on for you, have the possibility of being better. In "Rock Springs," when Edna says to Earl, "It's not a matter of not loving you," that's everything to me. Again, I don't want to talk about these characters as if they were real people. They're characters. I don't like other people to talk about my characters or their own or anybody's as if they were living, breathing people. You have options. They don't have any options.

Interviewer: You put them there.
Ford: I put them there.

Reconcilable Differences: The Play of Light and Dark Propels Richard Ford's Work

Gail Caldwell / 1987

First of two parts. From *The Boston Globe* 29 September 1987: 65–66. Used by permission.

It is the opening week of sage-grouse season in Montana, and Richard Ford—sportsman, novelist, peripatetic dreamer—is on his way to spring his five-year-old Brittany spaniel, Dixie, from hunting camp. "She held forty-five minutes on point last night," the trainer has told him by phone from Helena, so Ford is eager to see what she can do. For a man who makes a cross-country trek each winter to his other home in rural Mississippi—who has lived everywhere from backwoods pastorals to academic enclaves—this two-hour drive each way on a star-drenched Montana night seems about as strenuous as a trip to the corner store.

Jim Martin, the trainer, has done his job. When he sends up a ptarmigan to show off Dixie's skills, she comes to a dead halt on point until he releases her with a soft verbal command. Ford watches from a crouched position, impressed; his admiration comes through later, when he's coordinating hunting schedules with Martin. "I have to go on a book tour," says Ford, "and then I'll be ready to go."

"A what?" asks Martin. "A book tour? How long's one of them take, anyway?"

An hour down the road and halfway to midnight, the gas gauge on Ford's 1986 Cherokee is flirting with empty. What towns exist on this moonlit highway have long since shut their pumps, but we pull into Drummond on a half-gallon and a prayer. Ford reaches in the back seat for his baseball cap—logo: Mississippi Alligators—before heading for a well-lit bar. "Time for my good-old-boy act," he says, and walks across the street. Ten minutes later, the local sheriff has unlocked the gas pump, filled our tank and waved us on our way.

Standing six feet two inches with unalloyed blue eyes, Richard Ford is a commanding, soft-spoken man who shows a face to the world as mutable and eloquently spare as his fictional voice. He speaks with a stately, slow-pitched drawl left over from his native Mississippi, and he talks the way he writes: in simple compound sentences as careful as they are reflective. And he seems at home in this muscle-bound town near the Montana-Idaho border, whether he's cruising the Harley dealer for a softtail road bike or sipping bourbon at the local tavern—where Judy, the blond bartender, lights up at the sight of him on a slow night.

Set unsparingly against the mountains just west of the Continental Divide, Missoula is a brawny, sprawling town of 30,000, its neon promises—the Sweet Rest Motel, the Trail's End Bar—imposed upon a formidable landscape. Ford moved here with his wife, Kristina, in 1983 when she took the job of Missoula planning director; she now heads her own public policy research institute, and the two have just bought a house on ninety acres outside of town. Their split-level rental is a spacious wood-and-glass house set high in the hills beyond Missoula. The photographs lining the shelves are testimony of a writer's life, and what you'd expect from a man who juggles book tours with grouse and pheasant season: There are shots of fishing trips with Ford's editor, Gary Fisketjon (of Atlantic Monthly Press), and writers Raymond Carver and Geoffrey Wolff; of book-signings in Jackson, Miss., with Eudora Welty.

Frank Bascombe, the erstwhile fiction writer of Ford's highly praised 1986 novel *The Sportswriter,* concedes that one of the things he's learned in life is that "location isn't actually everything." And while Ford readily admits that the remote life suits him, he seems surprised to discover this about himself—at forty-three, he has lived in urban milieus from New York to California, as well as Mexico and Mississippi. "It simply is a matter of deciding to live on Elm Street instead of Birch," he says about the decision to stay in Montana. "I lived inside [the East Coast literary world] long enough to know that it wasn't an interesting enough life, and maybe I wasn't skillful enough to make it interesting. I liked the people I knew who were writers, but they weren't helping me get my work done. In a kind of glacial way, you gravitate to the things that you like, if you're lucky. And what I found that I wanted to do was live someplace where I could hunt and fish—and where I could have a nice view out the window. That's all it is to me."

The view out the window, from Ford's second-story study, overlooks the junction of the Clark Fork and Bitterroot rivers, where osprey and the occasional bald eagle soar at twilight, searching for trout. It is possible, in the early morning hours, to see the Northern Lights.

But this is also a vision of sublimity's darker side, for the Clark Fork is
the setting of the most wrenching story of Ford's new collection, *Rock
Springs,* where a man in a wheelchair goes night fishing in the fog and snags
a dead deer. Those osprey cruising downriver recall an earlier image from
Ford's first novel, *A Piece of My Heart*—when an osprey sinks his claws into
a huge rainbow trout and follows his prey to his death, beneath the waters of
the Mississippi River. "That osprey just chose more than he could chew,"
says the laconic Robard Hewes. "It was something that happened, so I suppose I made sense out of it already."

"I think that used to be a fairly potent image for me," says Ford, remembering that ill-fated osprey. "It probably is for many young writers: the image
of going after the thing you want, and getting completely sucked under by
it—to your own annihilation!" He laughs. "I do know some of the ways in
which drama emerges in things I've written, and it emerges from that kind of
source: in which someone renders himself vulnerable and gets annihilated.
And what you basically have to do—this is one of the things I've come to
believe—is recognize that it happens, and try to go on anyway. With a smile
on your face, if you can."

In three novels and one collection of stories, Ford has created four self-
willed works as discrete from one another as they are steeped in authenticity:
Nominated in 1976 for the Ernest Hemingway Award for Best First Novel, *A
Piece of My Heart* is a collision course with destiny set in the swamp-ridden
Mississippi Delta; its vivid metaphors and shifting narration have all the overtones of Faulkner's Gothic South. *The Ultimate Good Luck* followed five
years later, a bruiser of a novel replete with gunmetal dialogue and drug deals
gone sour. *The Sportswriter,* published in 1986, moved Ford beyond a quiet,
respectful reception to popular as well as critical acclaim: The book has sold
50,000 copies, and Vintage has just reissued the earlier novels. The first-
person story of thirty-eight-year-old sportswriter Frank Bascombe, the novel
is a large-hearted account of a man trying to reconcile his own sideline status
in the world. In looking back on why he abandoned a promising fiction career, Bascombe recalls that he "got gloomy in an attempt to be serious, and
. . . didn't understand the vital necessity of the play of light and dark in
literature."

That play of light and dark is the tension that both links and propels all
Ford's work, from the celestial irony of his first novel to the haunting, half-
reluctant narrators of *Rock Springs.* But the dichotomies have softened in the

later works, and Ford sees this as a logical progression from ten years ago, when he was surrounded by other writers struggling with similar demons. "We were living through some kind of existential shorthand: darkness for its own sake was the source of adequate drama," says Ford. "And I think it was native to me, and to these guys—a wonderful poet named Michael Ryan. Ray [Carver], Geoffrey Wolff. We talked a lot. And finally I popped out the other end of that when I wrote *The Ultimate Good Luck*.

"You hope that a thorough treatment of the dark side of human nature will necessitate, out of your intelligence and emotions, something balmy. And I think that's what happened to me. I just wrote out of that as far as I could write, until it became obligatory that I find some next step. And the next step was to find some consolation, which I think fueled *The Sportswriter,* and fuels all these stories in *Rock Springs*.

"We console ourselves with our ability to hope, even when it contradicts all of the facts of our lives."

Born in 1944 in Jackson, Miss., Ford lived an itinerant young life with his parents (his father was a starch salesman) and in his grandfather's large hotel in Little Rock. His father died when he was sixteen. This "kind of dicey life," as he now calls it, appears in his fiction, particularly in the character of Sam Newel of *A Piece of My Heart,* but Ford had no prophetic glimmer of the writer's path until he was already on it. He left the South in 1962 for Michigan State University, to follow his grandfather's lead and study hotel management. (He promptly switched to English.) Law school followed, but it proved unengaging. He found what he wanted in the English and creative writing department of the University of California at Irvine, where he took an MFA in 1970.

"I had not had, and have not had in the intervening years, much ambition—none that I can ever say drives me," says Ford. "When I left law school, I looked around and thought if there was anything I'd ever done that I liked doing, and I thought was worthwhile. And my mother asked me, sitting looking out the window—I was completely in despair, after my little attempt at having a career, fast going down the drain—she said, 'What are you going to do with yourself now?' How old was I, twenty-three? I said, 'I think I'm going to try to write stories.' And that was it; I never looked back."

After the sultry, bayou-ridden recesses of *A Piece of My Heart,* the inevitable label of "Southern writer" was bound to follow Ford, even though his work ranges from suburban New Jersey (*The Sportswriter*) to the hardscrabble Montana and Wyoming towns of *Rock Springs*. But his settings tend to

be muted stage sets for language, and he disdains the idea of regional literature, particularly when it ensnares the writer in all the old Southern cliches.
Making peace with a Faulknerian legacy has its own constraints—or, as Flannery O'Connor once put it, "Nobody wants his mule and wagon stalled on
the same track the Dixie Limited is roaring down."

"Nobody leaves the South and goes off to some very different place," says
Ford, "who doesn't spend some of his or her time puzzling about it. I think
it's in the spirit of having lived in such a very parochial and isolated place. I
mean, you go outside to what you deem to be the wider world, and it comes
back to you naturally: Now what was that again? Faulkner was wise enough
to know, I think, that [the South] was just a way to hang a novel in the air.

"I just realized that if you were going to write about the South—and I felt
I had to, that was all I had to write at that time [of *A Piece of My Heart*]—I
felt that you had to do all you could to get all of those rhythms, all those
ways of seeing the world, out of your life. And I certainly tried assiduously
to do that. I know *now* that I have succeeded. I may have succeeded less
excellently then than now.

"If you grew up in Mississippi, you almost couldn't see it except as a
literary landscape—it almost didn't have an existence but through the prism
of [Faulkner's] vision. That was the thing that drove me away from it—I
didn't want to think of the world in literary terms. If you do, then you're
almost doomed as a writer. Your work's always going to show the influence
of whom you've read, and that's not bad, I think—everybody does it—but
you have to finally find your own way.

"When the whole earth is a literary landscape to start with—every tree
has been described, every rise has been intuited—you'll do well to go someplace where you'll see it anew. So that's what I did.

"You have to trade on your ignorance giving rise to an imaginative response . . . I just see people: I see pictures in a newspaper, I see people walk
across a street, I sit in a bar and hear somebody say something, and then I
make up the rest." He smiles. "It turns out not to be so bad. People ask me
now [with the publication of *Rock Springs*] if I grew up in Montana, so some
part of the illusion is complete."

The Sounds of Success: Richard Ford Puts Each Sentence to the Test

Gail Caldwell / 1987

Second of two parts. From *The Boston Globe* 30 September 1987: 81, 83. Used by permission.

Missoula, Mont.—If *The Sportswriter* suggested literary stardom for Richard Ford, this month's publication of *Rock Springs* may confirm it: His fifteen-city book tour began a week before a laudatory page-one review of the stories appeared in the *New York Times Book Review,* and there have been murmurings from the film industry. Atlantic Monthly Press has issued a first printing of 30,000 copies. In Missoula, during an interviewing session before Labor Day weekend, the phone rings so insistently—calls from producers and solicitous editors—that Ford finally unplugs it. He seems unruffled, if pleased, by all the attention, and insists that he bears no grudge about "not being an overnight-good-luck recipient."

"I don't think that when I was young and writing I got bad treatment," says Ford, or that I was particularly overlooked. I was always quite reconciled to the fact that I just had to try to be a better writer, based on the kind of reception that I got. It does feel a little queer to have the books now be reprinted, and people deciding that they're better books than they were ready to admit ten years ago.

"What a writer most wants is to be sovereign over his work. It makes some kinds of fears and dreads less heartwrenching, and leaves room for other fears and dreads, which can be useful."

The small study with the view is lined with books—V. S. Pritchett, Henry James, John Updike—and a leather recliner overlooking the rivers below. Ford calls the neglected word processor in the corner "my amanuensis"; he writes in longhand at a small, almost spartan desk. He is in the planning stages of a novel called *Wildlife,* letting images and notes accumulate before he starts to write.

"Just to write a good sentence—that's the postulate I go by," says Ford. "I guess I've always felt that if you could keep a kind of fidelity toward the individual sentence, that you could work toward the rest." It's a purist's philosophy, equally apparent in the brutal, halting dialogue of the men in *Rock Springs* or the satiny musings of Frank Bascombe in *The Sportswriter.* It probably began, says Ford, with a reverence for poetry.

"A lot of my friends were poets. And [poetry] had a huge effect on me, most of it good. It made me a really close reader, and it made me realize how close a reader can read, if he wants to. It encouraged me to really listen to my sentences, to not write them once and think that they're fine. I mean, I don't think I write the most beautiful sentences in the world. But I don't think that there's anybody who *looks* at his sentences any harder than I do."

His wife Kristina is his first reader and listener. "We sit down someplace for three weeks and she goes over it line by line," says Ford. "As I read, she reads the line. And I say, 'Does that mean what I think it means? Does that sentence sound right to you? Isn't there a beat too many in that phrase? Do you hear anything in that sentence that you don't like? Tell me what it is.'

"I think it probably takes the patience of a saint to be able to do that for somebody else. I mean, I know she loves me, but you get outside the bounds of love pretty fast, doing that . . . So she has that kind of faith."

The Fords have been married for twenty years; they met in college, where Richard was a busboy in Kristina's dormitory. Kristina is a tall, striking woman whose energy rivals that of her husband. It is clearly a partnership of great and lasting affection. "I've really been lucky," says Ford when speaking of his mother, who died in 1981. "I've been raised, really, my entire life in the presence of two strong, wonderful women." He paid tribute to his mother, Edna Ford, in a stirring memoir in *Harper's* magazine last month: *The Ultimate Good Luck* is dedicated to both women, and the other three books bear the simple inscription, "Kristina." He laughingly allows that not having children "is rule No. 1 in Ford's 16 Rules on How to Conduct a Writing Life."

For all their diversity, Ford's works share a fractured sense of family, whether the men-on-the-run of his first two novels or the eroded nuclear unit of Frank Bascombe—whose young son has recently died, who keeps a distanced accord with his ex-wife. The solitary men of *Rock Springs* have unfaithful women in their pasts or young daughters in tow; too often, they're men for whom "trouble comes cheap and leaves expensive." Weary from the blind alleys they've stumbled down, even the most inarticulate characters of the stories succumb to a dreamy contemplation of their lot in life. "Somehow, and for no apparent reason," thinks a character in "Sweethearts," "your decisions got tipped over and you lost your hold. And one day you woke up and you found yourself in the very situation you said you would never ever be in, and you did not know what was most important to you anymore. And after *that,* it was all over."

Like Flaubert, Ford may live the emotionally stable life in order to explore its fictional alternative. "If your family or your marriage is happy," he says, "one of the things you're aware of is the possibility that it might not be. That's the dark side of one kind of bliss or another: that it will suddenly or irreparably end. And I don't think you have to have it end to know what that fear is. Maybe, in fact, you have it even more vividly when you have known things to be happy, things to be solid.

"I'm always interested in what happens after the bad things happen. Most functioning, balanced people can put up with the terrible tragedies: a life ending, the death of a child. It's what happens afterwards that's interesting to me . . . because it's a proving ground for drama. That's where the whole mentality of *The Sportswriter* comes from: What do you have to make anything good of, once you've perceived how much bad can happen?

"But that's the nature of fiction: fiction's linear, it's about cause and effect, about how the past impinges on the present and makes the future."

The Sportswriter is a heartbreaking novel, as much for its possibility as its despair, but Ford contends—that play of light and dark again—that Frank Bascombe is a happy man, or at least in the process of becoming so. The skeletal framework for the novel—a fiction writer turned sportswriter—came from his own experience when he was writing for *Inside Sports* magazine.

"*The Ultimate Good Luck* had fallen through the slats so profoundly," says Ford, "that I just thought to myself, 'maybe I'm wasting my time. And so I'm going to try to do something I've wanted to do all my life,' which was to be a sportswriter.

"I got completely engulfed by what I thought was the wonderful life of being a sportswriter: traveling from city to city, staying in nice hotels, going to ball games, coming home and thinking about them and writing notes, driving around and meeting ballplayers. And I thought, 'Well, if I ever write a book about a life that was a happy life, this would surely be it.' "

It was not a new dream for Richard Ford: fresh out of college, in the mid-'60s, he'd finagled an interview for a sportswriting job at the *Arkansas Gazette.* An editor handed him a clip file and told him to write a story. "Jesus, I stayed there for hours and hours," says Ford. "I didn't know what to do. I didn't know which items went together, or why. I tried to type, and I couldn't type very well. And I slaved and finally produced something for the guy, and

I went home and he never called. I waited and waited, and I finally called back and he said, 'Oh yeah, that stuff wasn't any good. We can't hire you.' "

Ford laughs. "If they had given me that job, I never would have been frustrated enough to turn to the last thing that anybody in his right mind would turn to: writing novels."

Hindsight offers a grand irony about all this: Ford wrote a book about a man who had abandoned a fiction career; in so doing, he salvaged, even exalted, his own. "I was thinking of [giving up on fiction] very seriously," says Ford. "I think of it all the time—at the end of books, I always think about just *not doing* this anymore—because it's too hard."

That disclaimer aside, he was already working on a few of the stories in *Rock Springs* while *The Sportswriter* was under way, partly due to an editor in New York who told him the novel wasn't any good. Both works draw their strength from a heartfelt authenticity, though Ford insists that his is a truth "with a little t, which is the way most truth comes." All four books cast a sidelong glance at the modern struggle between good and evil, whether the blunted sufferings of *Rock Springs* or the resurrection metaphor of *The Sportswriter,* which takes place over the course of Easter week. Like Ford, Frank Bascombe is a lapsed Southern Protestant. His creator nonetheless pleads ignorance as to the source of the novel's religious symbolism, calling it "crazy coincidence."

"And yet," says Ford, "it also has to do with the rather complete way in which, over centuries, an organized religion can account for every goddamn thing that you do. Everything! And you start tapping into those religions, those events, and you find out how complete has been man's enterprise over centuries to circumscribe and account for *all* our impulses.

". . . I think my religious background was utterly standard, just standard, I used to go to church, sneak out and steal cars." He laughs. "Church was always the one time you could get out of the house when nobody doubted where you were going."

"I guess I have always believed that there was more to livable life than the facts of it—that there was a spirit in one's life that cannot entirely be traced to the particulars. And in a totally secular way, that is the equivalent of a religious experience. But I mean a spirit that the word *zeitgeist* has more to do with than religious love . . . Still and all, you just can't live life totally in the facts. If you do, you run aground. There has to be some sort of air that you are buoyant on, to go on living.

". . . I think that a working skepticism about the unseen is a useful thing.

But I see great art created all the time from nowhere, and all the psychologists can't finally track down where the inspiration comes from to do something wonderful. I'm willing to believe that something could be existent in the world and I not know about it. So, that's a kind of optimism right there."

Ford looks outside before he smiles. "I am a fisherman, after all. There's no more hopeful enterprise in humankind than to go out on a river where you can't see below the surface, and hope you can throw this little thing out there and catch a fish."

For all his graceful amicability, Richard Ford says he is often perceived as a dour man—one who's "usually out in the world with my dukes up." It is true that, over the span of several days, a sense of gloom can pervade his spirit as unexpectedly as a Montana thunderstorm on a sunny afternoon. But on one brilliant morning, as we climb into the Cherokee that Ford has just been driving, the radio is turned full-blast to the sounds of Pavarotti. Ford looks almost sheepish. "The arias," he murmurs apologetically, but he waits for the opera to end before adjusting the volume. And somehow, of all the conversations and self-descriptions, this is the image that takes hold: a tall, angular man in a leather jacket, listening to a soaring Pavarotti as he glides over the switchbacks of western Montana.

The Life of the Writer: Lunch with Richard Ford

Wendell Smith / 1987

From *Versus* [Vanderbilt University] October 1987: 24–28. Used by permission.

"I remember one time I was in Jackson, Mississippi. I guess I must have been about six years old. We were standing at this steam table waiting to get served and get some food. My mother said to me, 'You see that woman standing over there?' I said yes. She said, 'That's Eudora Welty.' I looked across the room. I didn't know who the hell Eudora was. But I saw this ordinary human being standing there waiting in line to get her lunch, like my mother. In my mother's voice was this wonderful kind of affection and reverence for whatever it was she knew about Eudora, which was something that I didn't know. And that duality always stayed in my mind. That you can be that that she so wonderfully is, and also a human being walking on the earth."

I waited for Richard Ford by the elevator outside the university pub for twenty minutes. I worried that perhaps he hadn't been able to find the place. It was alright though, I reasoned. He probably had some important thing to do. Finally I went inside to save a table amid the lunchtime rush, and there he was sitting alone in a chair, looking lost in the crowd. He had been waiting *inside* for twenty minutes.

We sat in the warm September sun on the pub's outside deck. He finished his chicken burrito and began to pump new meaning into the term "self-effacing." The author of one of 1986's most successful novel's, *The Sportswriter,* and a recently released volume of short stories entitled *Rock Springs,* Ford is at a point where his career is taking off like a rocket. He also seems to have mastered the duality he recognized when only six years old. With him it is easy to get beyond the writer to the human being who walks the earth.

"I can't ever forget where I started off in life, which is that I was a bonehead kid living in Jackson, Mississippi, with parents who neither one went to college. In the process of having had a good life as a writer—I've been able to work hard and it hasn't been very discouraging—nothing has ever caused

49

me to think I wasn't just exactly like everybody else. I didn't start being a writer because I thought I was a genius or because I thought I had any talent. I don't think I'm a genius and I think you'll get plenty of corroborative testimony to that. And I don't believe in talent, really, because I don't know what it is. To believe in talent to me is kind of like believing in God. I kind of believe in hard work, which is what I always started out with, and a sort of affection for language, and having been lucky enough to be moved by literature at an early age. That's all I ever start off with.

"It makes life so much easier not to think of yourself as some kind of elite. The last thing I want to be is set apart from people. I depend on people to talk to me."

Ford is a tall man with a high forehead giving way to long dark hair streaked, prematurely one feels, with grey. He has piercing pale blue eyes. He is dressed in black—a black shirt, black jeans, and black Converse tennis shoes. He speaks in the amended phrases of one who chooses his words carefully.

"Calling yourself a writer is like calling yourself an outlaw. Somebody else has to do that. It's not for me to say that I'm a writer. It's for somebody else to say that I'm a writer and when enough people have said it then I'll maybe believe that I was, and finally I did come to that conclusion because I didn't do anything else. I wrote books and they did get published and people read them, so I thought all of the stations of that cross have now been finally established, and I could say without any particular pride but just in a generic way, well what I am is a writer because that's what I do.

"I remember when I finally figured it out was when it says on your passport, 'occupation.' I finally broke down with my first passport six or seven years ago and put 'writer.' That's finally at forty-three what I am. I don't want to say that I'm a bird hunter, or I'm married, or I'm a fisherman, or I ride Harley Davidsons."

The night before Ford read a new story of his called "Optimists" to an audience at the University. He stood at the lectern in a dark blue suit. His voice had the deceptive softness of a shy person's. When he began, the crowd in the lecture hall became very still:

"All of this that I am about to tell happened when I was only fifteen years old, in 1959, the year my parents were divorced, the year when my father killed a man and went to prison for it, the year I left home and school, told a lie about my age to fool the Army, and then did not come back . . ."

The boy in the story sees his father come home from work in the railroad

yards, where he has just seen a man killed under the wheels of a train. The
father tells of helplessly watching the man, cut in three pieces, bleed to death
in front of him.

Some in the audience laughed aloud when Boyd Mitchell, a guest in the
house, responds, 'You should've put tourniquets on." Boyd goes on to indirectly blame the father for the man's death. Enraged, the father hits Boyd so
hard that it kills him.

"Conventional moral judgements have always seemed to me to be a bit
posterior to the fact." Ford drained the last of his iced tea from the cup. I
have pointed out that he seems to write about people who are helpless wit-
nesses to disaster. There is a suspension of morality afterwards, I have said.

"We all act, if we are lucky, and at our best, in a moral way. But the
judging sometimes, the actual overlay of morality is very helpless. Judging
comes after the fact, when the moral overlay is never completely clear, so
that what we have to rely on as the instance ticked by us is affection for
people, a wish not to do other people harm, and hope that those things have
the correct moral consequence. In the instance of the boy's father, hitting
Boyd is almost a kind of Billy Budd act in which morality just simply isn't
useful there. In the face of just huge bad luck and huge disaster morality was
a helpless act. What he could do to mediate between that terrible event and
himself was to fill that gap with affectionate response. That really, for me,
takes the place of conventional morality in the stories. I would hope that in
all these stories that affection is always the one possibility, the one consolation that may get you off, that may save your life.

"When he goes to the dying man and kneels down and he knows he can't
do anything for him and the guy says, 'You're in Montana. You'll be all
right.' That's obviously not true but that's as good as he could do. And
anybody would want to be told that yes, I know that's as good as you could
do."

The police take the father to jail. The story traces the dissolution of the
boy's family afterwards until the final scene, in which years later the boy,
now a man, meets his mother in a convenience store. The audience clapped
enthusiastically when Ford finished.

"Kristina [Ford's wife] and I were driving from Mississippi to Missoula,
and we stopped off at a Seven Eleven in Billings, and I went in to get a coke
and find out what time it was and look up a restaurant name in the phone
book. And I saw an Indian woman walking around in there. She was quite a
handsome woman, and she'd obviously been drinking. I looked at this woman

and she had a man with her who was over in another part of the store, and they were kind of dressed alike, but he was not an Indian and she was. My mother had recently died. And something about her reminded me of my mother, and I thought: in this place in Montana, a person could meet his mother in a place like this absolutely unexpectedly. A person could be so estranged from one's own loved parent that you would meet her in a place like this and have her not recognize you. That's all it was. When I got back in the car I took a little napkin down off the visor, and I wrote that down in my notebook. That's how it came about. So, that's the way facts ascend truth. If I can say it and have you believe it and have it seem to be true of human-kind, then that's how truth gets made."

Ford is an enemy of labels and a champion of the essential undefinability of things, himself included. He says he hates to hem himself in with terms. Perhaps a life as a writer has taught him well how narrowly words can confine their subject. Although he sometimes does not take moving well he has lived in Michigan, Mexico, Vermont, and New Jersey, and currently lives in Montana. He rejects the notion that any writing should be spoken of as regional writing, and yet one of the main strengths of his own writing is his ability to capture places down to their most essential and individual detail.

I ask him why there are so many people writing about Montana these days and at first he rejects my framing of the question. We toss out names of authors until he concedes that maybe a lot *has* been written about Montana.

"I can only speak for myself. I went out there because my wife took a job out there. I was living in Vermont and was actually quite happy to be living in Vermont. She took this job and she had to drag me kicking and screaming out there. I was writing *The Sportswriter* and wanted to be near New Jersey, where I could go down there and take a look at things, see how the sun set and what the air smelled like. She said no, no, no, let's go on to Montana.

"And so I went out there and as soon as I got there I quit writing *The Sportswriter* for six months and wrote 'Winterkill.' And there was just some-thing about the place that seized me. I didn't go out there to work. I went out there in despair thinking I would never write again. And then suddenly, I just got gripped by some impression of life there.

"Inside that big landscape, civilized life is somewhat diminished in pro-portion. You can live in the East and feel like you live in a civilized world and men control everything. If you live in Montana you're well aware that this isn't the case.

"Drama always begins for me with some sort of fundamental conflict. Of course, the Montana that I write about is somewhat made up. Every writer has his own Montana that he makes up. I think it's just a landscape full of drama. It's a life just a little bit on the edge. You're always aware of what might happen to you. It *is* the Wild West.

"We're all liable to get annihilated. Any time. And our responsibility as human beings is to live beyond that inevitable observation about life. And to try to make ourselves happy with what we have. Make yourself happy with who you love. Make yourself happy in the landscape you live in. Make yourself happy having what few desires you can be satiated.

"It's a writer's obligation and his privilege to make up the terms of drama out of the experience he sees, or she sees. I don't know if it necessarily exists in the landscape or if it exists in human affairs, as much as you perceive it to exist. You make it exist.

"I remember four or five years ago when we moved to Missoula my friend Barry Hannah was out there—he's a good pal of mine—and we started talking about motorcycles. It occurred to me that all my life I had wanted a big Harley Davidson. I said to Kristina, 'I'm going to buy a great big 1300cc Harley.' And she said, 'Why?' I said, 'Because there's nothing in my life right now that could suddenly and immediately kill me.' If things don't go along dangerously enough I'll intrude a little bit. I like to be a little bit on the edge, but I can create the illusion of being on the edge without having to be there."

Ford seems to write one book about almost every place he lives. If *Rock Springs* is Ford's collection of Montana stories and *The Ultimate Good Luck* his Mexico novel, then *The Sportswriter* is his New Jersey novel. *The Sportswriter* is a unique achievement in recent literature—an unironic novel about life in the suburbs. The narrator, Frank Bascombe, is a man who loves what life has to give him. He is determined to take more rather than less pleasure in the facts of his life.

I ask Ford how it is possible to write about someone who is happy, when drama has to stem from some kind of unhappiness. He explains that he had to create some problems for Frank Bascombe to live through, and then steer Frank through those problems. Happiness, he says, is always measured against unhappiness.

"Every place my wife wants to go I go kicking and screaming, and every place I want to go, she doesn't go kicking and screaming. She thinks any place I want to go is a great idea. I think every place she wants to go is nuts.

But I go because I love her. I'd go to hell in a handbasket if she pointed the way.

"I went to New Jersey thinking: this is the end of my writing life. There's nothing here that would interest me. When I finished writing *The Ultimate Good Luck* I'd written a couple of stories. I'd gotten to that point I always get to, which is to completely rid myself of what I was doing before, sort of get the whole of it empty.

"I started looking around for something else to write about and I found that I had lived in New Jersey for five years and that's all I knew about then. After I wrote *The Ultimate Good Luck,* which is not about much happiness at all, my wife said to me, 'Why don't you write about somebody who's happy?' So I get set about writing *The Sportswriter* with that as something of a lead. If drama can happen in New Jersey it can happen anywhere, as far as I'm concerned.

"There are lots of things to dislike about the suburbs, and the New Jersey suburbs in particular, but people don't dislike them. And that's just the truth. The suburbs have been written about ironically so often that I thought it might be a more interesting surgery on the suburbs to talk about them in unironic terms.

"In every instance of the story when I found myself having Frank judge the world I tried to ask myself, 'Is this what I really think? Is this somehow tinctured with insincerity?' When I satisfied myself each time that it wasn't then I left it. I try to find language that is adequate to what I think, and what I feel. And that's what the book was trying to do.

"I tried to see if the kinds of consolations I take from my own life can be made palpable in literature. I wake up in the morning and I wonder what good is going to happen to me, even when I suspect nothing is. Whenever I'm sitting someplace and a pretty girl comes and sits down and talks to me, I record a small triumph. Or if somebody comes and says something nice to me, I find out that I have made a little advance on the day. Those are the kind of little moments that make your life livable."

After attending college at the University of Michigan, Ford attended graduate school in creative writing at the University of California, Irvine. He has taught at Princeton University and the University of Michigan. His short stories have been published in *Esquire, The New Yorker,* and *Granta.* His novels include *A Piece of My Heart* (1976) and *The Ultimate Good Luck* (1981). I ask him how he began writing, and he pauses for a moment before answering, as if no one had ever asked him that before.

"I started writing stories in college. I was always niggling around with writing one thing or another when I was a kid, but just in the most aimless way. I did that instead of being a jock. I wrote a couple of stories in college that my teachers liked. And then I was asked by one of my teachers if I would consider going to graduate school. I said no. I wanted to go to law school. So I went to law school, and I hated law school. I was always sneaking off across the quad at Washington University to listen to Stanley Elkin talk about literature.

"And one time Kristina and I were driving to Little Rock for Christmas— she had flown down to Saint Louis to meet me from New York—and all of my books got stolen out of my car. All of my notes, everything. Right in the middle of the year. And I said, after I had calmed down in a few days, this is some sign to me here. Someone is trying to tell me something. So I went back up and I made matters worse with my professors. They all said, 'Oh, that's all right. You're doing fine in school. We'll make all these things up.' I had to say, 'No, this is horrible. This is terrible. I can't do this. This is a disaster.' I was just trying to find a way to quit. So I just quit.

"I went up to East Lansing and saw an old professor of mine. I asked him if he still thought it was possible for me to write stories. He said, 'Well, you can if you want to. You seem to be relatively good at it, for somebody who isn't good at anything else.' So I went back to New York. Kristina and I got married and we went to New York [City]. I thought about it for seven months. I thought about whether I wanted to set off on that sort of tentative, experimental life. And I thought, why not? I've got nothing to lose. I've got nothing going for me except her, and that was enough. More than enough.

"So she quit her job. We packed up all of our stuff into a van and went to California. I went to graduate school, wrote stories there, and never looked back after that. Just did it. I look back all the time in one sense. I ask myself, 'Do I have any business doing this?' But I never ask myself, 'Is this a worthwhile thing to be doing?' It *is* a worthwhile thing to be doing. To get to do what Chekhov did? To get to do what Ford Maddox Ford did? That's worthwhile to be doing, if I never get a third as good as they are. It's a life that is dignifying. Better than I deserve."

Ford is scrupulously attentive to the tools of his trade. He is aware that the integrity of his language is intimately related to the place where he lives. For him every place has a language of its own.

We are talking about hunting and fishing. I comment that it is strange in a

Southern mind to see someone who is from Mississippi and writes about
Montana. He doesn't think it is strange at all.

"It's no stranger than Joseph Conrad learning English and becoming one
of the great writers in English. His first language was Polish. I figure as long
as that's on the books my little regional switches aren't really a menace.

"I came to some of young manhood through my grandfather and my father
and his relatives taking me hunting. It always stayed in my mind as a piece
of extant past, in a way kind of immutable. I never could figure out anything
to say about it. I could never say anything about it that would cause it to be
something interesting even to myself until four or five years ago. Somehow
it began to find its way into my work, and I was pleased because it did occupy
so much of an important time in my life, and I do it now. My wife and I both
hunt and fish. I just got old enough where I ran out of the other things I
wanted to write about and finally found what to me is always the key—a
language for it.

"One of the reasons I didn't want to stay in the South was that I didn't
have much to offer from the standpoint of language. My language, I thought,
was just like everybody else's language in the South. My access to it, my
reservoirs of it, were all pretty much literary inspired. I read Faulkner. I read
Eudora Welty. I read Flannery O'Connor.

"I wanted to go off someplace where I had to make up my own language.
When I had a language which was flatter, less inflected, I found I had a
language for hunting which wasn't Southern. All of that stuff I had in reserve
waited until I had a language for it. The language of the South was all used
up. But now I have a different language that's almost my own, which is that
kind of flat, uninflected language of the Great Plains, which I love."

At the reception after Ford gave his reading, bodies were packed in close
and hot. A circle of admirers waited patiently, almost timidly, to speak with
the man himself, in his dark blue suit. Ford spoke with each person in turn,
gave autographs and listened attentively to their comments and praise. Sweat
covered his brow. Somehow the subject of Nashville came up. Nashville is a
wonderful place, he said. I introduced myself and mentioned that we were
scheduled to eat lunch together the next day. Nashville gets pretty hot this
time of year, I said. Especially when you're wearing a suit. He agreed, but
said it didn't bother him too much. I went and held the door open to let in
some fresh air, and he spoke with the next person in line.

"I guess in my militant proletarianism about writers there is a certain
willingness to not believe in praise very much, for fear that praise will take

you away from your best instincts. For a guy who's an optimist, and I am an optimist, I am an optimist with a hard exterior about things like that. The good reviews will sometimes validate something that you hoped would be true, but all you are listening to is corroborative information.

"I take the bad reviews with a lot of bad temper. I think in some ways bad reviews find their way into that little sensor of my brain that says: learn something here. Find something of use to yourself here. I take the bad reviews very personally. I write the names of the people who review me badly on a little list, for future reference. I wouldn't go after them in the paper, but I will go after them personally someday. Someday I'll be at a party and someone will say, 'I'd like you to meet Larry McMurtry.' And I'll say, 'Hello, shithead. [He raises his fist.] You want this? That's what you get. That's what you deserve.' I wouldn't say that to a guy who's a professional book reviewer, but bad reviews from other writers, they've made an enemy out of me. My ears are alert for the name of Fred Bush or Larry McMurtry. My ears are singing with those names. If somebody says, 'Hi, Fred,' I'll always turn around and see which Fred it is.

"There's not much that joins writers, but a sympathy for each others' best efforts should foreclose any kind of meanness and niggardly spirit. I just wouldn't take time out of my day to say something ill in public about another writer, so as to say to a potential reading public: 'don't bother.' Maybe they want to bother. They deserve a chance to bother. His work, her work, deserves to be read. I don't want to be the guy who says don't do it."

We leave the pub and walk across campus. He has a book signing to do in the afternoon. He loves book signings. It delights him that people will take the time to come see him.

In *The Sportswriter* Frank Bascombe speaks of living within oneself, of rejecting self-consciousness. Richard Ford would object to being termed humble, and probably wouldn't listen to whoever told him he was a humble man. Humility disappears with the arrival of self-consciousness. He calls it self-psychologizing: somehow his marvelous achievements and a complete denial of the world's opinion of those achievements coexist in the same mind.

We walk up the steps to the English Department. It is time for him to go. It must take a lot of faith to do what you do, I tell him.

Richard Ford: From Freight Yards to Fiction

Joseph Steuer / 1987

From *W* Magazine 16 November 1987: 22–23. Reprinted by permission of Fairchild Publications, Inc.

In the early sixties, down south on the Missouri-Pacific Railroad, the Union men with drinking problems bid for night jobs in the switching yards, so their boozing wouldn't be noticed, and because it was safer than being out on the road—where someone might get hurt.

In Little Rock, Ark., around the three-hour mark, some of these men would get the shakes and have to get a drink. "Wanna run this thing?" they would ask Richard Ford, who had just graduated from high school in Jackson, Miss., and was in Little Rock living with his grandparents, working a summer job before starting college.

"So at age eighteen, I was running the big switch engines around the yards in Memphis and Little Rock, Texarkana, Poplar Bluff and all those places the Missouri-Pacific went," says Ford, now forty-three.

Ford, who has for the past dozen years been building a reputation as one of the foremost writers of American regional fiction, has just published his fourth book, a collection of short stories called *Rock Springs.*

"One time, I went to sleep at the switch engine with a guy who happened not to be one of those lax tosspots, and when I woke up, I was being picked up by my seat and thrown off the engine onto the ground," says Ford in a pleasantly forceful Southern twang. He never fell asleep on the job again.

In retrospect, Ford sees his job on the railroad as the genesis of his work habits.

"I try to be as responsible to my work as I can be, and not screw around. In some ways, that has been my ethic as a writer," he says.

After pausing to chew on an ice cube in his drink, he adds, "Because I have never thought of myself as particularly brilliant." He chuckles from somewhere deep inside his throat, suddenly becomes silent, thinks for a second, and then chuckles some more.

Some critics think Ford is brilliant and are calling *Rock Springs* his best work to date. Most of the stories, which take place in and around Montana, where Ford now lives, are about people living close to the edge.

The title story is about a man who is on the run in a stolen car with his girlfriend and his child after bouncing a series of checks. "Going to the Dogs" is about a man in a trailer park planning to skip his creditors, but he is temporarily waylaid by a couple of overweight party girls.

Most of the stories involve travel and tend to result in an epiphany of sensibility rather than an action-packed climax. The characters come to understand something about themselves, "which allows them to go on living," says Ford.

In 1962, after his job with the railroad, he went off to Michigan State. The first thing he'll tell you about college: "That's where I met my wife."

If you pick up any one of Ford's four books you'll find each is dedicated to Kristina, his wife. "Yesterday," he says, "when I saw my wife walk through the door of this place where we had this book-signing party, I thought to myself, 'Wonderful.' My heart leapt," he says in an emphatic whisper.

Crossing his legs, he stares into the middle distance for a second, as if meditating on her. "I have only two things in my life that matter," he says. "Kristina first, and then there's my work."

Before they married, he tried his hand at law school in St. Louis for a year, but then quit and moved to New York, where Kristina was working for IBM and modeling. They married in 1968. Since then they have been as footloose as the characters in his stories, living in, among other places, California, Montana, and the Mississippi Delta."

"Growing up in Mississippi," he explains, "makes you aware of how much about the country you don't know. And, it always seemed to me, particularly since I have begun to write, that unless I wanted to write just about the South, which I didn't, then I ought to go out into the world and see it," he says.

The Fords, however, live a life that is religiously removed from the visible writing establishment of New York. "I just like to clear away as much clutter, as much distraction from my life as possible, so that I can get down to what is important, my work. I have just reached an age in my life where I think I should be doing my hardest work."

Ford went to graduate school at the University of California in Irvine, studying with E. L. Doctorow and poet Galway Kinnell. He published stories and his first two novels (*The Ultimate Good Luck* and *A Piece of My Heart*) and taught at Williams College and Princeton University. "Teaching was taking my time away from my writing," he says, "I was teaching people who just didn't appreciate it enough. So, finally Kristina said, 'What are you teaching for? You want to write books. I don't care if you don't have a job— I'll get a job.' That was an offer I couldn't refuse."

"We were never rich. But then we were never poor, either," says Ford, adding that grants he received from the National Endowment of the Arts and the Guggenheim Foundation helped improve his fortunes.

"Being poor isn't all that it's cracked up to be for a young artist. It just makes you cold at night and worried in the morning."

Ford is rhapsodic about his new home. "Montana. You can probably picture it, and you don't want to believe it's as wonderful as it is," he says, sounding like a mystic. "It's your dream of what a place would be like. It's open. It's beautiful. The mountains are wonderful. What interests me is how life goes on in this setting. And life goes on in Montana in fairly dramatic ways. I am always looking for and finding some kind of human drama. And that is what I write about."

Richard Ford: From Mississippi to Montana, the Author of *The Sportswriter* and *Rock Springs* Crafts Fiction from the Heartland
Casey Seiler / 1988

From *TGIF* [*The Daily Northwestern*'s weekly arts and entertainment magazine, Northwestern University, Evanston, IL] 22 January 1988: 9. Reprinted by permission.

In Missoula, Montana, it's fifty degrees and thawing under a blue sky, and Richard Ford is wishing that he was in Mississippi. Ford and his wife, Kristina, have lived all over the country—New Jersey, Montana, Michigan, and Chicago (when I describe Lake Michigan's ice-paddy appearance to him over the phone, he says "I used to hate those: they always looked like scabs to me")—but Ford grew up in the South.

"I live in Mississippi part of the year—well, I have been in the past, though this may be the first in countless years that I haven't been back. But I've lived a long period of time there. In fact, I might be going back this week if the weather doesn't improve . . ."

Reading *Rock Springs,* Ford's recently-published collection of short fiction, it's easy to understand why a warm, sunny climate might put an ominous zap on his day. Ford writes about characters whose fortunes tend to turn on subtle events or quiet emotional nuances; an unassumingly nice day is just as likely to yield either a quiet afternoon spent at home or an unwelcome threat of violence and loss.

Ford's characters are, like the author, avowed fatalists, happy enough to get through a day without turbulence or tragedy. In his highly-acclaimed 1986 novel, *The Sportswriter,* Ford dipped into three fairly uneventful days in the life of Frank Bascombe, ex-husband, ex-novelist, and a man who longs for his fair share of grace and truth in an increasingly tricky world. Bascombe's distinctive tone of guarded sensitivity—a voice that he shares with many of Ford's narrators—makes him a bracingly honest spokesman for the isolated natives of a million suburban backyards. Ford's sportwriter is a rare bird in a day when most new fiction hands over its narration to characters who are a. drug dealers, b. flesh-jaded college students, or c. both.

61

Indeed, Ford himself is a strange case in a period when the most popular novels in campus bookstores come from authors (such as Bret Ellis and Jay McInerney) barely out of school themselves. Ford, who is now forty-four, had been writing and teaching for more than ten years before the publication of his first two novels (*The Ultimate Good Luck* and *A Piece of My Heart*) by Gary Fisketjon's Vintage Contemporaries line. *The Sportswriter* subsequently earned him notices in several Best-of-'86 lists, and now *Rock Springs* has been published by Fisketjon's new imprint, Atlantic Monthly Press. It collects several of Ford's stories previously published in such journals as *Granta, Esquire,* and Northwestern's *TriQuarterly.*

Ford was born in 1944 in Jackson, Mississippi, the son of a traveling starch salesman. In his essay, "My Mother, In Memory" (published in the August '87 issue of *Harper's*), he describes his youth up to and following the death of his father in 1960; it's an event that echoes loudly throughout Ford's work, and the pivotal point in the development of the artist as a young fatalist. He writes: "He had been everything to her, and all that was naturally implicit became suddenly explicit in her life, and she was neither good at that nor interested in it. And in a way that I see now and saw almost as clearly then, she gave up."

Ford went to college at the University of Michigan at Lansing, where he majored in literature and history; he went on to spend a year in Washington University's law school before dropping out to pursue teaching and writing full time.

Although his early residency in the South marks him as a writer doomed to comparison to the run of Southern authors (from the inevitable mention of Faulkner down through Flannery O'Connor and Walker Percy), Ford—partly due to his constant moving from one region to another—has no desire to be thought of as a "regional writer," and isn't fond of seeing his books subjected to such treatment.

"I suppose I've come to understand that term as a pejorative one," he says in a friendly mid-Southern accent. "Regional literature, that comes out of a small emotional and intellectual surround, and goes out to people in an equally small emotional and intellectual surround—I never have wanted to do that. As a writer, I just try to make my work as good as it can be . . . and have it apply to the lives of a larger and larger population."

"It's really interesting when people, particularly professors, credit you for some kind of influence which, as often as not, comes from a book you haven't read."

Ford is equally sensitive to larger questions of his literary "debts." This is understandable, as casual readers tend to have a knee-jerk Hemingway response when faced with many of Ford's stories—*Rock Springs* is thick with hunters, fishermen, and bar-room talk—while missing the fact that the two writers share little in terms of voice and compassion.

"That's a question that I would just as happily forget," he says. "I mean, I'm forty-four, but I didn't read anybody more than anyone else. You know, you write one book based on your past, and all of the things that you do up to the point that you write that book, and anything else you have to craft in fiction, you pretty much have to confect out of whole cloth.

"And no, you never get past the point (of being influenced); I think that everything that you read that's good makes a stamp on you. It's just no longer a *burden* for me . . .

"I think it's quite often true of writers—particularly novelists—that they're in a constant state of re-inventing themselves. Partly through the agency by which they get ready to do it, to make it possible for the person to sit down and write the next book—who is inevitably going to be different from the person who wrote the last one."

The past two years have seen Ford begin to receive the attention reserved for a major comer in American fiction. Along with his well-received earlier novels, *Rock Springs* has received glowing reviews (including a front-page review of the collection in the *New York Times' Review of Books*). One mention that Ford could live without was his positioning on *Esquire*'s grandiloquent "Literary Universe" chart in last year's annual summer fiction issue (Ford was mentioned as a "Rising Star," part of the "Montana Crowd," and on the client list of his agent). The writer could not have been less flattered.

"My name was on it a lot, and I remember somebody wrote, 'Don't get mad if you don't find your name on it.' Well, how about if you're mad that you did? (*laughs*) It's just not a dignifying position to be in . . . It's dignifying to a notion of human beings who are trying to practice their vocation as best then can, but then suddenly there's to be a pecking order, a ranking, and a quasi-mystical universe that we all occupy.

"That's totally anathema to what we do: it's anti-art, and anti-literature. And it doesn't, for instance, take into account the most brilliant writer in the world who's *about* to publish his best novel, who could really change a lot of reader's minds—but then there's that *chart* . . ."

It's no surprise, then, that Ford chooses not to name his favorite contemporary writers: "I'd be nervous about forgetting somebody," he says. "It's enough for me to believe that it's a wonderful time to be a writer, all across the board. To have a list of favorites, in a way, puts me right back into the ballpark with those people who want to make literary gods."

He takes a similarly egalitarian tone when discussing the fact that he shares publishers with other Vintage/Atlantic Monthly writers (most notably Jay McInerney) who fall under the much-maligned heading of "Yuppie Fiction."

"Well, that's somebody else's term," he says. "I'm the only one who breathes my breath. After a while, all those arbitrary terms—they never fit, but after a while, they just have no effect."

He does not believe that any affluent, college-educated business class is responsible for the recent upsurge in trade fiction, and likewise rejects the notion that the short story has become a "rediscovered form." "It may be," he says, "that for a moment the clouds passed from before the face of the sun, and editors realized that they could make a buck from it."

Richard Ford seems, in fact, to have little interest in the politics or economics of publishing, and no interest at all in the rhetoric of criticism. He sees himself as a craftsman like any other, who tends to shy away from the trite or demeaning aspects of his trade.

While discussing male/female relationships in his work (*The Sportswriter* was criticized by certain feminists), Ford makes it clear that such ideologies play little part in the writing: "The one thing that I have to give to all my male or female characters is the best line I have for them to speak, and the best lines that I've got to say about them. For me, there isn't any substantive difference between men and women in my stories. Now there is, of course, the biological difference . . . but I don't write 'men's fiction,' as opposed to 'women's fiction'—it's American fiction."

Ford takes pains to make it clear that he is, in the end, a classicaly regular guy who, in his own words, "worked hard and liked literature." He was not the seventh son of a literary ancestry, or a young prodigy bursting from the blocks of best-sellerdom; nor was he the product of any turbulence beyond that felt by the average forty-odd-year-old American.

"I never think in terms of metaphor," he says, when I mention one possible reading of the moment from one of his stories. "I think the difference is that I wrote it and you read it, and the fact of my writing it forever colors it for me in a certain way . . .

"But when the drums and Roman candles go off in my mind, it's always because of something rather smallish. Small, nice, pleasing moments."

"The important thing for me to think about, and to say to you," he says later, "is that to be a writer in this country is not to exist in a particularly specialized air. Read what you read, like what you like, don't what you don't—just like everybody else."

"Poet of Everyday Life" Has a Romantic Side

Paul Grondahl / 1988

From the *Times Union* [Albany, NY] 10 February 1988: C3. Reprinted by permission.

If the truth be known, Valentine's Day has a lot to do with Thursday's reading by novelist and short story writer Richard Ford at State University of Albany's Writers Institute.

Ford, it turns out, is a fool for love.

Next month, Ford—author of the acclaimed story collection *Rock Springs* and the novel, *The Sportswriter*—celebrates his twentieth wedding anniversary with his wife, Kristina.

"At least I did one thing right in my life," Ford quips. He was speaking by telephone from a hotel room at the University of Michigan where he was talking to students and renewing friendships made during his time there as an assistant professor.

Ford kicks off the spring visiting writers series at the Writers Institute. He will read one of his stories from *Rock Springs* Thursday at 8 p.m. in the Recital Hall of the Performing Arts Center on SUNYA's uptown campus. The event is free and open to the public.

Ford is really doing Cupid's work on his visit out here.

"This was a great opportunity to come East and find my wife the perfect anniversary gift," says Ford, who lives in Missoula, Mont. "I don't know what I'm going to get her yet, but I can only get it in New York, I think."

One would hardly guess Ford is the romantic, sentimental type, given his writing.

He has been called "the prose poet of everyday life of personal desperation" and his characters often are trapped in painful, purposeless relationships amid contemporary junk culture in a landscape littered with loneliness and broken dreams.

Yet out of this wasteland of 1980s angst, where life seems to have lost its meaning, Ford fashions a timeless art that has earned him a newfound following that has made him a major American fiction writer.

Michiko Kakutani of the *New York Times* called Ford "one of the most compelling and eloquent storytellers of his generation."

With the recent publication of *Rock Springs* by Atlantic Monthly Press, Ford, at age forty-three, reached a certain level of celebrity with glowing reviews and splashy cover spreads like the ones in the *Boston Globe* and the *New York Times Book Review.*

But Ford shuns the bright lights, big city of literary fame that could be his for the asking.

Instead, he lives on a ninety-acre spread on the outskirts of Missoula with his wife, who is director of the Montana Public Policy Institute, two Brittany spaniels, a fishing boat, assorted shotguns and fly rods.

It's not exactly the cultural capital of the world, Missoula.

In fact, if you dial the home telephone number for Ford listed on his curriculum vitae you reach Don Tripp's Wholesale Lumber in Missoula (a digit was inadvertently transposed on the resume).

"I live where I live because that's what fuels my work," says Ford, who has frequently been lumped in with Southern writers because he grew up in Mississippi and sets some of his stories in that locale.

He and his wife still maintain a home in the Mississippi Delta, where they spend winters so they can escape the brutal weather of Montana and also so he can fish and hunt ducks.

"I grew up in cities, so ever since I was in my late twenties, I've wanted to live someplace where I could walk outside and where I could keep bird dogs," Ford says.

But Ford's writing is not rooted in any geographical location. The settings for his books seem to change as his addresses do.

His first novel, *A Piece of My Heart,* published in 1976, was set in Mississippi. His third, *The Sportswriter,* 1986, is set in the Northeast, concerns a *Sports Illustrated*-type sportswriter, and was written following Ford's two years as lecturer and the George Perkins Fellow in the Humanities at Princeton University. Most of the stories in his latest book, *Rock Springs,* are set in Montana.

It is this story collection that has put the stamp of genuine article on Ford's writing and sent book reviewers scurrying for similes and superlatives.

Jonathan Penner in the *Washington Post* wrote: "One by one, these stories are fresh and free as new snow on the Clark Fork. . . . Richard Ford's stories are as candid as daylight, as inevitable as noon. Experience was never more closely observed. Nor was language ever more comfortable than the first-person voice prevailing here. You believe every word."

Carolyn See in the *Los Angeles Times* compared Ford's fiction to "a wave of prose as lurid and brilliant as the obligatory red neon that delineates small-town liquor stores in the Kansas winter-wheat belt."

Ford's hopes for how his writing is received are much more modest. "If I publish a book into the world, it just makes me very glad when people read it," he says. "My books have had a nice readership of late and that's all I care about. Nobody's printing t-shirts with my name on it."

Ford owes much of his recent good fortune to publishing whiz Gary Fisketjon, who founded Vintage Contemporaries and brought out Ford's books in those well-promoted, finely produced trade books of contemporary fiction with the slick graphics and striking covers. They've also been drubbed as "Yuppiebacks."

"I hope to die with my books in print with Vintage," says Ford, cutting short the suggestion they're aimed at Yuppies. "That's just stupid with a capital 'S.' It's a good scheme to get good books to readers. I don't know what else publishing is other than that."

Ford has since moved with Fisketjon over to Atlantic Monthly Press.

Ford doesn't do many readings like his SUNYA visit. "I never really got asked that much," he says, emphasizing that he's not a performer. "I've been bored so silly with poets yakking on about their work that I don't talk about anything. I just read. And my wish in reading a story is to speak it in a simple way, not to dramatize."

For the most part, Ford says, "My having any luck as a writer came after so many years I got accustomed to staying at home and I kind of like it."

At home in Missoula, he'll take pencil and paper and sit down from 8:30 a.m. to 5 p.m., and often again at night after a break, writing his stories.

"Writing is really all I have to do and I'm at the middle point of my life and I feel as though I should seize the time," he says.

When he needs a break, he'll get on the phone with his "very best friend," Raymond Carver, the short story writer and a resident of the Northwest.

Or he'll grab his fly rods and hike down to the trout stream he can see meandering below his house. Or he'll daydream about the kennels he wants to build so he can get more bird dogs.

But mostly, he gets his Brittanys and his shotguns and drives over to the property for which he holds a hunting lease, east of the divide, and shoots pheasant, grouse and partridge.

That's Big Sky country and it seems to possess all the magic Richard Ford's fertile imagination may ever need.

Ford Rejects Sentiment in Landscapes

Greg Booth / 1989

From the *Grand Forks Herald* [ND] 14 April 1989: 1B–2B. Reprinted by permission.

Two things matter to Richard Ford.

"I've been married to the same girl twenty-three years, and I write stories," the forty-five-year-old writer said.

It matters less to him that he lives in Missoula, Mont., or that he often goes south for the winter.

"I grew up in the '60s, and I'm a little suspicious about sentimentality in landscape," said Ford, whose latest book is *Rock Springs,* short stories set in the West.

Ford's characters, while not always shining examples, wonder about the lives of others. A character in *Rock Springs* even addresses the reader, wondering about the reader's thoughts.

"On the small level of life that I lead, I do champion human life," Ford said Monday.

Ford's stories don't always have definitive endings. In the story "Great Falls," Ford writes, "Things seldom end in one event."

"Fiction, by being a linear form, is about a linear sense of consequence," Ford said. "One way art lies about life is it makes endings to stories. Human life seems to have closure. One of the important things to know is it doesn't. I wrote, 'Things don't end because one man dies.' I've always tried to accommodate that."

Ford said his writing is often "a random accumulation of materials," and he tries to make his stories "as full as I can make them."

The Sportswriter, his 1986 novel, "seems like a big book," he said, though "it's not dedicated to some model of efficiency." When he began writing it, he said, "I thought, 'I'm not sure what I've got here.' "

His books are all quite different, Ford said. "I try to accommodate myself to find a form for the various stimuli that come along."

Ford will edit the *Best American Short Stories* collection next year, and is working on a novella.

Ford didn't read books much when he was young, in part because he was dyslexic. "I didn't start reading books until I got to college," he said.

Even now, he reads slowly.

"I read things I know will feed me. I don't read for pleasure. I go at reading hungrily, to learn things about the world. If I get in a bind, I'll go read Joseph Conrad or Ford Madox Ford. I like books about matters of life and death, and I like American writers."

Ford doesn't like book reviews, and his reading list comes from friends' recommendations and new books by authors he's liked in the past. He says he has opinions on contemporary writers, but doesn't like to drive anyone away from a book.

"If somebody reads a book and gets pleasure out of it, then literature's purpose is served," he said.

Man of Many Words: Writer Finds Himself Telling of Drifting Souls

Michael Sion / 1989

From the *Reno Gazette-Journal* 29 April 1989: 1D–2D. Reprinted by permission.

Richard Ford's stories deal with that rootless subculture of the West: the people you see every day in the cities and towns which scarcely interrupt the vastness of our region—driving pickups; drinking too much; getting divorced; going from job to job, town to town, and wondering how life ever got this crazy.

Folks—in fact—as itinerant as the Jackson, Miss.-born Ford himself, who had lived and written in the South, the northeast, and Mexico. But he only gained real literary success after writing short stories set in his adopted Montana.

Stories of families disintegrating through infidelity and *wanderlust;* of devil-worshiping bikers and disillusioned Vietnam vets; and of out-of-work, out-of-luck barflies fishing in the fog.

Via the stories, Ford, who is primarily a novelist, has gained critical acclaim and a wide readership this decade.

But he didn't set out by design to write them.

As Ford, forty-five, tells it, his wife, Kristina, was supporting him financially in 1983. When she landed a job as city planning director in Missoula, Mont., Ford headed west from Vermont where he had been working on his third novel, *The Sportswriter.*

Once in Montana, he started writing about the drifting souls of the West.

The stories were published in top magazines like *Esquire* and *The New Yorker.* And what resulted from the collection, *Rock Springs* (Atlantic Monthly Press, 1987; now in paperback from Random House's Vintage Contemporaries), was that Ford became something more than a fortyish writer with three tepid-selling novels and an unproduced screenplay under his belt.

He became, in fact, established as one of America's leading writers.

Critics chirped a chorus of praise. Joyce Carol Oates, for example, wrote, "Richard Ford is a born storyteller with an inimitable lyric voice, and *Rock Springs* is the very poetry of realism."

But despite his recent acceptance by the literati, and the ability to now support his wife, Ford, a straight-talking purist with a mild Mississippi drawl, still describes himself as "a lifelong amateur."

"I don't have an enlarged sense of myself," he says by phone from his rustic Missoula home, where he is working on a novella set in 1959 about a man returning home after fighting a forest fire.

The literal meaning of "amateur" really fits Ford when he says he has no more short stories in the offing, despite their big success.

"I have to please myself here—and that has nothing to do with satisfying a need for my stories," Ford says.

It comes down to a choice he made at the outset.

Oakley Hall, recently retired chairman of the creative writing program at the University of California at Irvine, remembers that Ford's life—as with the characters in his stories—had taken an irretractable turn in 1970.

Ford had an English degree from Michigan State University, had been mustered out of the Marines because of hepatitis, had taught a year, tried law school another year, and finally—realizing he wouldn't be good at anything else—threw all other ambitions out the window to live the writing life, and enrolled at UC-Irvine.

Hall, who is also a founding director of the Squaw Valley Writers Conference, says Ford's early potential has been fulfilled with the stories in *Rock Springs,* and that writing students are now studying Ford.

But while Hall lauds Ford's talent for writing of "the great dispossessed of the country," Ford himself testily defies categorization.

His work bears him out.

The first novel, *A Piece of My Heart,* published in 1976, was cited for carrying overtones of Faulkner's Dixie, and was set in the swampy Mississippi Delta and dealt with a sex-obsessed construction worker and a bored law student.

The Ultimate Good Luck, published in 1981, was a taut, Hemingwayesque action story of drug smuggling in Mexico. *The Sportswriter,* published in 1986, is an introspective, first-person narrative of a thirty-eight-year-old magazine sports scribe and failed novelist named Frank Bascombe, living in New Jersey suburbia and trying not to care too much about life.

Ford admits some acquaintances have criticized him for being presumptious in his writing. For unlike the chewed-up divorcees and cuckolds of *Rock Springs,* Ford has been faithfully married to the fair-haired Kristina, a former model, for twenty-one years. And Ford has never gone in for the occupations his adult characters are often stuck with—low-wage waitressing in diners, gritty seasonal labor, petty thievery.

Ford responds that hard knocks for their own sake never got anyone anywhere.

"Well, I've never understood where being down on your luck's been any good. You make your own luck," he says. "I never thought it'd make me a better writer."

In a similar vein, he turned down a chance to teach full-time on the faculty of the University of Michigan, realizing that it would only be trading time for money.

Instead, he seems to find the artist's reward in creating a powerfully resonant sentence.

During the interview, Ford flips to page 233 of the paperback edition of *Rock Springs,* and reads just such a line from the story "Communist":

"And I could hear geese, white birds in the sky, flying."

Ford repeats the line.

"That's a phrase to me, that's worth a lot," he says.

"Money is not the thing any of us is on the earth to aspire to. I never thought about money in my life."

Richard Ford: Despite the Dark Strain in His Work, the Footloose Author Says He Is an Optimist

Molly McQuade / 1990

From *Publishers Weekly* 18 May 1990: 66–67. Reprinted by permission.

In Richard Ford's fiction, characters wince at a painful moment, extract its grudging truth, and scramble to survive. Ford, whose fourth novel, *Wildlife,* is due out next month from Atlantic Monthly Press, writes about "the smaller lives," their redeeming aches, and the luck or grit his people need to know themselves.

"I'm an optimist," Ford insists, but is rueful about what he calls, with amused chagrin, his "solemnity." It is something that permeates his stories and novels and also makes its presence felt in the author's soft-spoken yet hard-bitten Southern drawl. "I would rather be the guy who says 'I'm happy,' " Ford avows, "but I'm not much of a hoper. Rather than hope, I try to do something."

Since 1968, doing something has meant writing, and it came about fairly innocently. "When I decided to write, it wasn't larky, yet it was quixotic," Ford says. "I didn't have any notions of making a life out of it. I had the idea of writing stories, one at a time." Briefly a law student at Washington University in St. Louis, he had grown dissatisfied with the "answers" the law prescribed. Having been away for a spell from his home in the South—he was raised a salesman's son in Jackson, Miss., and Little Rock, Ark.—and separated from his Michigan State University sweetheart, Kristina Hensley, whom he later married, Ford felt "itchy and curious." So he left the place where he was living and changed his life.

"Turning my life toward writing books was a pretty strenuous turn. I was wrenched around," Ford concedes. But by temperamental decree, the man seems to need to move. He has been called "peripatetic" with a swaggering romanticism that Ford fights shy of, claiming that such talk is "very tedious to me. I don't think I'm restless. I live in the U.S., and wherever I am, I am." (These places have included New York City, Chicago, Ann Arbor, Princeton,

Missoula, and now New Orleans.) Protesting that "your preconceptions about a place are not exactly what happens," he explains his roving by stating, "I need to be certain that I have new stimulus. New places give me something I can use." But the self-described fatalist grew up with "an awe of the unknown" that may have predisposed him to rapid transits. His awe, Ford says, "was useful. There were a lot of things I didn't understand, and I got accustomed to living with that. I discovered that the virtue of writing can extinguish the vice of ignorance."

Ford swears that "I wasn't an extraordinary young man at all, and I didn't strive to be. I liked to write because I could do it by myself." But he acknowledges the help he got—and the salutary boot out the door he received—from such mentors as E. L. Doctorow, with whom he studied at the University of California at Irvine, earning an M.F.A. in 1970.

Doctorow proved a useful teacher because, Ford says, he taught his students that once class ended, they had to make their own way in the world. "It seems like you're getting left out in the cold, yet you're supposed to be left out in the cold—and get your work done." A popular writing instructor himself at Princeton, Williams College, and the University of Michigan during the '70s, Ford quit in 1981 because his yen for "the cold"—and his wish to concentrate his energies on writing—got the better of him.

"I was always a hard worker when I was young, and my ethic was to work hard at writing. But to make literature your life's habit is a fairly fragile habit," Ford observes. "You get to the point where you're doing it the best you can, and then you can't do much else. It's like walking down a road that gets narrower and narrower. As you get further out on that limb, it becomes precarious, but writing is a precarious life—and all life is precarious." Or, as a character in Ford's acclaimed short story collection *Rock Springs* [Atlantic Monthly Press] puts it, "The most important things of your life can change so suddenly, so unrecoverably, that you can forget even the most important of them and their connections, you are so taken up by the chanciness of all that's happened and by all that could and will happen next."

Ford broods, "Writing is the only thing I've done with persistence, except for being married to Kristina—and yet it's such an inessential thing. Nobody cares if you do it, and nobody cares if you don't. And the way you 'make yourself up' to be the author of your books, especially when you're young, depends on the stars coming into alignment. Life tugs at you. It's not as if there's a profession for writers out there; there isn't even a fraternity. You may have friends who are writers, but they can't write your books. I don't think writers have careers—my work doesn't exist separately from my life." Ford's first book was *A Piece of My Heart,* brought out by Harper & Row in 1976, and nominated for the Ernest Hemingway Award for Best First Novel. *The Ultimate Good Luck* followed five years later; *The Sportswriter* was published in 1986. *Rock Springs* came out in 1987. All have been issued in trade paperback by Vintage.

As he has roamed, so have Ford's books. *A Piece of My Heart* was hailed by the *Boston Globe* as a Faulknerian "collision course with destiny set in the swamp-ridden Mississippi Delta." *The Ultimate Good Luck,* called by one critic "a bruiser of a novel replete with gun-metal dialogue and drug deals gone sour," takes place in Oaxaca, Mexico, and was completed while the Fords were living in Cuernavaca and Yahualica. *The Sportswriter* has New Jersey as its locale; Ford came to know Princeton well while teaching there. The backdrop of *Rock Springs* and *Wildlife* is Montana, where Ford moved in 1983 when his wife accepted a job as planning director of Missoula.

While Ford has changed addresses often, much of *The Sportswriter* and some of *Rock Springs* were written in a house in the Mississippi Delta, one of Ford's longtime favorite spots despite his reluctance to be classed as a Southern writer. Jackson, Miss., his boyhood home, continues to hold his affection—as does Jackson resident Eudora Welty—and many of his relatives are in northwestern Arkansas. Though Ford's attachment to Mississippi may be circumstantial (his parents settled there because it was located at the center of his father's sales territory), his ties to the South are such that his 1987 Mississippi Academy of Arts and Letters' Literature Award came as a special pleasure. Still, regardless of where he is, Ford aims "to write a literature that is good enough for America."

But no literature can be good enough for everyone. Ford recalls, with impenitent cheer, the reaction of "a famous New York editor" to the first hundred pages of *The Sportswriter,* later to sell upwards of 50,000 copies: "He told me I was wasting my life." Ford concludes, "I got bit there. But you'll always get bit." When his publisher, Simon & Schuster—for whom Morgan Entrekin had acquired *The Sportswriter* before leaving S & S—requested changes in the novel, Ford resisted. Gary Fisketjon, then at Random House, now Ford's editor at Atlantic—and soon to join Knopf—finally acquired the book as a Vintage Contemporaries Original. Agent Amanda Urban's entreaty—"You need a book that's going to do well"—was thus satisfied.

Not all critical response to *The Sportswriter* was ardent, but sportswriters made their enthusiasm known, writing fan letters to Ford (who, after college, had hoped to be a sportswriter for the *Arkansas Gazette*). Their testimonials? " 'I lay in bed with my wife and we read your book back and forth for a month," reports the author bashfully. "It hasn't made me rich, but it's made me read." Somewhat less gratifying was critic James Wolcott's fierce sally at Ford's accomplishments to date in the August 1989 issue of *Vanity Fair.* Deemed "a totally nasty piece of work" by Ford's publisher, "Guns and Poses: A Revisionist View of Richard Ford, the Lauded Novelist" was read by Kristina Ford, who told her husband not to try it. After letting fly with a few choice bits of invective, Ford philosophizes, "There are certain things that people are going to say about you that you can't redeem—you have to get used to it."

It was easier to get used to the praise of *Rock Springs* offered by such critics as the *New York Times*'s Michiko Kakutani, who cited his "wholly distinctive narrative voice . . . that can move effortlessly between neat, staccato descriptions and rich, lyrical passages," and novelist John Wideman, who lauded the way Ford fashioned a "concentrated, supple, ironic" prose style from "everyday speech."

In fact, some of the credit for that style should go, Ford says, to the poets he has read and admired over the years. Once merely "mysterious" to Ford, poetry became clarified when "I saw people doing it"—James Wright, Galway Kinnell, Gregory Orr, Charles Wright, Donald Hall. "I saw how useful it could be to exercise such care over phrases and utterances and lines." In his own sentences Ford seeks a comparable "level of intensity, an economy of language and maximum effect."

Ford's "maximum effect" will soon extend to film; he has just finished wrapping up post-production work on *Bright Angel,* an adaptation of two stories (and a new one) from *Rock Springs.* Starring Sam Shepard and Valerie Perrine, the movie was directed by Michael Fields and shot on location in Montana.

Also an essayist, Ford recently served as guest editor of Houghton Mifflin's forthcoming *Best American Essays 1990.* With typically gentle self-mockery, he recalls trying to say no to his first essay assignment, from Rust Hills of *Esquire.* The year was 1983, the magazine's fiftieth-anniversary issue was in the planning stages, and Hills approached Ford with the idea of writing a piece on Faulkner, Hemingway, and Fitzgerald. "Oh, you're making a big mistake," Ford dodged. "That's just an opportunity to hang myself." "Well," Hills countered, "you've been likened to Faulkner, you've been likened to

Hemingway, you've been likened to Fitzgerald." Besides, he added, "Philip Roth turned it down."

Other recent projects include Ford's introduction to *Juke Joint,* a collection of photographer-friend Birney Imes's work to be published in July by the University Press of Mississippi. And in January Ford was recognized for his lifetime achievements with an American Academy and Institute of Arts and Letters Award for Literature.

So he sits and works in his New Orleans townhouse, where the crime of the French Quarter is "scary." With his reputation as a "tough guy"—hotly disputed by Ford himself—and as a skillful evoker of male voices and violence, perhaps it's not surprising to hear Ford talk of a recent near-fistfight. "This man was threatening to beat up his girlfriend in front of our house. I just kind of stepped out the door and asked him to quit. So there we were, nose to nose. And the police came and wanted to arrest me. We settled it, though." Ford pauses. "Maybe I am a primitive and don't know it." He hunts and fishes "to forget about what's bugging me, because my father and grandfather did it, because Kristina likes to do it," and for the fun of raising bird dogs.

"Writers' lives are such pedestrian affairs," Ford complains. "You want to mine out everything you can, but then broaden your ways. In an effort to be demanding on myself, I create an aura of difficulty, in which things won't turn out right. But I would like language to be, in some secular way, redemptive. Writing is an act of optimism: you make a thing, make it well, give it to someone, and it has a use. They need it—though they didn't know they did."

Q and A . . . with Richard Ford
Terry Everett / 1990

From *The Clarion-Ledger* [Jackson, MS] 10 June 1990: 3F. Reprinted
by permission.

Delta State University English professor Terry Everett interviewed Jackson
native Richard Ford—who now lives in New Orleans—about his new novel
Wildlife. Ford, who has won numerous awards for his work, is the author of
A Piece of My Heart, Rock Springs, The Ultimate Good Luck and *The Sportswriter*.

Q: What do you think you accomplished in *Wildlife* that you had not
accomplished in your previous work?
A: I think once I finished writing those stories in *Rock Springs*—*Wildlife*
takes up some of those same concerns—I really wanted to write a longer
trajectory. I felt like those stories, even as I have high regard for them myself,
opened up certain kinds of necessities in me to continue the lives of the
characters longer. And novel length seemed appropriate, in order to be able
to extend these lives to a point of complete resolution, particularly regarding
human family relationships. I wanted to write something about a family that
came apart and came together again.

Q: Does *Wildlife* in any way grow out of the materials you are working on
for your forthcoming essay on your father?
A: I don't think so, unless it is that one of the challenges to writing this
essay is myself—to find a language that is apt for the kinds of affection that
I felt for him, him whom I only knew until the time I was sixteen and he was
fifty-four. How do you express love for a man you didn't know as well as
you would have known him another six months? So, an incomplete father-
hood sort of bournes a very complete affection. How do I find a vocabulary
for that? Well, for me, the form of the essay is the appropriate rhetorical
strategy because I'm trying to find that vocabulary.

Q: How's that coming along?
A: Actually, it's coming along slowly, but I have had these other things
that have gotten in the way. But it's always easier to write about my family,

79

my parents, when I'm living in the South. And New Orleans is sort of the South, as we all know.

Q: Sort of.

A: It's very far south, but in some ways the Delta is much farther south.

Q: Percy tried hard to take it out of the South, but he didn't succeed. Speaking of those other things that have taken up your time, I've learned that you've written another play.

A: Well, I haven't written another play. I should have written another play. I owe the Actor's Theatre of Louisville a play, and I fully intend to write it. It's just that with moving down here from Montana in the last year and being really in the grip of this book until February, I just didn't have time, and also, you know, I wrote a movie.

Q: What's happening to it?

A: Oh, it's ready to go. It'll be released in the fall.

Q: We can look for it?

A: Well, I'll go see it. I'm determined that I'll go see it in a moviehouse. I don't want to be the guy that gets a special screening. I want to see it next to my fellow Americans.

Q: What else is in the works?

A: I'm gonna write, if I live long enough, a sequel to *The Sportswriter,* to be called *Independence Day.* I've been doing what I do with books, which is to say, I sort of conceive a long time in advance that I want to write such a book. I was impressed with the fact that I still had language for a book that I thought would be like *The Sportswriter.* So I have been making copious notes for almost two years now. I think maybe at the end of this calendar year I'll have time to really direct myself toward it and do that. I think it will take a while. While I only took from start to finish of the first draft of *Wildlife* from October to the following June, I really think *Independence Day* will take longer. It's a bigger book.

Q: I know you've spent a lot of time in New Orleans over the years and it's one of your favorite places. How does it feel to be living there?

A: It actually feels just exactly the way I thought it would, which is to say because I have been here so long and so many times, it feels very ordinary, which I like. And I don't feel I'm living in an exotic world that care forgot. I feel like I'm living in an American city which is close to where I'm from

and where I like it. You know all we do basically here is work. So, I don't
have much of a sense of the city that's different from the old sense I've ever
had. I haven't discovered new things about the city. It could very well be I
won't live here long enough to discover new things about it. I have this
yearning to move back up to the Delta, and I have a very clear sense that I
will.

Q: I remember you did awfully good work while living at Coahoma.

A: And I also had an awfully good time. I loved living there. I think if the
truth be told that we moved away in part because we were so comfortable
there.

Q: Ah! That's an extraordinarily interesting remark.

A: We got along so well there. We liked it so well. I think that at least at
that time in my life I needed a little strife. Oh, boy, I found it.

Q: To shift ground, I liked your tribute to Kristina in the June *Esquire.*

A: It was an opportunity to write a little love letter to her. That's what it
was. I felt sheepish about doing it in one way. I didn't want it, as I said in the
essay itself, to seem to be bragging. You can't really be said to be bragging
because you love your wife. But on the other hand, she does so much for me,
and is, in addition, quite apart from me, such a wonderful girl. There really
isn't opportunity enough for me in my life to express that.

Q: I've heard you and Kristina talk about how you worked together sometimes on the final draft of *The Sportswriter.* Did *Wildlife* work that way?

A: Oh, yeah! You know we moved into this house without any furniture,
and I read all of *Wildlife* to her, sitting upstairs in a lawn chair and on the
floor. The house was completely empty for practically the entire months of
January and February. So, we just did it day after day after day after day. We
were living in some friends' house down the street—some friends from Jackson—and we would sleep down there and then we'd come up here every day
and work on the book as long as it took.

Q: So, she helped you find "surprise" words?

A: Oh, yeah! She let me read things over and over. And she read things
over and over. We just did things that we've always done. I have no sense
that a book is finished until I've done that. That's what finished means to me,
when I can read it to her and be reconciled with her about that book.

Q: Several of your works, "Empire" and now *Wildlife,* beautifully present a wisdom about how strong, but wounded people can move beyond crises in their lives. Isn't this the heart of your tough-minded optimism?

A: I think so. I'm glad you say optimism. It is, to me, optimism. Bad things come to everybody. We don't get out of it. And the real important, the real interesting optimistic side of all bad things, is what we do in consequence of them. And, for me, I think if I could find satisfying drama in other kinds of events besides human crises I would be happy to find them. But I don't really. I'm always waiting for matters of life and death to arise and then see what we do as human beings. For me as a writer, I want to see what I can say as a writer, make people say, make them think as a consequence of human acts.

Writing Now a Way of Life

Linda Quigley / 1990

From *The Tennessean* [Nashville, TN] 20 June 1990: 1E–2E. Copyrighted by *The Tennessean.* Reprinted by permission.

Richard Ford is often compared to Ernest Hemingway, but his hero is Eudora Welty.

He's a novelist and short story writer who takes his work very seriously, but he's profiled in the July issue of the trendy fashion magazine, *Mirabella.*

His work is also coming to your neighborhood theater, starring the ever-so-sexy Sam Shepard. The film, *Bright Angel,* based on Ford's original script, is due out later this year.

And *Wildlife,* his fourth novel, is getting "probably the best reviews of any book I've every done, but it also got a couple of very perplexing kicks in the ass, too," he said in a telephone interview from Jackson, Miss., his boyhood home and now a stop on his promotional tour for *Wildlife.*

So, as *Mirabella* suggested, Ford's "career, of late, certainly seems to have reached a state of grace." If that's true, he's got a good life, because "writing for me is not a career, it's a life.

"All I hoped when I was twenty-four and starting was that when I was forty-six I'd be doing something that I liked and married to the same girl, and I've got that," he said. "Life throws you too many uncertainties, and I don't have wide, expansive plans."

He does, of course, plan to keep writing, with *Independence Day,* a sequel to *The Sportswriter,* his third novel, in the planning/writing stages. He said he's "going to write some stories and a couple of essays between now and the end of the year."

He expects to continue his life with Kristina, his wife of twenty-two years. She's an urban planner, "who makes my life seem worth living—that's why I dedicate all my books to her."

She's also a buddy in his active outdoor life—one of the qualities that sparks comparisons with Hemingway. (But, he told one reporter, "I don't hunt dear—I don't own a rifle. I know certain journalists have made me out to be a guy who likes to bite the heads off chickens, but I'm really not even much of a meat eater.")

83

If Kristina brightens his life, she also brightens the work that is so much a part of his life. "When I was writing the first two books (*A Piece of My Heart* and *The Ultimate Good Luck*) . . . they were darker visioned books.

"When I wrote *The Ultimate Good Luck,* a *Newsweek* reviewer said he thought I wasn't getting into the humors. I paid attention. I had been going along looking for drama. If a thought worked its way into my mentality that said darkness for its own sake is sufficient to hang a book on, I did.

"About that same time, my wife said, 'Why don't you write about somebody who's making a happy life?"

He's done that in *Wildlife,* set in Montana in 1960 and told, later, in the words of Joe Brinson, who was sixteen that summer when his father, a small-time golf pro, lost his job and went off to fight a forest fire, and his mother "met a man named Warren Miller and fell in love with him."

It is a book, according to its publisher, that "reveals the world just as it is: not an easy place, but not necessarily a bad one."

To write this book, Ford said, "I had to develop beyond my early efforts, to learn that literature is in some small way consoling and redemptive."

And, most of all, literature is acceptable.

On that recent day in Jackson on his book tour, he was having lunch with another native of Jackson, Eudora Welty. "Knowing her and having her like my work has been one of the great cherishable events in my life," he said. "Writing stories and writing essays are really received habits, and who I received them from is her.

"Living in Jackson and being around her made it perfectly plain that being a writer was quite all right. Those kinds of things instilled in you at an early age, even unspoken, are quite valuable," Ford said.

"In 1968 when I considered writing, I didn't even have to think 'But, OK, is it even worthwhile.'

"I knew it was worthwhile because Eudora did it."

Forget the Hemingway Comparisons: Richard Ford Is an American, Yes, But He Has His Own Voice

Steve Paul / 1990

From *The Kansas City Star* 8 July 1990. Reprinted by permission of *The Kansas City Star.*

Richard Ford has a word or two for all those readers and critics who saddle him with the label of Ernest Hemingway's heir.

"I never think about Hemingway," he says. "I never read Hemingway."

In fact, in an essay for *Esquire* in 1983, Ford pronounced the venerated writer inferior in almost every way to his contemporary, F. Scott Fitzgerald.

It is the plight of any writer in any age to be compared with those who came before him. Ford, in the fourteen years of his published life, has been no exception. It's just something to be endured for someone who strives to reflect, as he calls it, "the American experience expressed in language" and who proudly plants himself in the tradition of such Americanists as Sherwood Anderson and Willa Cather.

"If that's going to be where I start," Ford said in an interview last month at the American Booksellers Association convention in Las Vegas, "I think then inevitably people are going to compare me to other people. I know that everything I read, particularly everything good I ever read, becomes part of my literary experience.

"Am I unique among contemporary writers who get compared to other people? No. Ray Carver got compared to Hemingway. Tom McGuane gets compared to Hemingway. Everybody who ever designed to write a short story or aspired to write a short story gets compared to Hemingway.

"The only thing that ever annoys me is that in comparing me, or tracing influences to me or to my colleagues, there doesn't ever seem to be the recognition that you can't write a good story, you can't write a good novel, on the strength of influence. You can only write a good story or a good novel by yourself. . . .

"Anybody's style is their intelligence. Their style is just a natural incarnation of their intelligence. You can't imitate someone's intelligence. You can't be somebody else's mind. You might learn a trick. But it finally has to gear itself in to your own intelligence and make something worthwhile, or it's useless. And if it does gear itself into your own intelligence and make something worthwhile, then it's yours."

As for Ford's style, it is testimony to his desire as a writer to expand his horizons that his work has ranged from the near-Southern gothic in his first novel, *A Piece of My Heart* (1976), to the gritty realism of *The Ultimate Good Luck* (1981) to the voluble introspection of *The Sportswriter* (1986) to the stripped-down narratives of his story collection *Rock Springs* (1987). And now, in his fourth novel, *Wildlife,* Ford offers his leanest profile yet.

Wildlife shares both the Montana setting and the spare, vernacular-voiced tone of the *Rock Springs* stories. It is reminiscent especially, in its structure and theme, of one of those stories, "Great Falls."

Wildlife dwells on the observations of a sixteen-year-old confronting the failure of his parent's marriage. In "Great Falls"—like the novel, a first-person narrative recounting youthful angst from a later perspective—a fourteen-year-old boy must figure out what it means when his mother goes off with another man.

When the narrator in the story says, "I thought to myself that my life had turned suddenly, and that I might not know exactly how or which way for possibly a long time," he is prefiguring the confusion and upheaval expressed by Joe in *Wildlife.*

"I was never particularly aware that *Wildlife* was responsive to 'Great Falls,' " Ford allowed. "I knew it was responsive to certain stylistic impulses in me, and to certain kinds of dramatic situations, but that's all. And I knew it was set in Great Falls, too. But I knew at that point in my life, a year ago last October, if I were going to write a story about the circus coming to town, the town was going to be Great Falls. It was just in my blood to write that."

Great Falls, Mont., had been a recent grounding point for Ford, a peripatetic writer, born in Mississippi, who now lives most of the time in New Orleans (Ford, forty-six, spent much of his youth on the road. His father was a salesman in the South for the Kansas City–based Faultless Starch Co.)

"I felt that when I wanted to write *Wildlife,* I could still write the sentences with some of the same cadences of . . . some of the stories in *Rock Springs.*

"My feeling is if you find something that, by luck or by however, is working for you, use it up and try your very best not to repeat. And if you're going to use some of those resources, try to make it more comprehensive, try to make it more sympathetic, more intellectually complex, try to include more.

"With that as a set of aspirations, then the novel became almost incumbent on me. . . . I wanted to write something bigger and to take something I already knew much further than I already knew them.

"I think that a tripartite relationship—a woman, her husband, and another man—is fairly basic human drama in life in America. Having that observed by a child, I think, is also very basic, both in literary terms and in experiential terms. Kids see their parents do all kinds of things."

There is something else about Great Falls that Ford likes to talk about, something that illuminates his overriding concern for the details that create good writing and for the sheer pleasure and sense of accomplishment that comes with creating a sentence that works.

"I have loved writing about Great Falls," he said, "because of just the town itself, because of where it is in the world and on the map, and also because it has that wonderful name. The name was just magic in my ears. I like the way it has a long 'a' and short 'a.' I like the way it makes a kind of iamb in your mind's ear—*Great Falls, Great Falls.* I like the idea of things going downhill. I like the idea that 'falls' has a huge force in it, a regenerative force.

"Those kinds of language-determined things are much overlooked in the ways people talk about literature—the affection a writer has for any one isolated piece of language, a word or a phrase. Whenever I see Great Falls on the page, it has a little brio about it and I immediately want to start writing something after it."

Ford will be leaving his fictional world of Great Falls when he takes up again the story of Frank Bascombe, the suburban New Jersey sportswriter of the earlier novel. He is planning a sequel to be called *Independence Day.*

It was *The Sportswriter,* about Bascombe trying to come to terms with his life after his divorce and the death of his son, that first brought Ford wide attention and gave him the confidence to go on as a writer. His reputation has continued to rise, partly because, as in *Rock Springs* and *Wildlife,* he has given voice so eloquently, so sympathetically to the lives of ordinary Americans.

It is the fiction writer's duty, Ford said, to put into words what people can't always express for themselves.

When, in *Wildlife,* Joe's mother realizes that she will leave her husband, she tells her son: "Your life doesn't mean what you have . . . or what you get. It's what you're willing to give up."

"Jeannette at that point was realizing she was giving up a lot," Ford said. "I think it seemed to her that in every choice you make which you think is for your own good, there is a concomitant loss, a real loss, a loss you're not easily willing to sustain. . . .

"One of fiction's or any art's responsibilities is to take the pat answers by which we normally go through our lives and reinform them by exposing them to actual experience, which then becomes truth.

"We all walk around using a set of what we generally think of are conventional wisdoms, which probably at sometime had been true, but which need to be updated all the time so that our responses don't become inadequate to the demands of experience."

Ford Just Wants His Books to Be Loved

Ginny Merriam / 1990

From the *Missoulian* [Missoula, MT] 22 June 1990: E6, E14. Reprinted by permission.

In one of those odd, circular turns of life, last week Richard Ford stayed at the Holiday Inn across from his old junior high school in Jackson, Miss. He was interviewed Friday morning as a literary luminary on his hometown television station, where he practiced the advice given him by friend Tom McGuane: "Just answer the questions." Later, he was off to lunch with friend Eudora Welty.

Fresh from two days at the American Booksellers Association convention in Las Vegas—where he was a featured breakfast speaker with John Updike and Amy Tan—and an appearance on *Today,* Ford is in the middle of a thirteen-city tour promoting his new novel, *Wildlife,* published June 15. With nine cities under his belt and four to go, Ford has the book foremost on his mind.

"I'm happy," he said in a phone interview with the *Missoulian* from Jackson. "I'm happy that this book is in the world, and that people who are reading it seem to get it."

In the middle of the flurry of attention and reviews given well-known writers with new books, Ford is still judging the reception of *Wildlife;* as he puts it, "The waves are still crashing over the sides of my boat."

"I've gotten the best reviews of *Wildlife* of any book I've ever written," he said. "People have been saying encouraging things. I've also been hearing some off-the-mark and some of the most unflattering things with this book."

Ford, known for his occasionally blunt manner, wastes no time on those who hate his work: "I wish them ill health," he says.

And he has little care for reviewers he doesn't respect or who don't grasp the work. The *New York Times* reviewer of *Wildlife* simply "missed the book," he said.

But that's not to say he doesn't care about reviewers.

"What I always want to hear from book reviewers is whether or not I'm

89

getting all the resources I have for writing fiction on the page," he said. "I other words, is the book rich enough? Beyond that, you want to hear if you're doing a good job. Is this a book people will read?"

In this case, the answer is apparently yes. Ford's last book, a collection of stories called *Rock Springs,* brought him true national attention. Reviewers called it "cause for celebration" and a "stunning volume of stories." With this new book, the spotlight is on. Ford is regarded as one of the leading voices in American fiction today.

He's also one of the most written-about writers around. His bad-boy/ charming-boy image, his penchant for moving, his devotion to his wife, Kristina, and his quick, literary wit make him fascinating to readers and to journalists. As his publicist writes of him, "He is widely considered to be one of the most attractive, witty, learned, and charming personalities on the literary scene."

During an interview, he's focused on the chore at hand, always "on" and aware he's on. He'll call a "moron" a "moron" without flinching. He never backtracks or asks not to be quoted, and he speaks in straightforward, compound sentences.

The catch phrase "former Missoula resident" doesn't quite fit Ford; it's more appropriate to say he and Kristina alighted here for a few years in the late 1980s. They have lived all over, and they don't stay long.

"I never could get really buckled down," Ford said. "I get bored easily with places. I get nervous with permanence. I was happy once in this old house in Mississippi, I couldn't stand it."

Ford counts his years in Missoula as some of his best and most productive.

"I felt when we got to Montana that writing was the thing I should be doing in my life," he said. "Not until I got to Missoula did the idea of writing and being nothing but a writer become a possiblity."

After leaving Missoula last September, the Fords rented a place in Dutton through the fall.

"I lived in Missoula for quite a long time, and I was happy there every day," Ford said. "But I came to love central Montana more. I like it because it's farm land, and it's big and I can go bird-hunting there."

Now that they're living in New Orleans, where Kristina is working as the principal city planner, the Fords are shopping for a place in Teton County.

"We think maybe this is a chance to really try living in two places," he said.

While Ford sees landscape and place in his own life as "basically inert, kind of postcard-ish to me," he said, a definite sense of place is vital to his fiction. He has set stories in central Montana, and the new novel is set in Great Falls, a place that fascinates him for its position at the junction of the plains and the mountains.

"It's like Dick Hugo said. Great Falls has been for me a triggering town," he said. "I certainly felt very attached to the place in writing *Wildlife*. And by that I don't mean that town on the Missouri, I mean the place I make it."

Within the setting, Ford is interested in families: "What are the possible permutations of people who love each other, who want to stay together?" Ford asks. He's also interested in "re-threading the old Tolstoy vision that all happy families are alike," and in looking at Henry James's interest in fiction, "the connection between blish and bale."

Ford, who wrote the screenplay for the movie *Bright Angel,* filmed near Billings and scheduled for release in November, is planning to write some essays and short stories before delving into a novel that's "a little beyond the note-taking stage." He thinks he has more left to say within a central-Montana setting, and he doesn't appreciate the notion that he's an outsider.

"It pisses me off that some people think I shouldn't be writing about Montana because I wasn't born there," he said. "I tend to say, 'So, do it yourself.' But part of me—a larger part of me—wants to try to do it even better, to improve on it. My attitude is I'm an American. I'll write about anything I want to. If you can do it better, do it."

But the long-term goal is simple: "I'd like to write books that everybody loves."

Richard Ford's Creative Spark
Michael Schumacher / 1991

From *Writer's Digest* May 1991: 33–35, 76. Reprinted by permission.

The last time I spoke to Richard Ford, he was hard at work on a new short story that he was calling "Inferno." He knew what he wanted to do with his story, but he was having a difficult time with its opening.

"I spent five days trying to write the first sentence," Ford said. "When you're up against a story and you know you're ready to write it—you know what's out there to be written about and you know the things you'd like to get to—writing the first line is like standing in front of a huge wall, behind which is everything that you want, and you have to build the perfect door."

Two years later, Ford makes it clear he found everything he wanted behind that metaphorical wall. "Inferno" had escalated from a story to the novel *Wildlife*.

"I wanted to write a story that had a forest fire in it. I started off thinking that it would be a story because I didn't want to take on the notion of writing a novel. It was always meant to be something longer than, say, a 5,000-word story—I hoped it would be of a long, but not defined, length—but I didn't know what it was going to be."

One of his main considerations was continuing the thematic progression he'd been developing from his first novel on—but not at the cost of plowing through a lot of old turf. Throughout his career, Ford has focused on how ordinary people face crisis, especially in matters of the heart, then move on. In his early novels, he chronicled the lives of people who were looking for love; in his later books, his characters were in danger of losing it. In *Wildlife,* the issue is love lost, then regained.

"I was very, very concerned about going beyond things I had done before and not repeating myself," Ford says, adding, in hindsight, that "I couldn't have ever written the novel if I hadn't written three of the stories— 'Communist,' 'Optimists,' and 'Great Falls'—in *Rock Springs*. Those stories have to do with moments in which families come unglued, as seen through the eyes of a surviving son.

"I realized I wanted to write a story in which a family went through the states of unity, disunity, and back to unity again, but I don't think I would have wanted to write the last movement of that structure if I hadn't satisfied myself on writing about how families come unglued, and how that unglued condition can be seen sympathetically. One of the primary appeals of those three stories, I suppose, is the narrator's sympathy for himself, his parents, and his life that's gone. I wanted to see beyond that, to push it into the next little mini-epoch: Could I find a language for families coming together again?"

When you talk to Ford, you are likely to hear plenty of discussion about language and writing good sentences; language, he says, is a large part of what brings a person to write, and it is also part of each writer's signature. Ford has dedicated his writing life to the composition of individual sentences, and everything else—theme, meaning, usefulness—rises from those sentences. It's a point Ford can't seem to emphasize enough.

"The sentence is where one important, immediate individual experience of literature takes place," he says.

The sentence is also the point at which Ford's work really originates. He doesn't depend much on elaborate outlines or plot structures; instead, he begins with an incomplete idea and painstakingly develops a story or novel from a single line. That sentence might not wind up being the opening line of the published story or book, but it is the line that inspires the continuation of the story itself. In *Wildlife,* that line was *My father went to fight a forest fire.*

"When I write a sentence like that, or even think it in my head," Ford says, "I think to myself, 'Yes, that's dramatic. That's interesting. Use that. Take it someplace.' Everything starts at a level in which small things *feel* important to me."

From such a line, the building process begins. Each word suggests characters or actions to explore. *My father* points to two characters, including a first-person narrator, who can be developed. The past tense (*went*) indicates the structure of the narrative—the narrator is looking back on an important time in his life. *Forest fire* offers specific points of drama.

Ford admits his devotion to language and the individual sentence makes for a slow—and occasionally frustrating—writing process, but he also maintains that it helps him bring realism to his books.

"When I started writing this way, in 1970, I was living in Chicago, and I thought to myself, 'This is going to be a difficult way to write books.' I had begun earlier with a rather conventional notion that stories often come in big masses—that is to say, you had a whole or half of a story in your mind at the beginning—but I was realizing that I had to bring everything back to sentences, lines, and details. I thought, 'Oh God, what a clerical nightmare this is.' But I've managed to write books that way, and I've managed to exert the amount of attention and care to the books that I wanted to. This last is important to me.

"I also have the somewhat self-flattering notion that this is the way we all live our lives: in often isolated events. Details. We get out of bed, we come downstairs, the door opens—we don't know what's going to be out there. We somehow have to connect what we did before we got out of bed to what we do the rest of the day. We're always connecting, trying to make our lives seem logical. The way anybody makes sense of his life is by choosing the things he finds most interesting to do, choosing a way to lead himself from one event to another, creating a logic that is his life. That's the way I write stories. So, then, if I want someone to set fire to a house at the end of *Wildlife,* which was my plan, what I have to ask myself is, 'Why on earth would I do that?' Then I have to imagine an answer in language and in the story."

The answers come from any number of sources. Ford continually jots in notebooks he carries with him everywhere; those notations—mostly snippets of overheard conversation, interesting bits of research that catch his eye, and sentences written independent of a specific writing project—constitute an invaluable part of his writing process. These are the raw materials for a story or novel, the "sentences, lines, and details" that help him piece together his work. Ford has kept notebooks for twenty-five years, and he estimates that each novel relies on seven or eight years' worth of notes. The opening for *Wildlife* resulted from sixteen pages of notebook snippets.

"I take notes because I don't trust my memory very much," Ford says. "I know there will be things that I will notice or think or say, or that somebody else will say, that I'll never hear again if I don't write them down. My work depends on lived life, and the source of my work is in the conversations and lines I've collected or made up, lines I've written, pieces from here, pieces from there."

These snippets will eventually appear in lines of dialogue spoken by his characters, or in the characters' actions, or even in some of the seemingly minute details that add dimension to the characters or the story. If he's especially fond of a snippet, Ford will hang onto it for a long time, working with it like a puzzle piece, trying to insert it into different stories or novels until he finds its perfect fit.

Such was the case with one brief yet striking passage in *Wildlife.* Through-

out the novel, Ford describes the ways one's home, ordinarly a place of comfort, safety and security, could also be the site of terrible betrayal. (The book
centers on a boy's witnessing his mother's affair while her husband is off
fighting a forest fire.)

This phone conversation between father and son introduces a small, yet
important anecdote.

> I thought he must be calling from the restaurant where we'd been last night.
> "We don't have any control over anything here now," my father said loudly
> over the noise. "We just watch everything burn. That's all. It exhausts you. I'm
> stiff all over from it."
> "Are you coming home?" I asked.
> "I saw a bear that caught on fire, Joe,"my father said, still loud. "You
> wouldn't have believed it. It just blew up around him in one instant. A live bear
> in a hemlock tree. I swear. He hit the ground squalling. It was like balled light-
> ning."

Later in the same scene, Ford discovers what might seem to be the point
of the passage, though he doesn't do so in reference to the bear episode:
"Regular life doesn't exist out here," he said. "You have to adapt."

For readers, a scene like this looks like good planning, a significant piece
of creative writing inserted at precisely the right moment for maximum effect. It is this, of course, but it also has a history that illustrates how Ford
develops his notebook snippets into fiction.

When he was researching forest fires, Ford ran into a description of how
bears often make the mistake of retreating to trees for safety during fires.
That description brought to mind a notebook snipped Ford had been trying
to work into the novel.

"Three or four years ago, a guy told me a story which I put in my notebook. He told me about going out on his front yard one day and seeing that
his yard dog had treed a little black bear. It was early in the morning, and the
guy called his son at work and said, 'There's a little black bear treed here.
Would you like to shoot it?' And the son said, 'Well, yeah, but I can't come
'til the end of the day, when I get off my shift.' So the guy sat out on his
front porch all day, about seven hours, with the dog barking and keeping the
bear up in the tree, until his son could come back from work at four o'clock
and very calmly shoot the bear out of the tree. Bears, to me, are sympathetic
animals. Bad things happen to bears, and it's affecting when something happens to them. It feels important.

"So that went in my notebook. I kept coming back and coming back around to that story, but it just wasn't fitting. I couldn't set up the story around an event because it seemed too static, and I couldn't get anybody to *tell* the story—I just couldn't make it work."

And it didn't work until, in another book he was using for research, Ford came across an account of a fire that occurred near Superior, Montana, in 1910. The reporter wrote about hearing a bear squall in the midst of a fire, and this reminded Ford of the story he'd heard and tried to use.

"Maybe it would never have caught my attention or made it into the book if I hadn't already had this disposition to put a bear story into the book," Ford allows, "but I thought, 'Why would a bear squall? Maybe he was up a tree.' I knew this happened to animals, so I made up that part of the story. That's how particulars get into books: They get transmuted and altered and shortened and elaborated."

Ford used notebook particulars throughout the book. At the beginning of *Wildlife,* the father loses his job, which puts him in the position of signing on to fight the fire, thus creating the tension that leads to his wife's affair. An important part of this narrative—the father's job prior to being fired—was the result of Ford's interest in occupations, and a two-line notebook snippet. (*My father was a golfer. A teaching pro.*)

"As a writer, I've always been interested in what people do for a living, though not in a romantic or even sociological way," Ford explains. "If people are going to have a body, a presence, in a work of mine, they're going to have a profession, because in my little value system you don't live very long on this earth without having something to do to make a living. So one of the big challenges for me is always to figure out what people *do.*

"*Wildife* had golf in its beginning because my friends in Missoula—Bill Kittredge and Jon Jackson—used to go out and play golf, and I'd think to myself, 'There's something wonderfully odd, quirky, and dramatic about playing golf in Montana.' I've always associated golf with warm climates, but my friends would go out and play on these chilly golf courses that were just kind of converted range land—flat, with some sort of anemic little trees sticking up. When I wrote *He was a golfer. A teaching pro,* I pictured a man being on a golf course in Montana. It seemed odd. I liked it as a thing to have in my story."

The snippet was written well before Ford began his novel, but when it came time to find an occupation for one of his main characters, all he had to do was consult his notebooks. The existing lines provided a logic and order to the character he was creating.

"I begin by trying to connect those little, very unconnected and raw pieces of literary impetus. I try to find words and phrases that connect those things or add to them. It's funny. I don't always say to myself, 'Is this a line calculated to have this effect on a reader?' I might do that as a last stroke, when I'm going back and looking at things. I'm mostly doing these things intuitively and then exerting some cognitive control over them later. The style of a book almost comes out of something entirely intuitive—something proportionate to the material, something commensurate with the importance of the actions."

Despite talk of intuition and the unusual method by which he pieces together his books and stories, nothing is serendipitous or sloppy about the way Ford crafts his fiction. A working professional in every sense of the word, he labors, often at great length, to meet his own tough standards for good literary writing. While strong fiction can be entertaining to readers, Ford suggests it holds at its core a much higher purpose.

"I'm trying to write a story which is useful to people, to teach them or instruct them or console them about their own lives. You don't need to go to fiction to see life the way it is; you don't need literature for that. I think one of the reasons people go to fiction is to get away from their everyday lives, to find something that is made and shaped as perfectly as it can be.

"In *Wildlife,* when Joe tells the story about those days in his sixteenth year, he's saying, 'I can tell you a story about my family coming apart and coming together. I will try to tell this story, make it up even, in a way to make it have a shape, to make it useful and, in the process, give me the opportunity to hear individual lines, see lives described, conclusions tentatively drawn, which maybe you can use in your own life. I'll tell you something that happened to me and that something will be useful to you.'

"Well," Ford concludes, "to hand someone a useful line, to give someone a made story, is good. I think that's 'a small, good thing,' as my friend Ray [Carver] used to say."

Ford's deliberation in piecing together logical and useful stories is echoed in his handling of the mechanics, as well as the more esoteric elements, of writing. He spent two years writing *The Ultimate Good Luck,* his second novel, only to devote another year to changing its point of view from first person to third person. Not only was the work difficult, but it came at a time when he was trying to follow up *A Piece of My Heart,* his 1976 novel that had been nominated for the Ernest Hemingway Award for Best First Novel.

"I was anxious," Ford recalls, "because here I had written my second book and it hadn't worked out. I wondered if it meant that, basically, I'd had it. When you're young, and you're always working against those fears that you're a 'one-time writer.' "

The Ultimate Good Luck is a short novel, but the unpublished draft, written in the first person, was even shorter.

"When I wrote it in the first person, it was awfully short, and even though I didn't want to write a long book and eventually didn't write a long book, there just wasn't enough in the draft. The book was just too austere. There were a whole bunch of things that I knew about in advance, and that I wanted to be able to discover more about in the telling of the book, that I wasn't managing to get in. I wrestled with trying to find ways to get more of the stuff in there, but I couldn't do it.

"Finally, I was in Vermont—it must have been the summer of 1978—and my friend Geoffrey Wolff read the manuscript. After telling me that he thought it was a good effort, and a lot of other things he knew were not going to make me any happier, he said that maybe what I ought to do is change the point of view. I think he did it with a great deal of hope that it would help me, but also with a certain amount of trepidation, knowing that it was going to cost me.

"At the time he said that, I was naive enough to think that it was not going to be as hard as it turned out to be. You don't just go through and change the pronouns; you take the novel as written and throw it in the trash can, keeping only what you can use again. It's not going to be the same book. It's not going to be your story done differently; it's going to be another piece of writing entirely. It was very hard, but I just bore down on it, thinking to myself, 'Well, I'm going to have a book here at the end. I'm not going to let this one throw me.' And it didn't."

Ford brings this kind of dedication and determination to all facets of his writing. After you've talked to him for a while, listening to him speak in his serious, utterly focused manner on a variety of topics, you get the idea that somehow, through the experiences of trial and error, Ford has successfully married the ideal and the pragmatic; he's found a way to conform the mechanics of writing to his hard-nosed standards. Ford might shrug and attribute it to his work ethic, but for many writers, especially novices, striking the balance between the practical and the ideal is a difficult task.

That balance is clear when Ford speaks of the terse, almost spring-loaded dialogue that he writes for his characters. Pedestrian dialogue, or dialogue that's used as filler, is not for Ford.

"I try to make every line have the necessity of representing a human being," he says. "Every line has to have some kind of impact, even if it's a small scale or proportional impact. No free ones: Very little 'How do you do?' 'Oh, I'm fine, how are you?' None of those. I'm not trying to write dialogue which is actual to life. I'm trying to write dialogue that refers to life in an economical way. There's a difference.

"As I said, I don't think readers need to go to my stories—or anybody else's—just to have life rehashed. Stories should point toward what's important in life, and our utterances always mean something. Out utterances are almost always things that we have to take responsibility for, even if we think we don't. Our impulses can be understood by what we say. I want to write dialogue in an economical—but not drastically economical—way. Fewer lines, greater impact."

For all the hard work that his writing entails, it is the involvement with language that keeps Ford writing. It is there at the beginning of a novel or short story ("The ideas come to me out of language") and it is there at the end, as he reads aloud to his wife, Kristina, soliciting her reactions and advice, checking the rhythm and sound of his sentences. Sentences must mean exactly what he intends them to mean, Ford says, but the language in a sentence is just as important, and he will rework a sentence if it seems to have one beat too many, or if it doesn't sound correct to his ear.

And, in a way, it is language that keeps him on the move. Labeled "America's most peripatetic writer" by *The New York Times,* Ford has lived in Mississippi, Arkansas, New York, New Jersey, Illinois, Montana, Mexico, and Europe, to name just some of the locations. There's more to his movement than wanderlust or the inability to stay in one place for any length of time; many of these locations have turned up as settings for his fiction.

"I go out of curiosity," explains Ford, who is now living in New Orleans, though not for very long by his estimation. "I go because I can hear another idiom and can see a different landscape to which I can dedicate language."

Ford isn't inclined to relax or take root in his writing, either; like a man who's spent a lot of time on the move, he knows where he's been but is uncertain where he's going. He refuses to look at his career or his books in terms of progression, which is just as well, because at times it is difficult to believe that the person who wrote *The Ultimate Good Luck* was the same person who wrote *The Sportswriter.* Ford would probably tell you, and with a straight face, that he wasn't.

Nor is he inclined to set goals in terms of what he'd like to accomplish. He modestly allows that he would like to "widen his grasp" and leaves it at that.

He may have best answered the question when he was struggling with the opening of what would become his fourth novel. He was working to get from Tuesday to Wednesday, trying to put marks on a page that was at once an enemy and his reason to live, and any discussion of goals carried with it a sense of immediacy.

"When I start a story, I want to finish it," Ford said then. "I don't like unfinished things. I don't like parts of stories lying around in desk drawers. When I started writing novels, I was deathly afraid that I wouldn't finish the first one, and after that I have always been almost unusually anxious about making sure I finish.

"I guess I set the standard goal that most writers set: I want to write as well as I possibly can. But have I set goals for the number of books that I'll write? No. Length of books? No. Did I ever have the aspiration to get my books reviewed on the front page of *The New York Times?* No. Getting rich? No. I mean, I try to do the best I can, and I think that if I'm good enough, people will read my work."

An Interview with Richard Ford

Ned Stuckey-French / 1994

From *Speaking of the Short Story: Interviews with Contemporary Writers.* Eds. Farhat Iftekharuddin, Mary Rohrberger, and Maurice Lee. Jackson: University Press of Mississippi, 1997. Used by permission.

Richard Ford has written four novels and a collection of short stories, as well as a screenplay and several essays, articles and reviews. His first novel, *A Piece of My Heart* (1976), helped its author win both a Guggenheim Fellowship (1977–78) and a National Endowment for the Arts Fellowship (1979–80). It was followed by *The Ultimate Good Luck* (1981), a bruising, cinematic portrayal of Harry Quinn's attempt to get his girlfriend's brother out of a Oaxaca jail. In *The Sportswriter* (1986), Ford chronicled an Easter weekend of crisis in the life of Frank Bascombe, a funny and reflective New Jersey sportswriter who is recovering from a divorce precipitated by, among other things, the death of his son Ralph. *The Sportswriter* was in many ways Ford's breakthrough book of realism. Recently, he has published a novella, *Wildlife* (1990), and edited and introduced *The Granta Book of the American Short Story* (1992). In 1996 he was awarded the Pulitzer Prize for his novel *Independence Day.* Richard Ford was born in Jackson, Mississippi, in 1944 and has taught at The University of Michigan, Williams College, Princeton, and Harvard.

Stuckey-French: A few years back in your introduction to the *Pushcart Anthology,* you said that when you were first starting out you wrote many short stories and sent them out, but had to face the rejection time after time and decided to heck with this, I'm going to start a longer project so I can get some more sustained time to write.

Ford: That's right. That's exactly right. I began writing *A Piece of My Heart.*

Stuckey-French: What finally led you back to short stories and when did you start writing them again?

Ford: I started writing short stories again in 1979. I was teaching at Williams College, and Ray Carver and I were great friends. He and I were kick-

ing around and went to the dog track down on the Vermont-Massachusetts
line, with Kristina. I had been thinking the dog track was sort of intriguing;
but Ray really loved to gamble. He'd gamble on most anything—in a kind of
sporting way. Nothing serious. I remember the three of us in the stands at the
dog track, and Ray was continually going off to make a bet. And of course
he knew nothing about dogs. We'd bought these little tout books they sold
you when you came in.

Stuckey-French: Which don't tell you much anyway.

Ford: They don't tell you *very* much. They tell you about the history of
an individual dog, and its weight and age and where it was from. But that
was all the inside dope he needed. And I'll never forget; he went down and
made his bet, and he won. Then he went back down to get his money. This
was in 1978, I guess, '78, '79. But when he came back up those concrete
stairs, I saw a look in his eye of, sort of, wonderful, low-grade fury and
frenzy. He had not been long from drinking at that time, and he still had a
sort of wildness about him. But seeing that look made me think I'd like to
write a story where somebody had that look. It was so vivid. I didn't really
have an idea for a story, because I was at the time working on *The Ultimate
Good Luck* and had pretty much put story-writing out of my mind, thinking
that what I was was a novelist and not a story writer. But here was some little
spark to seeing that look in Ray's eyes. God knows what its components
were: avarice, pleasure, surprise, a glimpse at a life in which you were routinely a big winner. He liked thoughts of being a big winner—and he was
one. But I went home to this big converted barn I was living in, and I thought
to myself that I hadn't written a short story now in probably five or six years,
or even tried. But I thought I'd try to write one, my first, all in a day. And so
I sat down and I wrote it all in a day. It's a pretty short little story called
"Going to the Dogs." It's about a man and it's not really about Ray, but a
man who hatches a petty scheme to make a lot of money, and then doesn't.
Ray's look, I guess, inclined me to that man.

Stuckey-French: So what was his anger about?

Ford: Oh, it wasn't anger. It was an ecstasy. He'd been having a few years
of losses then, and this was different, and he liked it very, very much. It was
sweet, really, and also funny. He pissed all the money away eventually that
night.

Stuckey-French: By the sixth race it was gone.

Ford: By the sixth race, right. But anyway, I wrote that story and then

didn't write another story till 1981. The stories all came one at a time. All
the stories in *Rock Springs,* except for maybe the last two, were written one
and two years apart. I wrote several of them during the time I was writing
The Sportswriter, when I'd come to a patch of time when I wanted to stop
and didn't know what else to do but wanted to keep writing. Kristina and I
were living in Montana by then. And I would write one more story. And over
time I began to think, as the stories accumulated, well maybe I can do this,
whereas before I didn't think I could. And I thought it was natural in the life
of a writer: that you at some point can do some things and at some other
point you can't. Now, since 1987, I've written two stories, one of which is a
novella-length piece and the other is a long story called *Jealous.* And I
thought in each instance that those were going to be short stories, of some
short story length. But they weren't. They were longer. So, short stories
weren't available to me at first, and then they came, and then they went away
again. It's not mystical, at all. But I don't really want to belabor the point.
Maybe they'll become available again. Who knows?

Stuckey-French: So the most recent stories outgrew themselves?

Ford: Well, I'd like to write stories again. At the tag end of a long novel,
novels seem like such a long thing to do. I'd like to do something that is
somewhat less hard. And stories—for me—are less hard.

Stuckey-French: A novel is such a long project, such a big commitment
of yourself and your time that it seems you must believe in it, believe that
it's really going to hit, that this one's really going to work. But, with a short
story, is it easier to believe that you have a little more leeway?

Ford: Well, if stories fail, then they don't make a short story. It's like
bread. Either it's a loaf of bread or it's doughy goo. And you can put it away
and not think to yourself you've just pissed away two years of your life, or
lost your whole purchase on your vocation. I've never written a story I didn't
finish though.

Stuckey-French: They always feel like a loaf of bread?

Ford: Yeah. I haven't written many, though.

Stuckey-French: Each one at the end, it feels like it's a winner?

Ford: Well, it's a finished story, anyway. I've really only written twelve
short or slightly longer stories in my life—that is since I decided I might
could write them at all. And what I do, which in a sense addresses what you
just said, is try to compensate for the lesser status of a short story by over-

preparing, by considering it at the time I write it as the most important thing in the world. I don't think other people are like that necessarily. Some probably are. But some can write stories perfectly well from one side of their desk, or one side of their mind. But I've found it most expeditious to really clear my decks completely and concentrate only on the story at hand, which makes it as important as I can make it.

Stuckey-French: That sounds in a way like what I've read about the way Ray Carver worked too. I remember reading about his desk one time and that he kept a very neat desk and that each story was in a folder and that he only had the one folder on the desk at a time.

Ford: Maybe. I don't know. I saw Ray's desk a few times. It didn't make a big impression on me. It was just where he wrote.

Stuckey-French: Not that neat?

Ford: I don't remember. That's the side of a writer's life that doesn't much interest me. This business of how you go about writing—your desk, etc.—doesn't seem to reveal anything very interesting. And when it does seem to reveal something interesting, I finally think it's trivial. It's the stories that are interesting. The other, I suppose, is an amateur fascination whose implication is that the "magic" of literature can somehow be penetrated by examining the rather inert artifacts of its making. Of course, maybe I'm wrong. That's always possible. Maybe you can get at something that way.

Stuckey-French: So in the generation of a short story you say you really prepare. Yet, you say that first one, the first one when you started again, "Going to the Dogs," came in a day. Do you usually feel that they just come in a rush now, once you're ready to write?

Ford: No. It took me about five days to write "Rock Springs." It took me thirty days to write "Empire." One of my continual wrestling matches with myself is to work harder, longer, have more concentration—the Protestant virtues of selflessness. And I'd like to get back to the point that in writing stories I *could* write them in a day, or write them, you know, in four days— some succinct time. But, I probably overprepare, which makes writing them a longer proposition. I habitually want to ward off a day when in the course of writing a story or a novel, I suddenly don't have anything else to write about and I'm only two-thirds through. That's more concern to me than writing a story quickly. It's hard completely to explain but I think it's me trying to be better, me trying to take my work more seriously, to prepare more, to get more into stories. But it's possible, I suppose, to reach a point of diminishing returns where your preparation and your wish to be serious begin to turn on you slightly.

Stuckey-French: I remember talking to Scott Russell Sanders—I don't know if you know his work, but he's written both stories and essays—and he said that the difference for him between an essay and a story is that for an essay he takes a lot of notes. He's an ex-scientist so he even numbers the notes; whereas for a story, it is more likely to grow out of an image, like the image you mentioned of Ray Carver coming back with the money from the window. Sanders said that for him a story almost writes itself, it comes in a rush, it comes at once, whereas an essay is more assembled. Is that some of what you're talking about when you say you want to guard against overpreparing? Do you want to move your stories away from being assembled and back toward the image?

Ford: The idea of an assembling is not foreign to the way I write essays, or to the way I write anything—stories included. I think of stories as constructions, and their logical, sequential nature is an achieved quality: the process of first putting one thing next to one thing, then putting the next; all of which creates, if you're lucky, the illusion of a cohesive story. You create the illusion of a told tale, and you create the illusion of naturally occurring linearness. I think I know what he means by things coming in a rush, as though they came to him and found their existence on the page in an already cohesive shape. That might be good if the story was full enough. My way at least lets me put whatever I want into a story and work at making it fit; instead of becoming, early on, submissive to a wholly formed, "naturally occurring" story whose structure is difficult to fiddle with.

Stuckey-French: Another example of this phenomenon is that Faulkner said that when he sat down to start *The Sound and the Fury,* all he had was the image of a little girl crawling out of a window and he could see her drawers . . .

Ford: If that's true. I guess he said that. Who knows if it was true. Why would he tell the truth?

Stuckey-French: Isn't it pretty to think so?

Ford: Well, to fit myself into that idea, it's possible that my recollection of what provoked "Going to the Dogs" is just a convenience of my memory. I'm sure I had other things circulating in my notebook, or so to speak, in my thinking, and I'm sure I wanted to work them into the story. That's certainly typical of me, and it's truthfully and fundamentally the way stories come into being for me. There all these things that are accumulating in my head or my notebook, things I like or am interested in, and what I want to do is get them into stories. That's my use for them, and that's my understanding of what literary art is. I want to find or make a context in language and logic into which this detail, this line of dialogue, this concept will fit, and which context will, by making them contiguous and interactive, develop in all into something unforeseen, something that is actually new, larger than the sum of parts, and useful and perhaps pretty. And so, for me, it does slightly belie how stories occur when I say they originate in an image. Beyond that, stories originate in my life because of the inherited form of the short story into which I fit my practices. If that makes any sense.

Stuckey-French: Sure.

Ford: So that first there was a thing called the short story, and I work, and I find a way to inhabit it.

Stuckey-French: It makes lots of sense, and I guess, thinking about that, in looking for that linearity that the short story as a form has or is supposed to have, or does have.

Ford: Sometimes.

Stuckey-French: Right. It seems to me that in your stories often one of the things that kickstarts that line is an allusion to violence, or the threat of violence. That is often there and then the story unfolds.

Ford: I suppose.

Stuckey-French: Claude's father yanking him by the hair out of the car, that kind of thing. And then we wonder how bad can this get? Or how do we keep this from getting so bad it's just too awful?

Ford: My notion about what I guess you could call the ontogeny of fiction is that fiction is about (it is, anyway, when I write it) what we do as a consequence to dramatic acts. Much of our lives is spent dealing with the consequences of our own and others' important acts; trying to make virtues out of vices, trying to make normal things that have happened against our will and against all logic, seem normal, survivable. And so, for me, at least up to now, it has seemed that what stories can be about is how people put their lives in order after rather dramatic, sometimes violent, percussive events. And because I know those things happen to all of us—or if they don't happen to us literally, they happen to us in our ambient life—I know we're curious about them as determinants. We're natively curious about events that change even small personal histories. So, insofar as a story of mine might be instructive, it's that it is about what people do when bad things happen. For me, what's mostly threatened in the stories I've written is the fabric of affection that holds people close enough together to survive.

Stuckey-French: And that there might at least be the hope then at the end that that fabric of affection can be regained somehow?

Ford: In some fashion. At least it can be glimpsed by the reader, if not always the characters.

Stuckey-French: Or at least we can see some understanding of how it was lost?

Ford: That's right, and in that understanding, achieve some kind of reconnection. I mean I know you can't ever put things back how they were. But maybe you can put them together in some way that they could never have been otherwise. There's a little moment at the end of "Optimists" when a man whose family has gone completely kaflooey sees his mother in a convenience store. She goes over to him and kisses him on the cheek and basically, implicitly, tells him that she loves him. And people have said to me, "God that's such a bleak view of the world. That's such a small grain of solace to have." But I think, well no it's not, because if in the midst of your hectic life you can unexpectedly see your mother, and she comes over and says, "You know, I loved your father and by extension loved you," well, gee, that's a lot to me.

Stuckey-French: Right, and if that's all there is, then that has to be enough. Certainly, it's a memory you could hold onto, that could help carry you through life from then on.

Ford: I'll tell you one part of the origin of that story too. I was once in a convenience store in Billings, and I was in getting some Cokes for Kristina and me. We were, as usual, driving somewhere, I don't know where, and I saw a woman, who was clearly an Indian woman. But, she was quite done up in the way that you sometimes see Indian women. That is to say, she had on very tight jeans, and she had on very shiny boots, and she had on a lovely Western belt and brocaded white shirt. She had her hair done very slick and pulled way back strictly off of her forehead, and she looked very, very sleek. But she was also pretty drunk, because she was reeling a bit in the aisles. I looked at her and it was only a couple, three years after my mother had died, and I thought to myself as I looked at her—she was a woman of about sixty—I thought, that's somebody's mother, even though she seemed utterly independent of anybody around.

Stuckey-French: The outfit had served to make her not a mother?

Ford: That's right, but maybe she was. At any rate, I went back and I sat down in the car and wrote out some notes on that story just sitting there in the car.

Stuckey-French: You talk about the preparation you do for your stories. In that case it seems like maybe you had been preparing for that story, but you needed that image of her to bring those things together. The convenience store gave you something.

Ford: Yeah, you gotta pay attention.

Stuckey-French: I wanted to ask you about the end of another story, "Rock Springs," and how its final moment of understanding is arrived at. It seems to me to be the same kind of moment of understanding and recognition, but it also seems to work a little differently because of the move into direct address at the very end. I guess direct address is always implicit in a first person narrator. I mean, there is always a "you," but . . .

Ford: Yes, but it had only been implicit up to then.

Stuckey-French: Right, and there it becomes explicit, and it's a way to summarize those understandings such as they are at that moment. They are there in a list of questions.

Ford: I think it comes less into that story as a rhetorical strategy than as a gesture of sympathy; the story trying to find a way to connect itself with whomever might be reading. It's saying, "we're alike."

Stuckey-French: Exactly, and that's the way I read it from the get-go. I just think it's a wonderful ending and that it really works that way.

Ford: It was just an act of God, with me doing God's bidding. I wrote that story sitting in a little loft in New York in February of 1981, with no heat and with construction going on. Kristina and I were living in this illegal loft on Greene Street, and the Streets People came and said, "You're using PVC to conduct gas into your apartment and we're going to cut you off." And they did. They cut us off. We had rented this apartment, and we had no place to go, and I had to sit with a little space heater in just the most remote place you could be from Rock Springs and I wrote that story then. In some ways, I think, if that story has any intensity in it at all, it has the intensity of wanting very much not to be where I was. In a way, emphathizing with myself for being in a really bad situation which I didn't see anyway of getting out of, and then writing about a situation in which a guy was in a bad situation which he doesn't see any way of getting out of.

Stuckey-French: My wife has taught that story and occasionally, she'll run into a student who just . . .
Ford: . . . hates him.

Stuckey-French: . . . just doesn't like the . . .
Ford: I know.

Stuckey-French: . . . who says, "Don't say 'you.' I'm not like you."
Ford: "I don't steal cars."

Stuckey-French: Exactly. I don't know the source of such a mis-reading. Well, I hate to call it a mis-reading . . .
Ford: Well, they're youngsters for one thing, and that is definitely not a youngsters' story. You know, I remember when I read *The Moviegoer* by Walker Percy I was living in New Orleans, on leave from the University of Michigan, and I couldn't wait to get back to Michigan and get other people to read it. Joe Blotner and I taught it, and the graduate students at Michigan could not understand why anybody in the world would be the way Binx was in that novel. They were just too young.

Stuckey-French: It's a wonderful book.
Ford: Oh, one of the great American books, I think. But, here is a guy turning thirty at Mardi Gras, and these graduate kids were smart, but they were not thirty and they weren't melancholy and it wasn't the '50s, and they had no purchase on that story whatsoever and it doesn't denigrate it in any way as a story. And I think that in "Rock Springs" you may have to have a few miles on you for that story to have the resonance that it could conceivably have.

Stuckey-French: And I wonder too if you have to have, in some way, stepped into that class, or have been in that class. Not that you have to have stolen cars, you know, but that you somehow need to have felt that desperation, that need to get out. In that story, it seems to me, a lot of it is not just getting out of that place, but getting out of that . . .

Ford: . . . mentality . . .

Stuckey-French: Right, or that economic situation.

Ford: Well, the story would, if it could, establish a sympathy for a person like that. And I've had that same sentiment expressed to me about my stories: "I don't like these people. These people are marginal and they're crooks and they're sort of lowlifes." And I think to myself . . .

Stuckey-French: Try to have some heart?

Ford: Yeah. This story says you have to have some sympathy for these people, and maybe it strains the point to say that you have to have some sympathy because you are like them. But, basically it says you have to have sympathy because they are on the earth here beside you. And if you don't have that sympathy, in my view . . . you ought to.

Stuckey-French: I agree. Somewhere, perhaps it was in your introduction to the Granta collection of American short stories, you mentioned that there could be such a thing as a Republican story . . .

Ford: (laughter)

Stuckey-French: . . . a story that tells you what it's like to be a Republican and why one should be a Republican, and thankfully, I think, you shuddered at such a thought, but do you write democratic short stories with a small *d?*

Ford: Yeah, I do. I think my playing field is broad and level. Though not everybody agrees with me about that. I don't think that's the only way to write stories. People have said to me, "Well, you didn't grow up lower middle class. You didn't grow up in those circumstances." Though I did grow up in circumstances of life in which my family had grappled themselves up out of that other stratum into one where there was some clear air to breathe. And I think one of the things that I grew up realizing was that they were terrifically fearful that something was going to happen that was going to drop them back down into worse circumstances. That's dramatic, I think.

Stuckey-French: I remember reading somewhere the adage that in our society every woman is just one man away from welfare.

Ford: And I believe that, and I think it about myself, about being a writer. Nothing's promised. I know my father felt that way. Maybe I inherited it from him.

Stuckey-French: He was a salesman. I thought of that in *A Piece of My Heart* where I guess it's Hewes who is talking about what that work can do to you, which I think a lot of people aren't aware of. Even those who've read *Death of a Salesman,* maybe they don't think about the hemorrhoids and . . .

Ford: . . . closing your hand up in the door and all those nights alone in motels and years and years of that. The thing I couldn't figure out was why he loved his work so much. He just loved it. I would think about all the particulars—loneliness, drive, drive, drive, hot, hot, hot. It was before the days of air-conditioning. I couldn't figure that out. Still, really, in a way can't. It's a fit subject for art, I think; to investigate that unknown.

Stuckey-French: So what did he love about it, do you think? The independence?

Ford: I don't know. He loved my mother desperately, and they had had this wonderful life together for years before I was born . . . fifteen years . . . and my mother was a really interesting person and compelling in a way, and I can't imagine what it would have been like to have had all those years together with her and then suddenly for me to have come along and for his life then to start out in a slightly different tack, which is being mostly alone. Maybe it is just that he wasn't a very sophisticated man, or maybe he just liked new beginnings every week, and the end of the week was the beginning of the weekend, and the beginning of the following week was the beginning of another week in which he didn't know exactly how things would go. And maybe, it was on that low level of satisfaction. Or maybe it was something entirely unknown to me. But really, when in a piece of fiction a writer says he "investigates" something, he is really just inventing possible answers— obvious ones and less obvious, fanciful ones.

Stuckey-French: And I guess part of those new beginnings is that you are just constantly meeting new people and you have that opportunity to talk.

Ford: That's right, and he did. A kind of endless, almost unhierarchical diversity. Once again, you go along this flat plain and you're constantly like a pinball being baffled back and forth among people, and maybe he just liked that. I don't know. I'm going to write an essay about him next year.

Stuckey-French: Are you?

Ford: I wrote a long essay about my mother. And I'd like to write something about my father. But the problem is that he wasn't around after I was sixteen, because he died, and I don't want to write the absent father essay. I'll have to figure out something different.

Stuckey-French: I noticed that *Wildlife* and "Great Falls" and, I don't know, a couple of other things that you've written are all about 1960–61 and a seventeen-year-old narrator. Is it important for you in some way to return to that moment when your father died?

Ford: Probably, but not I think in an autobiographical way. One of the things writers do is contend that their life is just like everybody else's life, and if something happened to me when I was sixteen that changed my life forever. . . .

Stuckey-French: . . . everybody had something that did?

Ford: At least it is possible they did. Women and men too. Obviously there are limits to that contention, but I think it is true that when boys, and girls too, reach that age, they're beginning to leave adolescence or childhood and heading into adulthood, and all kinds of important things happen. And I thought for me it was crucial, and I thought all kinds of other things happened to kids all over the country that were crucial. So it was just the natural kind of writerly participation in the lives of others, which originates in my participation in my own life. But I didn't write anything in those stories there about fathers dying, because I didn't want to write about that.

Stuckey-French: Right, they're not about that.

Ford: I was interested, as I said before, in what happens beyond some crucial event, which even though it changes life it also lets it come back together, maybe in a more interesting way. I wished to have as many participants survive the event as can be. So death of the father didn't figure in.

Stuckey-French: Those stories, it seems to me, are more about the relationship between the boy and the mother, and how they're both at some turning point and have to get to what's next.

Ford: That's right. I guess I'm just interested in the whole configuration; from one permutation to the next at a particular age, or at least I was. I don't know if I'll write about it anymore.

Stuckey-French: The whole country turned at that moment too, I guess.

Ford: Well, the fifties officially ended. But I'm not sure the fifties ended until Kennedy was killed, really. But at least if you set something on the cusp of '59–'60, the reader now can look back at that time, and, through the focus of a story, history can be made to seem more intelligible, or at least seem to have implications that weren't immediately apparent then.

Stuckey-French: So, do you feel a responsibility or a desire not only to try to understand what happened on a personal level, but also . . .

Ford: In a historical way? No, I don't think so. I think history for me is a convenience, which is of the same kind of convenience as time-setting *The Sportswriter* on Easter was or time-setting other stories of mine: that is, they're set on days or years that are recognizable by the reader—on holidays or Halloween or Thanksgiving, or precise years. I like to set events at a time that the reader has some memory of. The reader then is more easily convinced to participate in the story's illusion, and the story then begins to inform that time for the reader through the agency of his memory. But I don't myself pretend to have any particular purchase on that time. I'm using it just as a mnemonic. Somebody asked me when I was in France a couple of weeks ago, what I took to be a theoretical question . . .

Stuckey-French: Well, you were in France.

Ford: . . . which had to do with my sense of history, and my view of it. And if I hadn't been respectful of the guy, I would have laughed, because I have almost no sense of history. But, in a way that the French might appreciate, I have a kind of existential freedom regarding history. I convert it. Traduce it. Change it. Maybe that means I have a sense, after all.

Stuckey-French: A sense of moment?

Ford: Yeah, or a willingness to change it, a willingness to say, "History's like this. For me, history's like this. I'll bet it was like that for you." And all I have to do is get you to agree that it was, because that's basically the nature of literary truth. If you and I can posit an important possibility and agree to it and live in accordance to it, I'm afraid it's on the way to becoming truth.

Stuckey-French: So, for instance, it can be Thanksgiving [in the story "Going to the Dogs"], but also on this other vector coming in it's the time I had to move out and stiff this guy on his lease?

Ford: That's right.

Stuckey-French: By bringing those two things together it's that much more memorable or believable?

Ford: You get a whole package of memories and a whole package of responses, which you otherwise weren't going to get if you had it be the 5th of November. We story writers need all the help we can get. And yet, when people say about *The Sportswriter* "You set it on Easter because it's a story about redemption, isn't it?" I think to myself, yeah, maybe that's right, maybe that's right. But the *real* reason I set it on Easter was that's the day I began writing it. Easter Day in 1982. And I think I began it then because

Easter just struck me as a very memorable holiday—one anybody in America had some vivid associates with. Plus, I was looking for a short period of time in which a novel could take place and I thought "Well, Good Friday to Easter. That's a nice short little course that you can set a novel in." So that's what it was. That it became interested in redemptive issues was really after the fact.

Stuckey-French: So, it wasn't a question of trying to resurrect Ralph?

Ford: No, but I'll tell you, as I've said before, if you start monkeying around with these Judeo-Christian myths, you're in over your boot tops in a hurry. You better be up to it. They have remarkable potency, whether you're acquainted with them or just are a novice, as I was.

Stuckey-French: You better be ready for some readers who know it better than you?

Ford: R. Z. Sheppard in *Time,* when that book was reviewed (and he liked it), said he thought I had made it have fourteen chapters because there are fourteen stations to the Cross. But that was the first time I'd heard there were fourteen stations to the Cross.

Stuckey-French: I remember reading an interview where Bill Gass talking about how his story "In the Heart of the Heart of the Country," which opens with the allusion to "Sailing to Byzantium," "And so I have sailed the seas and come . . . / to B . . . / a small town fastened to a field in Indiana." Then it's written in those sections, you know "People," "Weather," whatever, and some critic counted the sections and said, "Ah ha, 32 and 32 lines in 'Sailing to Byzantium." And he [Gass] said the same thing you just said, "I'd never thought of that."

Ford: On the other hand, it's sometimes nice to think that you plugged your finger into a hot current, even if by accident. Only a fool would argue much.

Stuckey-French: What about some things that I wondered if you do put in a little more consciously? For instance, humor. It seems like you really enjoy writing something funny.

Ford: I'm actually quite bereft if I write a story which doesn't have any humor in it; and for various reasons: one, that humor finds its way into any piece of literature as a relief, and also because I think often people actually say important, serious things under the guise of not being serious about it. One of the purposes of any story is to ask the reader to pay attention to this which she or he might not have paid attention before, and, indeed, pay attention to it in this degree of particularity, whereas in ordinary life things flow by and we don't pay much attention to them. So, I want stories to draw the reader's attention to something and say, "This is important." And humans always make jokes when they aren't joking at all. So, it has at least two sides to it and maybe it has other sides too—one of which is that writing something funny pleases *me*. Nothing makes me happier than when I can be writing a story and make myself laugh. I call that a triumph, even if I later throw it out, and I often do throw it out.

Stuckey-French: So what are some of the funniest moments for you?
Ford: I can't remember.

Stuckey-French: Well, I was thinking when you were saying that humor can instruct . . . that in "Winterkill" when the woman . . . ah, is it Nola?
Ford: Yeah, Nola, who just came out of the song, you know, "Walking along a thoroughfare." Do you know that song, "Nola"? That's the only reason I used the name. I have a friend in Chicago who can play "Nola"—the song—*on his head,* by hitting the top of his head with his knuckles and moving his open mouth in and out. Possibly you'd have to see it to think it was funny. In fact, I'm sure you would. But I thought it was very funny.

Stuckey-French: I would love to see and hear that. In the story, Nola's talking about when her husband knew he was going to die and he spontaneously decided that he wanted flank steak, and Troy connects right with it. He says, "I know. I thought of lobster when I was lying there dying." And I laughed there.
Ford: I wanted you to. I thought Troy was a comic character. But, in that story anyway, Troy seems comic in spite of being wrecked physically. Ultimately, too, of course, he isn't comic, but rather noble.

Stuckey-French: He's sad, and yet he's such a wonderful audience to her.
Ford: He's so thrilled to get to talk to a woman, whereas ordinarily he might've just been cast aside. I remember when I wrote *The Ultimate Good Luck* and Walter Clemons, who I'm sorry to say just died this summer, reviewed it in *Newsweek.* One of the things he said about it was that he liked the book, but he said I'd managed to write a book that short-circuited something I could do—which was to be funny. He'd liked another book of mine, *A Piece of My Heart,* which had comic parts. And that made an impression on me, and I just thought that I wasn't going to write anything else that short-circuited humor. (I've since broken that promise a time or two). But one of

the things that you want to do as a writer is to get everything you know and are capable of as a writer onto the page so that you can exceed it in the act of writing; gain access to something you couldn't otherwise ever have gotten access to. That's a problem for many young writers; they tap into only part of their abilities. It's something you can overcome with hard work, of course.

Stuckey-French: I'm thinking a little more about the humor in your stories. It seems like one of the agents for bringing the humor into your stories is children.

Ford: Oh, yeah, because I sometimes see them as such malevolent little creatures who rule (and often not benignly) the lives of adults.

Stuckey-French: Yeah, like Cherry imitating Paul Harvey. There's something wicked about that.

Ford: Yeah, well I think kids can be wicked by not knowing wicked.

Stuckey-French: They're not expected yet to have a conscience, or manners, or something.

Ford: That's a very Victorian idea. If you read Hardy and you read kids in Hardy. Or, if you remember in *Wuthering Heights,* there's a scene which occurs in a kitchen, and the children hanging puppies by a string off the back of a chair. And Father Time in *Jude the Obscure* comes into the book as a child but ages unnaturally fast and speaks only as an adult, speaks runically, speaks rivetingly to Jude. I think that's where I determined how to use children. You use them as extremely potent characters, rather than as bothersome non-entities (which they mostly are in life); little oracles who speak as adults or who affect events in large ways yet remain deceptively "innocent." You know, if you have to have children speak as children, they won't say anything very interesting. They don't know anything.

Stuckey-French: It's when they're imitating adults or trying to horn in on the adults' conversation that they get spooky, because there are these adult voices coming out of their mouths.

Ford: Truthfully, though, I'm only interested in adults. I think that's the only time when life begins to make any difference; when you can take responsibility for your actions and your actions can have a consequence which you can oversee. So, children are, for me, little condiments in stories. You know, you shake them in to spice it up, but the real events take place in the lives of people who are responsible, who bear the consequences of action as fully as it can be borne. I think that would probably get me in trouble with the Pope. [laughter] But he probably doesn't read my stories in Italian—or, really, know much about real life. I mean, he's a priest.

Stuckey-French: I don't know. He's laid up now with that broken leg. Maybe he has the time to read some fiction.

Ford: I want to know how he broke his hip. I want to know how he got down on the floor in that bathroom. That's what I want to know.

The *Salon* Interview: Richard Ford

Sophie Majeski / 1996

From *Salon*.com, Inc. 18 April 1996. This interview originally appeared in *Salon*.com. Reproduced with permission. www.salon.com.

Richard Ford, whose novel *Independence Day* was the first ever to win both the Pulitzer Prize and the PEN/Faulkner Award and had just about every critic in America breathing words like "mastery," "genius" and "tour de force," once told an interviewer that "writing is the only thing I've ever done with persistence, except for being married." Much has been made of his habit of moving around—his most recent home is on Bourbon Street in New Orleans, where his wife of twenty-eight years, Kristina, is executive director of the city planning commission—and *Independence Day* plays beautifully with the idea of impermanence.

The novel is the sequel to Ford's highly acclaimed *The Sportswriter,* which was the story of a man named Frank Bascombe who, devasted by the death of his young son, dropped quietly out of his own life. In *Independence Day,* Frank Bascombe more or less returns, moving into his ex-wife's old house, settling permanently—after a fling in France with a woman some twenty years his junior—into the suburbs to reconnect with his family and to sell real estate, which becomes for Bascombe a heady metaphor for the nature of attachment. He has moved into what he calls his "Existence Period," a tenuous equilibrium that seems to depend on keeping people and his own feelings at a comfortable remove.

Over lunch in San Francisco at the beginning of a fifteen-city tour to promote the Vintage paperback edition of *Independence Day,* Ford says that he personally prefers the sometimes disastrous habit of feeling to Bascombe's more defensive strategy. Attractive, intensely engaging, very funny, all soft Southern charm—he was born in 1944 in Mississippi—Ford asks for a quiet table, thinking of the tape recorder, and though he eloquently and cordially answers every question, no matter how personal or banal, he asks polite and probing questions of his own, including the first question of the interview.

RF: So do you think *Independence Day* is more of a man's book than a woman's?

118

SM: Hardly. The women in the novel seem to know so much more than the men.

RF: Yes, they have a line on things.

SM: Do you think that women really do know more about what's going on than men do?

RF: Well, I know that by living thirty-two years with the same woman my view of the world has been remarkably changed, certainly in a way it would not have been if I had lived alone or not been with this wonderfully forceful, smart woman who doesn't miss anything. She makes it appealing to try to widen my view, for instance, to be sure that you're not thinking out of only one part of your brain.

SM: Which part would that be?

RF: Oh, the part you grew up with. Being a Southerner it's very appealing to think that you are who you are, that your character is fixed. It's very much a notion attuned to the conservatism of the South, that old tradition of the South being what it viewed itself as. But the fact is that when you have another person in your life, someone you care for and want to accommodate, your view and sometimes even the rudiments of your character will change.

SM: I loved the line in *Independence Day* about conservatives being people who make the same mistakes over and over again.

RF: Yes, and don't admit it. I've been doing what I've been doing for so long that I can't remember when it finally dawned on me, but I try to give women in my novels as many good lines as I give men, which is a way for me to confer on those characters the control of their lives. Language in a novel is action, it's where values reside, and so what people say in a book, particularly when there are not going to be sword fights or firefights or cavalry charges—when human interaction *is* the action—becomes very important as the determinant of who they are and how other action will take place. So I always want to make sure women have good lines.

SM: So it was a conscious choice?

RF: I'm not sure. It was either a thing I recognized that I wanted to do and then did do or it was a thing I was already doing and finally recognized. My assumption as a person who writes about moral issues is that women and men are alike. And in terms of their consequential acts, they have to be responsible for what they do in pretty much the same way, and the differences that are perhaps inspired by gender are subterior to what is more important to me—how men and women treat other people, how they act in ways that bring about consequences in others' lives.

SM: So there is something essential about us that is beyond gender?
RF: Yes, I look to the end line. Do they *die* any differently? I watched my mother die, watched my father die, and I thought to myself, that's where life ends, and it's very much the same. There are some things that are beyond gender. I've discovered it in a long relationship with one person, which isn't to say that it's magic or that you have to have a long relationship with one person—maybe it's just taken me thirty-two years to get it in my brain. But there are qualities in human life that perhaps only literature can define, which are more fundamental than those other distinguishing qualities among us, like gender, age and sex. There is something else.

SM: Do you have any idea what it is?
RF: It's probably not a thing for which there is a diction; it's probably something literature can only allude to. I was riding up here with this kid who was interviewing me earlier today, and he was talking about Frank, saying he was shaving the truth to get women into bed with him, and I said, wait, wait, *wait* a minute. Maybe there are moments when Frank would *like* to go to bed with somebody, but it really has less to do with seduction than with wanting to be close to somebody, with wanting to do whatever you can to narrow that space Emerson calls the infinite remoteness that separates people. And maybe that's as close to describing the thing as I can get. The need to be able to touch somebody. And not even physically. Because I know in long relationships between people, when they get old and physicality begins to seem less crucial, there is still some closeness that physicality does not describe. I've seen it with my parents particularly. And even closeness is just a metaphor for something else. Language would always be dealing in its metaphorical representations. It is something for which there is no language. You might even see it best in one-celled animals, in amoebas. Or in Pleistocene creatures who don't have the confusion of thought to complicate things.

SM: Do you feel as if writing novels is a sort of alternate existence, that you get to play, for instance, with having kids?
RF: I wouldn't have said that about it. It sounds almost illicit when you say it like that. But there is that aspect of being a novelist. You get to participate in other lives through the agency of language. There's a line from Randall Jarrell, who said that poets are not people who have the experience they

write about but people who need to have it. Through your work you do get to meet certain needs.

The other thing is that it allows you to live life over and over again. That's one of the reasons I wanted to write this novel in the first person, and in the present tense. The novel gets to say we're present tense here, and yet we can read the present over and over again. Which is quite a nice thing to do, we'd all be better off if we could not stop time but slow it down a little bit, and live the pleasant things more pleasantly and live the incautious things more cautiously. And being a novelist does let you do that with the work you invent, you get to go over it and over it and think about it: Do I want this to happen? Is this a good thing? Do I want to be responsible for having a character think this? It really helps you pay attention.

SM: Do you think novelists are responsible for what their characters think?
RF: Well, they're responsible—they're not necessarily answerable.

SM: I was thinking, reading this novel, how there's both pleasure in doing what you're not supposed to do and pleasure in doing what you're supposed to do. Frank gets pleasure out of both, so how do you balance it?
RF: Your life is how you balance it. There's that moment when Frank is kind of looking for somebody to give him dinner and lets himself be momentarily bewitched by this scullery maid, during which time he thinks, maybe I can just abandon my kid for the night after toting him all that distance. There's a lot to be said for doing what you're not supposed to do, and the rewards of doing what you're supposed to do are more subtle and take longer to become apparent, which maybe makes it less attractive. But your life is the blueprint you make after the building is built.

SM: So everything is hindsight?
RF: When you're talking about how you balance it, yes, it certainly is.

SM: Do you think things just happen to us?
RF: Yes, they do, but it's one of the real schisms of emotional life that you have to take responsibility for them. I mean, if your mother dies, that is obviously not your responsibility, but with most things you have to look inside yourself and think—and this is really kind of novelistic thinking—that this happened to me because I did this and I did this and I did this and I was in the way of this. It's a worthwhile kind of ethical route to follow.

SM: Do you think too much has been made of how much you've moved around?

RF: Yes, I do. My wife was just asked to apply for the job of planning director out here, by the way.

SM: Would you want to live here?

RF: No. I love to come to San Francisco, but it just doesn't appeal to me as a place to live. New Orleans was a really good example of that, a place I really loved and so we moved there and now I don't want to live there. It's a little like the old adage of being careful about what you want. I don't like living in New Orleans. In fact, I've just basically kind of quit living there.

Kristina's declared herself out of the loop, she's made the decision by fiat that she's staying in New Orleans, and I have yet to come around to that decision, so I have other houses and other venues and I can still sort of strike off and go to Montana as I am now. I'm going to stay there until the end of the year.

SM: Where do you think you might want to live?

RF: I have discovered where I like it for now. I like the northern tier of Montana. I like it in the Delta of Mississippi and I like it in Paris. So I can live in those places at this time in my life. And one of these days I'll run out of bucks or I won't want to do it anymore or I'll get sick and die or a hundred things will happen, but at this particular moment that's what I'd like to do. But the really, central thing is that, no matter where I move, I always write and I'm married to the same girl. All that other stuff is just filigree.

SM: What were you thinking about when you decided to write about *Independence Day?*

RF: A couple of things came to mind at once. Sometimes I get interested in words, and I found myself writing in my notebook about independence. The word kept coming up in one context or another, and there's this great line of Henry Miller's one of the most interesting things I've ever heard anyone say: "Never think of a surface except as a volume." So when I see a word that I'm interested in, what that means to me is that the word has a kind of density to it, and if I can dedicate some language to it I can invent something. So I decided to write a novel in which I would use this word a lot, and maybe even write a novel in which it would be a primary concern. And then it seemed natural to set it on the Fourth of July. I was very attracted to Bruce Springsteen's song "Independence Day," in which a son sings a kind of lament to his father, especially the line, "Just say goodbye, it's Independence Day." I hadn't ever realized that independence in the most conventional sense means leavetaking, putting distance between yourself and other people, getting out of their orbit. So then I wondered if that's what it has to mean, so I thought I'd write about it and see if I couldn't make it mean something else, if independence could in fact mean a freedom to make contact with others, rather than just the freedom to sever oneself from others. Anyone can sever ties, and it's part of my general scheme to try to write things that are affirming. It's always easy to write about things that fuck up, things that go kaflooey, and people leave and the door slams and that's the dramatic end. But I'm always interested in what happens after somebody walks out the door. I'm interested in what they do later. The most constructive impulse in my life is that I don't ever walk out the door; I don't do exits.

SM: What do you mean?

RF: I mean I don't say "fuck you, goodbye." If I love you, you're going to have me forever.

SM: Why do you think that is?

RF: Because people left me when I was little. I never thought it was better to be alone than to be with someone you loved.

SM: Because your father died when you were a child?

RF: Yes, I knew what that was like, and that wasn't so good. The other thing is that I like setting books on holidays because I think all Americans have very patented memories for Easter, very patented memories for the Fourth of July, so if I set my book on that day, I would tap into those memories and engage people at some very primary level. And holidays are often when people want to be most themselves, when they want to be the best they can be—school's out, it's a holiday, let's be happy—and often circumstances intervene to make you miserable or frustrated, so it's a very good little proscenium for a human drama in which the reader can recognize the terms and be engaged.

SM: As you were writing, did independence come to mean something different than how you had originally conceived it?

RF: It's really kind of interesting to me; I don't know how interesting it is to anyone else. But when I started writing about Frank at the beginning of the book, I kept thinking to myself, what the hell is at issue here? You lope off into what you think is going to be a long novel and there's always a period at the beginning when you're facing a lot of things you don't know the nature of. Because he was past those crucial points in his life when there was crisis, so I thought to myself, well, he has an equilibrium in his life which he has paid the price of isolation to maintain, and that's when I invented the Existence Period, which was that period after the crises have subsided. You've survived, and you're nominally happy, so the issue has become—and this is the kind of novelistic thinking one does—what price have you paid to attain equilibrium? And what I figured out was that the price Frank had paid—and it was a high price—was that he was isolated and had achieved independence only in a conditional sense. And what was at issue in his life was how in the process of maintaining that equilibrium he could ever touch somebody. How could he run the risk of complicating his life by engaging people he cared about? So that is what the book is about. How does he engage his son, how does he engage his ex-wife, how does he engage the woman he might be in love with, how does he engage his profession? And that's a fairly fundamenal human challenge.

SM: I was just thinking about people who've found equilibrium by going to India or Thailand to meditate, having enlightenment experiences but being unable to share them, unable to maintain that equilibrium when they engage again with other people.

RF: You lose the sensuous part. You have to have things coming in and the only way you can have things coming in is for there to be other people around. We need the unpredictable.

SM: But why can't we have the equilibrium and the relationships?
RF: Because we want things.

SM: What do we want?
RF: More. All of the things that get me into trouble are instances of me wanting more than I can deal with. It drives me crazy, it makes me neurotic and compulsive and wild and keeps me up at night dealing with those things I have wanted and have gotten. But I would rather go down to blazes that way than go to blazes in some abstinent state. I'd rather live than exist.

SM: So you want to feel everything.
RF: I do. This is a silly corollary, such a male thing it's probably almost perplexingly stupid, but I have a big Harley-Davidson motorcycle which I bought in 1989 and kept for about a year. Then I put it in storage because life changed, and it stayed in storage for seven years and I would sometimes think about it in that storage bin in Missoula and think to myself, "This is the nature of my whole life. I did this thing and then I built a box around it

and shoved it back in there and it just keeps every once in a while looming up at me shouting, 'Mistake, mistake, mistake.' " But then last week I got it out of storage, and I took it up to Great Falls and I took it to the Harley shop and they got it started up, they got it cranking and I went back to see it two days ago and I thought, "Here you are you sucker, I'm ready for you now." And it made me the happiest man in the world.

Seeking Shelter from the Storm: Richard Ford Pays Homage to Central New Jersey

Richard Shea / 1996

From *The Princeton Packet* 21 June 1996. Reprinted by permission.

Before *The Sportswriter* was published in 1986, Richard Ford was an unknown. He'd written two favorably reviewed novels, but they didn't sell. He'd also given sportswriting a shot, but his employer, *Inside Sports,* folded a year after he was hired. Perhaps being a full-time writer, he thought, wasn't meant to be.

But his wife, Kristina, who'd supported him from the start, suggested he try writing another novel, this one about someone who's happy." Mr. Ford was happy as a sportswriter, so he gave his main character, Frank Bascombe, the same job. And he set the novel in a then-unlikely literary landscape, one where the Fords had resided for six years: central New Jersey.

"The only way you can [write about New Jersey]," Mr. Ford said, speaking from his home in Montana, "is to take the conventional wisdom about New Jersey, which is that it's kind of an unappetizing place, and reverse it, actually write a book that is kind of an homage to New Jersey."

Both *The Sportswriter,* which put Mr. Ford on the literary map in 1986, and its sequel, *Independence Day,* which won him this year's Pulitzer Prize for fiction and the PEN/Faulkner Award, are, indeed, homages to central New Jersey. But they're a whole lot more. Like John Updike's "Rabbit" books, they are commentaries on the United States and, in particular, their middle-class suburban residents, with central New Jersey serving as microcosm.

When Mr. Ford began writing *The Sportswriter,* he was, by that time, living in Montana, where he still has a home in Chinook, "a little town, way out on the prairie," he said. But from 1976 to 1982, he and his wife, an urban planner, lived, off and on, in Princeton, the town he used as a model for his character Frank's hometown, Haddam.

Those familiar with Princeton will certainly see the similarities between the two towns, but there are differences. There's a theological institute but no university in Haddam. The street names are also different, and, while

126

some of the surrounding towns are given real names—Hightstown and Lambertville, for instance—others are made up. Mr. Ford mixes fact and fiction for a reason.

"It's like writing about real people," he explained. "If you write about real people, if you have actual models for your characters, when you want to deviate, or when you want to just completely depart from your models, then this sort of persuasiveness of actual human beings makes that deviating hard.

"So, really, what I think I do—both with human beings and with places—is, I take what I need and leave what I don't and invent what I can't find."

Independence Day begins several years after *The Sportswriter* ends. It's 1988, and Frank Bascombe is no longer a sportswriter, but a successful real estate agent. He is, however, divorced and living alone. His two children—Paul, fifteen, and Clarissa, twelve—are living comfortably, but not exactly happily, in Deep River, Conn., with their mother and her second husband, a wealthy architect. Trouble, for the Bascombes, began when the oldest child, Ralph, died of Reye's syndrome at the age of nine. Frank spends much of *The Sportswriter* in what he calls a "dreamy" state, removed from the pain associated with the loss and, at the same time, trying to pick up the pieces.

In the new novel, Frank is back in action—or, at least, he thinks he is—this time cruising through "the Existence Period." It's a time when, scarred and made wise by experience, you're better able to handle life's problems and content in the knowledge that you can't solve them all.

So, yes, Frank is a "happy" character, and his living in Haddam, the cradle of suburban New Jersey, seems only fitting. Scenic, historic and safe, it's a slice of real estate to which out-of-towners flock, searching for their dream houses. And Frank, as a realtor, sincerely wants to help them. It's his way of "being useful," a term Mr. Ford applies to himself as a writer.

But Frank, like Mr. Ford, is a realist. He knows that people like the Markhams, an older couple from Vermont who, after seeing forty-five houses, are still not happy with the choices, are going to have to face up to facts. The Markhams want a pre-war, three-bedroom, charming Cape, something close to a middle school, for about $150,000. But deals like that, Frank notes, "are history. Ancient history."

Mr. Ford, who's lived in many places throughout his life—which means he's spent lots of time with realtors—admits that Frank doesn't make finding your dream home look easy.

"But that's the scariness of being adult," he explained. "It's true in fiction, it's true in life: That it's not so much what happens to you, it's what you do about what happens to you."

The only son of a traveling salesman and a homemaker, Mr. Ford was born in Jackson, Miss., the middle of his father's territory, in 1944. Country folk, Parker and Edna Ford wanted a better life for their son; so they sent him to good, suburban schools and encouraged him to take advantage of the cultural offerings in Jackson.

By the time he was a teenager, Mr. Ford was getting into the kind of trouble adolescents often do. The police were acquainted with him, and his father, who was often on the road, considered sending his son to military school. But one morning, when Mr. Ford was sixteen, his father had a heart attack. Mr. Ford tried CPR, but to no avail.

"He died in my arms," he recalled.

While Mr. Ford was saddened by his father's passing, he was also relieved.

"Probably his not having been around as much as he was not around hastened my feeling that, even though I loved him, his departure from my life set me free," Mr. Ford explained. "So there was a real bittersweet feeling to it."

Suddenly, Mr. Ford was a man, a fact his mother, who died in 1981, made clear by demanding he find a job. After he graduated high school, Mr. Ford worked for the Missoula-Pacific Railroad for a couple of years, put himself through Michigan State University, then started law school in St. Louis. But living alone, and "deeply in love" with his wife-to-be, Kristina, whom he'd met in Michigan, he was feeling restless.

Then, during exam time, right before Christmas, his law books were stolen from his car. Mr. Ford and Kristina headed down to Little Rock, Ark., where his mother was living, and discussed his situation.

"It became clear to me that I was having a little crisis in law school," he recalled, "and over the next two or three weeks, I just decided, 'Well, f— it, I'm not gonna go back to law school. I cannot make myself go back to law school. There are too many compelling things in life that are pulling at me."

When his mother asked him what he would do, Mr. Ford replied, "I'm gonna be a writer."

Soon, he and Kristina were married. They lived in New York City for a year, then went out to California, where Mr. Ford got a master's degree in literature at the University of California in Irvine. In 1970, they moved to Chicago, where Ms. Ford had been offered a job. While there, Mr. Ford began his writing career.

It may sound like a fantasy-come-true kind of life, but Mr. Ford believes that he and his wife simply made the kinds of decisions everyone, in his or her life, has to make. Rather than believing the grass is greener on the other side, they set out to make it greener at home.

"One of the qualities of being a writer, I really believe is, that there is no calling, except that you do it," he said. "There isn't any potential energy that you have to seize. My own metaphor for it relies upon the notion that you have to invent your whole personality as a writer, invent your whole self as a writer and that, if you don't do it, that self is not waiting out there for you to occupy it; it doesn't exist.

"So I try to console young writers—as much as I can, 'cause I don't teach—by saying, 'If you don't write this book, who cares? Don't feel it's a loss if you can't do something. It only matters if you do."

The happy house Frank Bascombe inhabits in *Independence Day* was built on shaky ground. Frank's talent for wrapping emotional issues in neat little packages, for giving names to the phases of life, is not enough to protect him from the unexpected. He learns this soon enough, as he attempts to help his troubled son, Paul, work through his problems with the law and his life in Connecticut, a life without a full-time father and an older brother.

Over the Fourth-of-July weekend, they drive to the basketball and baseball halls of fame, all-American backdrops rendered vividly and, often, beautifully by Mr. Ford. In Cooperstown, N.Y., home to the Baseball Hall of Fame, however, things go terribly wrong, due partly to Frank's reluctance to meet problems head-on.

"I think that the Existence Period started out in Frank's mind as a period in which he thought he was rather independent, life was pretty much in balance and he had freedom to do what he wanted to do. Then, what he discovered . . . [is that] the Existence Period is purchased at the price of isolation, and that if you're going to work hard at keeping the world at arm's length, you're going to—as he says to [his girlfriend] Sally—fall outside of affection; you're gonna not greet the complex issues of your life complexly. And, in fact, maybe you really can't hold the world at arm's length."

What makes Frank Bascombe such a likable, sympathetic and, inevitably, powerful character is, he's a typical middle-aged, middle-class suburbanite with an atypical gift for articulation, for putting into perspective what so many of Mr. Ford's readers experience.

"Primary to my understanding to what's going on in American life," Mr. Ford said, "is that there's a general sense that there's a wild world outside our perimeters. And the suburb is one response to it; there are all kinds of other responses.

"Basically, what [*Independence Day*] is about—and it takes on a larger sort of stature in the book as you go along—is, people wanting to find shelter, people wanting to find shelter from something."

An Interview with
Richard Ford

Elinor Ann Walker / 1997

From *The South Carolina Review* 31.2 (1999): 128–43. Used by permission.

I met with Richard Ford on the morning of March 18, 1997, in Chapel Hill, North Carolina, where Ford had been invited to be the Morgan Family Writer-in-Residence. In that role, he met with undergraduate and graduate students as well as interested members of the community on a daily basis. The day preceding our interview, in fact, he discussed his fiction with a panel of scholars and answered numerous questions from a varied audience. During the course of our interview, when either of us refers to "yesterday," we are referring to that occasion. I am indebted to the English Department at the University of North Carolina and the committee in charge of the Morgan Family Writers for inviting me to participate in that week's events.

E.A.W.: I understand that you have been a fan of Bruce Springsteen.
R.F.: I have.

E.A.W.: I know that Bobbie Ann Mason has written a number of stories in which she has incorporated Bruce Springsteen lyrics and other references to pop culture.
R.F.: I didn't know that. Good for her.

E.A.W.: And she has been criticized for that. Do you think too much has been made of a distinction between real culture or literary culture and pop culture?
R.F.: I don't know much about cultural distinctions. I only know that Springsteen's lyrics, and also his phrasings and his music in general, have meant something to me personally. So that must mean it or he fits into whatever level of culture being a story writer is in America now. They seem to exist on the same plane, or at least compatible ones. His great song, "Independence Day," this great anthem to leaving home, was probably the first thing that moved me along the path to writing a novel called *Independence Day.* The title for my book comes as much from his song as all the other

sources that that name could come from. I'm sure there are plenty of kinds of music that I wouldn't be as comfortable with, but I wouldn't want to say they don't enter the culture where my stories and I enter the culture, the literary culture. I certainly don't have any qualms about Bobbie Ann—whom I hardly know—using those lyrics. I wouldn't do it myself because I know I'd have a hard time overcoming their particular authority. If I struck a Springsteen lyric into a line of mine or a scene in the story, I'd be afraid that I'd never be able to reauthorize the scene, that the lyric would just suck all of my particular authority out of the scene and into a Bruce Springsteen ethos, and that would be it for me. In fact, there's a scene in *The Sportswriter* that takes place pretty close to the Jersey shore in which Frank [Bascombe] is in a phone booth, where he actually gets hit by a car, and a girl comes over from the root beer stand. A carhop. And when I got her over to where he was, I write that she was wearing a sweatshirt, and I really wanted to put some catchy Springsteen lyric on it, or else put "Springsteen Tour 1985" or something like that. But I thought, no, no, no, you keep that out of there, because it'll just gobble up your scene, in addition to making me look like I was poaching, which I probably was. But I thought the detail might make the scene not be about what I wanted it to be about.

E.A.W.: Well, certainly, people have argued that Springsteen is a kind of spokesperson for America or a truly American voice. . . .

R.F.: Well, they've argued that about my novels, too, but I don't think they are.

E.A.W.: No?

R.F.: America, thank God, is a lot of voices, and I'm just one voice in a chorus, you know?

E.A.W.: It's interesting to me that *Independence Day* is diffuse—it's a big novel—but it's also a very contained story, set just around those particular days in the life of Frank Bascombe. You don't conceive of Bascombe's voice as an utterance of some testimony to American experience?

R.F.: I think that might be a reader's judgment. I think of him as being very specific to what I was able to make him do. I'm not unaware that he occasionally looks over and sees something and then makes a pronouncement which a reader could say was a more general pronouncement about American culture. But I always try to make those kinds of remarks from him sufficiently double-edged so that they are at least as humorous as they are serious and don't make me seem like what I'm not—a know-it-all. If I would seem to be getting pontifical, I'd hope my own sense of absurdity would bail me out of it. I heard somebody say that as writers get older, they tend to get more and more general in their pronouncements, and I wouldn't want to do that. I will *never* write another Frank Bascombe book if I feel like I'm impelled to do so by some sense of national responsibility. How silly. I'm really only interested in the specific word, the specific deed, the specific actions in the book.

E.A.W.: You've said that too much has been made of your own penchant for relocation. . . .

R.F.: Yeah. It's a dull subject. But maybe there's nothing else about me to talk about.

E.A.W.: The same questions over and over again. . . .

R.F. And I keep trying to come up with interesting answers, but I get tired of my own interesting answers. I mean, if you live some place and stay there, do you want to talk about *that* all the time? My sense of locatedness is actually just a matter of where I work, and the contact I keep with the people I love. That's as much location as I feel is absolutely essential. Other people seem to feel differently about it.

E.A.W.: Another thing that people have spent conversation and ink trying to figure out is how "southern" a writer you really are, and I know that you've talked about that some, too. I read somewhere that when you published *A Piece of My Heart,* critics and reviewers could only say that it was neo-Faulknerian, and at that point you decided, no more southern writing. . . .

R.F.: I did. That's right.

E.A.W.: And you haven't set a work in the South since.

R.F.: That's exactly right. I'm a southerner, obviously; I like the South, I still live some in the South, but the South is just not a subject on which I have any interesting things to say or any curiosity about, and probably having made that decision back in the mddle '70s, my southern experience is even thinner now. And the subject of the South bores me, really. To me, the South as a regional entity or identity represents one of a number of unpalatable things. It's either the chamber of commerce boosterism, the sort of chest-thumping "how great we all are," which I of course know isn't true. We southerners aren't particularly great. Or else it's a notion representing some kind of encoded white self-regard, which I don't like either. It would seem to me that if the South could find a vocabulary adequate for all of its equal component parts, it would quit being the South and just become part of America. But by insisting on itself the way some wanton southerners enjoy doing, what it's basically doing is resisting useful change. So Centers for the Study of Southern Culture make me tired. I don't see enough black faces in those groups. I don't see enough Asian faces, Native American faces.

E.A.W.: It's too self-referential?

R.F.: It's too white.

E.A.W.: You've traveled a lot. Do you find in your travels that people still have very strange conceptions of the South?

R.F.: Oh yes, the French do. I seem to stay a part of the year in France, these days. And I spend a lot of time trying to rethread their views about the South. They're even more willing than we are to segment the South off and romanticize it and ignore unacceptable racial attitudes. In my life, by my witness and testimony, if I am willing to say that I'm a southerner, then maybe by my life I'll represent, or be an example of, things that you can both be, and not have to be, to be a southerner. It's true that people often say to me, "Where are you from?" And then I'll say, "I'm from Mississippi," and then they'll say, or go so far as to say, "Oh, you are not." And I'll ask why they think that, and they'll respond, "Well, people from Mississippi don't sound the way that you sound," and my answer is always, "Well, you'll just have to revise your sense of what Mississippians sound like." I guess I think I'm not typical of what the French think southerners are, and yet I am from where I'm from. So maybe they can use me to expand their . . . what? Views?

E.A.W.: The French *are* fascinated by southern writers.

R.F.: I know, often by all the wrong things. [Laughs]

E.A.W.: What do you mean?

R.F.: Well, they're saturated by what they think of as the "gothic," but not many could describe what the gothic was (well, I suppose the scholars could). But if they finally did describe what a theory of the gothic was, then it would probably exclude most of the literature of the South. Maybe they're thinking about Poe and certain fragmentary parts of Faulkner—of Miss Rosa Coldfield talking about Colonel Sutpen and all the generations of miscegenating Bonds; or Wash Jones, or "A Rose for Emily."

Because of my association with the University of Rennes, where I'm a board member and director of the William Faulkner Foundation, I have tried to widen up their palate a little bit.

E.A.W.: All that symbolist yearning. . . .

R.F.: Well, at least I'm responsible for getting Ernest Gaines to the University. I don't know if they [the French] really see Ernie as a southerner, or whether they just see him as a black writer rather than as just a writer, the way I think of him. Maybe seeing a culture from a distance makes categorizations irresistible. But it's hard to get people to open up and let in what they are so happy not to let in. I've also gotten Barry Hannah over there; he'll certainly widen their palate.

E.A.W.: Give them a taste of violence. . . .

R.F.: Yeah, a taste of violence, cultural cynicism. Some of his characters are racist. Those are his subjects, all right. And often quite, quite funny, too. He mediates those things pretty well.

E.A.W.: Even though *The Sportswriter* and *Independence Day* are not set in the South, plenty of critics have found Frank Bascombe housed firmly in the tradition of a Walker Percy character, a Binx Bolling, a Will Barrett, or even a Robert Penn Warren character such as Jack Burden.

R.F.: I think that last is a stretch. And it's closing the field too narrowly. Frank's also in the tradition of a character like the speaker in Joseph Heller's book *Something Happened,* or the speaker in John Barth's book *End of the Road,* so it's a narrowness to say it's southern just because it's like these, even though it is. But it's also a literary contrivance, this first-person narration with present tense verbs. God knows I was strongly affected by Walker's books, but I was equally affected by Joe Heller's books, too. So I guess I just have to discount the dominant southern whatever.

E.A.W.: I guess part of it comes from Bascombe's. . . .

R.F.: Being a southerner?

E.A.W.: Yes, and cataloguing things and naming predicaments, in the tradition of Will Barrett's "suck of self". . . .

R.F. Yeah, but that line I quoted yesterday was from Sartre: "To name something is to take it out of the well of the unmediated and bring it up to the level of notice." OK, those characters do that, but it is in the tradition of Western literature to do that. Not just the South. It's hard to beat down. But I will.

E.A.W.: And of course Percy was reading Kierkegaard and Sartre. . . .

R.F.: Oh yeah. Those things have to be freed from the grips of "southernness." They're in the full middle of the Western canon of narrations in which characters hypothesize and speculate and make fun of themselves. Walker did it wonderfully, and so did a lot of others.

E.A.W.: Yesterday you said that if you were smarter you'd write philosophical novels. . . .

R.F.: But I'm not. . . .

E.A.W.: Well, don't you find that tone of Frank Bascombe's a musing, philosophical. . . .

R.F.: Dalliant. I find him dalliant. [Laughs.] Not to be taken so seriously. The first question that you asked me yesterday was about all of those names [such as "dreaminess," "factualism," "literalist" that appear in *The Sportswriter*], and I don't know if, even if I sat down with the books, I could completely plot them all out. But I would think if you were an ardent and skillful philosopher that you'd be able to make all of those things dovetail. I might could. It could be that at one time I had them all nicely dovetailed. I can probably explain the "Existence Period" quite nicely, and I can explain "dreaminess." As concepts they're provisional ways of getting experience released from mute sensation and giving them a name. That's what writers are supposed to do.

E.A.W.: Examining that vocabulary turned out to be a great teaching exercise: my students tried to define all of those terms, but the outcome was that the terms resisted, finally, some all-encompassing definition.

R.F.: Paul West wrote once that language can never with utter authority reveal the nature of anything. So there's always at the edges of those defining gestures—trying to find language for sensate experience—a certain lack of perfection. But, on the other hand, I think that anybody probably knows what a "factualist" is; I think anybody knows what "dreaminess" is. The idea is to authorize the reader—with more accuracy than convention provides and/or than his own internal language is equipped for—to recognize what's going on in his own life.

E.A.W.: Percy very much believed that part of the aesthetic function of the novel was to name the condition or have that moment for the reader to say, "I know that." Part of countering isolation, I guess.

R.F.: Sure. Walker maybe took that more seriously than I do, but I think he took a lot of things more seriously in a philosophical way than I do. Maybe that's why he's a better writer. The years in his life that I knew him the little bit I did, he often seemed very serious to me. Or maybe when he was around me, my presence made him joyless. Maybe he knew I was learning things from him. Maybe it makes one uncomfortable; I don't know. I remember one time I saw him in the lobby of the Walthall Hotel in Jackson—he and Mrs. Percy. And I ended up carrying his bags out to the car. I think, on the one hand, he wanted me to do it—thought it was nice if slightly strange. But, on the other hand, I think he wished to hell I'd go away. [We both laugh.] I don't blame him. I wish a lot of people would go away, too.

E.A.W.: You've said that Percy has been telling us through his novels that southern regionalism has had its day, and you've said also that the South is not a "place" anymore. It's become anonymous; it could be anywhere. Do you think the term "southern writer" is an anachronism?

R.F.: I always thought it was at least unininteresting. It long ago outlived its usefulness in encouraging the work of the broadest reference. I mean, Eudora [Welty] doesn't think of herself as a "southern writer." I've talked to her about it many times. I think it's a thing that writers would never have dreamed up for themselves if some Louis Rubin–type hadn't come along and hung it on them. There is, though, a certain comfort zone around it; you can kind of slip into it and think, "Well, if I'm not this, if I'm not Dostoevsky, then maybe this is what I am: a southern writer." In my view, that's a wish for comfort that writers may feel, but it's one we might very well resist. I'd rather be a failed Dostoevsky than a highly successful regional writer. That comfort gives people a sense of their place on a map when their place is only their work. But basically I don't like those critical impulses that section people off from a larger readership or create a language system that only a certain kind of people can really truly appreciate. It's not even elitist. I don't think it helps writers.

E.A.W.: Well, you've just touched on my next question. "Southern writing," the label, was generated out of a specific critical white male perspective. But southern literary scholar Fred Hobson has written that it is in the work of Ernest Gaines and Alice Walker, actually, that we now find what he has called the "old power" of southern writing. You've observed that when we try to fit African American writing into a formula linked with a southern tradition, the "tradition" becomes a slippery term as well.

R.F.: Yes, it [the term "tradition] should just slide beneath the waves. I mean, I don't agree with Fred Hobson probably about that and a great deal else. Why does it have to be either/or? The world is *not* bifurcated that way;

southern or not-southern doesn't represent the world in a sufficiently complex and interesting way to say now that they [Gaines and Walker] are equipped with the old fire, the old power. Bullshit. They're just as good as they are, and we don't have to measure them in terms of a spurious something that's not as good as they are.

E.A.W.: It does seem to be a problem for contemporary southern writers—that critical propensity to name and label and compare. "They're like Faulkner, or they're trying to parody Faulkner because they can't be like Faulkner". . . .
R.F.: Critics do that. Then weak-kneed writers take it up. Ugh.

E.A.W.: They do. So black writers and women writers who write about different things and whose definitions of tragedy are of course very different are then labeled *more* insignificant, or not *as* powerful.
R.F.: Those kinds of distinctions are just not native to me. I think that at a young age critics and scholars and reviewers begin to have their minds narrowed in behalf of some spurious precision fostered by what I don't know. The job market? Cynicism? Boredom? You almost never see a critic with a wide spirit. You see plenty of them, of course, who've read more than you have. But that's different.

E.A.W.: Well, if there is a ghost of a writer leaning over your shoulder, who would that be?
R.F.: I dunno. There's a zillion of them. I've got a shoulder full.

E.A.W.: They're weighing you down?
R.F.: No—they're holding me up, with their little wings. [We both laugh.]

E.A.W.: That's a nice way to put it.
R.F.: No, really. Lots of people. I'm happily at ease thinking that I've been pushed along, held up, propped up by all kinds of wonderful writers. It's no surprise that it was a big deal to be growing up in Jackson with Eudora Welty in town. It was a big deal to me before I even read a story of hers. Her being there provided a sort of silent sanction that it was actually okay to try to be a writer. Or having E.L. Doctorow as a teacher when I was twenty-three years old. Writing stories has been my life, and my life has intersected with all sorts of people who've all been generous and whose work has affected me. And they haven't all been southerners, and the southerners I met didn't always exert a "southern" influence on me, and the ones that did certainly

didn't exert a salutary influence. One time, long time ago, Walker asked me if I were going to get a place down in Louisiana. And I said yes. And he said, "Oh don't get a place in New Orleans. Come on across over here to the suburbs where it's nice." And I thought that was wonderful. You could have been talking to somebody in Cleveland or Akron or the Twin cities. There was nothing southern about it.

E.A.W.: It seems that we [critics] have some propensity to over-classify fiction, to put it in a category, to call it one thing or another. Why do you think it is that we try to see works as products of regionalism? It's not just in the South. There's been a new school of "midwestern fiction." Why do you think it's so important for us to see fiction not as a product of America as a whole but of a particular region?

R.F.: Dim-wittedness. Careerism. An unwillingness to take on enough, an unwillingness to get outside of a tiny little boat and swim in deeper water. Not that my life is illustrative of somebody's who's done that, but when I go to spend part of my year in Europe, one of the things that I'm most moved by is the lack of distinction between European fiction and American fiction. It seems so similar rather than being distinctively, importantly French, for instance. But it's just part of our American heritage to exclude. White people came to the American continent to exclude ourselves, and as soon as we got here we started excluding everybody else. It's this whole spurious idea of independence. The American practice of independence is premised on the notion of "get away from me, because I'm better off when I'm here by myself and can be seen; or, my independence or my worth is more easily proven when I'm not somehow diluted by you."

E.A.W.: Like Thomas Paine.

R.F.: Yes. All of those founding fathers, really. The whole way in which Western expansion or manifest destiny was lived out in American history is just the story of that: get away. Don't tread on me, or for that matter even get very close to me. Most of us have it in our make-up; maybe it's human—Native Americans probably have it, too—but it's particularly rife in the white American landscape. That's what my book *Independence Day* is about: the eventual sterility of cutting yourself off from liaisons with other people, from attachments, affinities, affiliations with other people. Finally the end of the line for independence is sterility. So you have to redefine independence to aid you in making these connections. But I do it, we all do it—categorize and exclude. I'd like to do it less.

You should read the wonderful Richard Blackmur essay called "A Critic's Job of Work." In it he makes the argument—lost now among critics—that critical categories, critical exclusivities—are really only provisionally useful, and that eventually after you've used one (Freudianism, for example) and ruled a book off with its strictures and looked at things closely, you must put the book back together again, restore it to its great complexity, because that's how it truly exists. It's possible to delude oneself into thinking the book anatomized is the book put in its truest light. Well, it's not.

E.A.W.: Murdering to dissect?

R.F.: Alas.

E.A.W.: Undergraduate students, too, are very hungry for *the* answer.

R.F.: Good luck. Law school taught me that if I was going to find that, I'd need to make it up myself.

E.A.W.: Students can be particularly obsessed with finding *one* right answer, which sometimes a literary text simply doesn't provide. It's very disconcerting to them when you say, "This is just one way to look at it, and here's another way to look at it."

R.F.: We deprive them of their passionate innocence when we give them a system for things. I remember when I first started to teach in graduate school, I had a wonderful teacher who was a young colleague at Kenyon of John Crowe Ransom's. Anyway, Howard Babb was his name, and he was the director of the class that I taught, and he would come in and pick out the angle from which we would approach the story we were to teach that week. He used to look at stories in terms of their formal features. And he'd choose one: point of view, or imaginistic patterns. And one day after class I asked him, "Mr. Babb, how do you know which one to use?" And he said, "I don't. I just look at the story one day, and that's what seems to me to be interesting about it. But then I'll look at it the next year, and something else will be interesting. There's no key to it; you're just trying to open the story to the students, and sometimes you open it from this end, and sometimes you open it from that end. It's not the key; it's the opening." Jesus, how important that was to me. Sad to say, he's gone now.

But I do also credit my own unwillingness to categorize, as much as I have such an unwillingness, to studying the law, to being a law student. Coming into class and having cases presented to me, then the next day other cases, and all of the strategies that we learned, the keys, the protocols for the case before, were gone the next day, and you had to wing it.

E.A.W.: You quit teaching, didn't you, at some point? Or even several times?

R.F.: I never really started again, after the first time. I taught at Williams College; that was my first job teaching full-time, and I just couldn't stand it. I loved my colleagues, I liked my students, I liked it up in Vermont where I lived; I taught myself a lot from trying to teach them. But I couldn't stand the routine. Writing is enough routine for one human.

E.A.W.: But you do still teach?

R.F.: I just finished ten weeks at Northwestern [University in Chicago, Illinois], and one or two other places before that. I'll probably do another ten weeks at Northwestern.

E.A.W.: Why do you keep teaching, then?

R.F.: Well, to change the water in my bowl. Every now and then I get to feeling like I'm too isolated, and an offer will come along. I'm a pretty good teacher, because I'm always afraid, and then I work really hard, so I do give it my best shot. But I think if I had to do it a lot, I wouldn't be any good at it.

E.A.W.: Teaching takes quite a bit of energy.

R.F.: It's a real vocation. It's hard. Much harder than being a writer. Not that it shouldn't be.

E.A.W.: Do you fall prey to your character Frank Bascombe's "seeing around"?

R.F.: I see around a lot of things, but I don't see around literature now. It takes up the whole picture for me. But I had to graduate to that view. When you're young, and you have a lot of possibilities and you have a very tenuous hold on what you're doing, you're always slightly aware of what's out there in your peripheral vision—other things to do. Now I no longer think that there's anything specifically out there on my periphery that I could or should do. Which isn't to say that it won't happen, or that I'll keep writing forever. Maybe *Independence Day* was the best book I'll ever write, so if it is, I just hope I know it in time to save myself humiliation and to go and do something else.

E.A.W.: I'm very interested in the way that you use the word "location." You've said that you've "tried to contend that locatedness is not a science of the ground but some quality within us." And your character Quinn in *The*

Ultimate Good Luck uses the word "located" oddly, so that the sentence's syntax requires that it function as a noun. Here he's speaking of working alone at night: "It made you feel out of time and out of space and located closer to yourself, as if *located* was the illusion, the thing he'd missed since he'd come back, the ultimate good luck" (italics mine). Could you comment about that word "located" and "locatable"? You use the terms in other writings as well.

R.F.: Well, I've thought so much about these things that I don't know where I've written what I've thought, or if I've just thought it and not written it. But, anyway, I think one's sense of locatedness represents the claim you make on place, rather than the claim it supposedly makes on you. Think about a poem like [Percy Bysshe Shelley's] "Mont Blanc." The speaker of that poem talks about seeing that mountain, and he ascribes to its otherwise inert, rocky self animate character. He hears it "speak," and the streams make sensible sounds to him. Likewise, if you read the beginning of *Walden,* [Henry David] Thoreau talks about the forest in terms of animate behavior. My view—not that it's original with me, God knows—is that those things are not animate, that they never speak. Okay, I know it's a figure of speech. But in talking about sense of place, or locatedness, or the importance of place, or how we feel about it, that figure of speech gets made perplexingly literal sometimes, and in that transaction personally responsible for how one feels, and what's important about place gets shed or lost. Therefore, my view is that anything you feel about a place, anything that you think about place at all, you have authored and ascribed to some piece of geography. Everything that defines locatedness is then something that you yourself generate. So if it's a sense of place you experience, you're just expressing what you feel and which you say the place has created. So when Frank says, "Place means nothing," in *Independence Day,* what he means is, "this place ain't givin' me nothin,' and I want something from it because I've been here, I've felt things here, and now I'm here again, and I don't feel anything." He's just realizing what I just said: that places don't have characters and don't literally give us anything.

E.A.W.: Do you think that "place" then finally is almost more of a metaphysical construction?

R.F.: Well, there are real places, obviously. But the way we *feel* about them is largely a confection of our own. I mean, I live in Montana, and it's a very beautiful place. But I see lots of beautiful places. It's like Frank says:

it's similar to looking at a picture postcard. I don't feel warm to it or get anything from it except what I let myself feel or create out of myself.

E.A.W.: Do you miss places?

R.F.: [Pauses] I miss them all about equally. I don't miss any one of them more than the other. I really don't. That's something that was instructive to me, when I realized that I missed places just about equally, and what that meant to me was that the places themselves were just about equal. It's we who credit them differently. And that in itself goes against the whole notion of primary place. When Frank talks at the end of *Independence Day* about where he wants to be buried and can't figure out where he wants to be buried, that was basically my making a joke out of the "sense of place." Because you would think that if you knew where you wanted to be buried, then you could almost begin to invent a theory about where you belonged. I said to Kristina [Ford's wife of thirty years], "If I died, where would you bury me?" And she said, "Well, I don't know; I guess I'd bury you in Mississippi." And I thought, no, not there, but I didn't know where, and I still don't.

E.A.W.: Scatter a few ashes over Montana?

R.F.: Well, to cover all the places that I've liked, you might need more ashes than I'll make. What I finally decided was, just bury me no farther than four feet from where I drop.

E.A.W.: In *Wildlife,* you tell quite a poignant growing-up tale.

R.F.: It's my favorite book—of those that I wrote, that is.

E.A.W.: The sixteen-year-old son in that book, Joe, makes adult observations about loving his parents. . . .

R.F.: Well, he's an adult when he tells the story.

E.A.W.: He has to recognize his parents as separate entities, that they are finally unknowable, and come to terms with the loneliness evoked from this kind of love. Would you call the inherent loneliness of the human condition one of the main themes in your work?

R.F.: It's what Emerson in his essay on Friendship (interestingly enough) calls the "infinite remoteness" that underlies us all. But I also think that that predicament is a seminal one; that is, what it inseminates is an attempt to console that remote condition. If loneliness is the disease, then the story is the cure. To be able to tell a story like that one about your parents is in itself an act of consolation. Even to come to the act of articulating that your parents

are unknowable to each other, unknowable to you, is itself an act of acceptance, an act of some optimism, again in that Sartrean sense that to write
about the darkest human possibility is itself an act of optimism because it
proves that those things can be thought about.

E.A.W.: When Joe's father burns down Warren Miller's house in *Wildlife*
and Joe nonetheless thinks that he "loved him in spite of it all," the scene
reminded me of William Faulkner's "Barn Burning." Were you thinking of
"Barn Burning"?

R.F.: No, I was not. The *last* thing I'm thinking about is some other guy's
story. I mean, who's to say that I would ever have thought of setting Warren
Miller's porch on fire if I never had read "Barn Burning," even though I've
only read it once. But who's to say that I wouldn't? You're plotting a book
out. You're thinking what can the father do when he gets to this guy's house?
Well, he could kill him, but I didn't want to have him do that, because that's
not quite the level of his rage. So you go on through a short list of possibilities. These decisions come much more out of the puzzlement of trying to
construct a scene than they ever come directly out of something I've read. Of
course, it could come *indirectly* out of something I've read, without my
knowing it. What's corrupting about making those kinds of critical pseudo-
connections between works is that doing this makes the reader think that the
creation of literature is different from how it really is. Less random. Less
adventitious. Less—finally—exciting and breathtaking.

Literature is much better understood in this kind of limbo of providence
and almost unassigned impulse. Literature is actually something that you
appreciate more when you understand how provisional it is. How most stories
are exquisite because they *almost didn't get written,* or just accidentally got
written. If everything has to be relatable to something previous, the whole
enterprise is—to me, anyway—rather enervated.

The other day Ruth Moose told me that she liked a little story I wrote
called "Privacy" that was in the *New Yorker.* We were talking about it, and
she said, "That's such a good story, almost a perfect little story." And I said,
"It took me forty-five minutes to write." She said, "Oh my God, don't tell
anybody that. I want my students to think it takes weeks and weeks." And I
said, "No, it didn't." I said, "Forty-five minutes start to finish." She said,
"Oh, I don't want to know that." And I thought to myself: *do* know that.
Know that. I just went up to my room one day without a clue, sat there and
thought, Gee I haven't written anything in a long time. I wonder if I'm ever

going to write anything again. So I looked in my notebook and the first thing my eye fell on was that little kernel or grain of a story, and I sat down and zipped it out. Not that it's a great story. It's just whatever it is. But it was just, you know, very spontaneous. I thought it was a story, in a way, that was kind of a spoof of a [Milan] Kundera story.

E.A.W.: I want to ask you about Frank's fleeting sensation at the end of *The Sportswriter,* when he speaks of a solitary epiphany, the "glistening one moment." He's talking about being out from under that film of life— recognizing, though, that his sensation may not possibly be sustained, that this is *the* moment, this is how it is. But then at the end of *Independence Day,* Frank feels the "push, pull, the weave and sway of others." Is that to indicate that Frank has changed over the course of those two novels? That he is now, somehow, not so estranged?

R.F.: Absolutely. When I wrote the ending to *Independence Day,* what I originally wrote was very different from the ending that's in the book now. When I originally got to the end of the book, I had some ideas about what the ending would be, and I used them, wrote them out. And it was wrong— just wrong, wrong, wrong, wrong, wrong. I actually realized that I really wasn't up to writing the end of it. I had a hard time even making myself write it. But when I did, I showed it to my editor at Knopf, and he said, "This is great, a wonderful ending," and I thought, no it's not, no it's not. Actually in January of 1995, I was in New York working on the book still, trying to see it through production. And I said, "I don't like this ending; I'm going to write another ending," by which I meant the last page or so, and my editor said, "Well, I wish you wouldn't." But I did, just sort of muscled up, ganged up on the ending.

The first ending left Frank alone in the car with a doctor's drawing of his son Paul's wounded eye, and I thought that was a wonderful image, visually very strong, but it didn't register the end the way I wanted the end to register; it seemed wrong that Frank was alone in the car and I wanted a feeling that was different from how he felt at the end of *The Sportswriter.* Without question I wanted the ending to represent Frank moving into affiliation with others—which it does—now—with Frank walking up into the crowd watching the Fourth of July parade.

E.A.W.: Inclusion and not exclusion?

R.F.: I didn't think of the ending of *The Sportswriter* as exclusionary. I just thought that sometimes you just rise briefly out of the murk and morass of life, a moment in which you kind of feel out of the mess, and it's a wonderful feeling. I never really thought about whether that feeling was "sustainable" or "unsustainable," those terms you used. But it was an unsustainable moment, and yet it was *just* a sufficiently sustainable moment to make the reader think that all is not lost, that life isn't permanently a function of messes and murks and down drafts. I mean life isn't sustainable, finally, right?

E.A.W.: Those moments almost only come to a person when he or she is alone.

R.F.: The ones that come to you with somebody else are different. At least from my particular philosophical Emersonian view (see, I think that's who my great influence is: Emerson), the kinds of rapport you have with others are totally supported by some kind of wholeness of self.

E.A.W.: One more question about *Independence Day*. You write out the sounds that occur in that book: "boom-Haddam, boom-Haddam, boom boom ba-boom," and "slip-slap, slip-slap, slip-slop." What effect are you trying to achieve?

R.F.: Mostly I think it's funny and interesting on the page, though I am trying to find words that accurately represent sounds, too. I think that when you see those words, you sound them in your head, and it's pleasurable. It's small potatoes stuff, really.

E.A.W.: Like a poem?

R.F.: Yeah. Like a poem, exactly like a poem. I want the reader to make those sounds in the mouth and hear them in the ear. I think it's fun.

E.A.W.: Do you read Wallace Stevens?

R.F.: Yes, all the time. I quoted him yesterday: "In an age of disbelief, it is for the poet to provide the satisfactions of belief with his measure and with his style." That's what I understand literature to do.

A Conversation with Richard Ford

Huey Guagliardo / 1997

From the *Southern Review* 34.3 (1998): 609–20. Used by permission.

This interview was conducted on July 25, 1997, in the relaxed atmosphere of Ford's townhouse on Bourbon Street in New Orleans, a residence that in its rich and eclectic appointments reflects Ford's nomadic existence over the last two decades. Ford had recently returned from a three-month stay in Berlin, where *Independence Day* had been translated into German. *Women with Men* had been published earlier that summer, and so I decided to open the conversation with a series of questions about that book.

HG: Let's begin by talking about your most recent work, *Women with Men,* a collection of novellas. I'm interested in why you chose this form, which a reviewer for *Time* referred to as "the orphan of contemporary fiction. Too lengthy for modern magazines and too short for penny-pinching publishers."

RF: I think probably that alone was an inspiration, to try to write in a form which seems to me highly serviceable, a form in which a lot of wonderful literature has been written, and yet that doesn't get a lot of use by American writers. Magazines do dictate much of what is written. I had just finished a long novel, and was not in the mood to go back to writing, serially, short stories. I wanted to write something the long story form perfectly suited, a substantial piece of work that is not a novel but is longer than a short story.

HG: The first two stories of the trilogy were published previously—*The Womanizer* in *Granta* and *Jealous* in *The New Yorker*—and yet the three pieces are woven together beautifully. All explore human loneliness and the complexity of human relationships. All involve marriages that have fallen or are falling apart. The most important link, however, seems to be the characters' inability to bridge the loneliness and connect with one another. One character declares in her suicide note that she will "die knowing nobody." I kept thinking of a famous line from *Cool Hand Luke.* "What we have here is a failure to communicate." In your mind, how do the novellas fit together?

RF: I think they fit together in the way you just described. They are also about varying degrees, varying sorts of human solipsism. The thing that de-

147

feats affection in each of these stories is one person's inability really to look outside him- or herself, so much so that the needs, the preferences, the well-being, the sanctity of others are, in effect, completely ignored or misunderstood, causing calamity. All three stories have at the end some calamitous event that is a somewhat hyperbolized version of modern life. In a cautionary value they would basically say what realistic fiction, if not always, at least often says: Pay closer attention to what you're doing or bad things will result. They also make the claim that this is a Western phenomenon, in the broadest sense of West: all of us Anglo-Saxons and Germans and French and so on suffer some sort of solipsism, a way in which we cut ourselves off from people. It is unmistakably, as a theme or set of concerns, a variant on some of the concerns of *Independence Day.*

HG: Do you see the middle story, *Jealous,* which takes place in Montana, as a kind of center panel that bridges together the two longer stories, both set in Paris?

RF: They're published in the order in which they were written. I always meant that there would be two Paris stories and then there was this Montana story which came in between. No, I wouldn't say that the middle story bridged it; that would probably be arguing for a more meticulous structure than I had. I was interested in stories being, as I said, variants on some principal concerns of mine; and so it would probably be using retrospect too liberally to say that I see it as such. But on the other hand I do believe, as you suggest, that those stories are actually quite well united, and how one relates to the other could be something that falls under the aegis of stories not finished until they go outside the control of the writer.

HG: Were you alluding to Hemingway's story collection *Men Without Women?*

RF: In no way.

HG: You don't think then, that it's possible to view Larry, the young Montana boy in *Jealous,* as a sort of Nick Adams character?

RF: Not to me. Unless all teenage characters going through the first throes and pangs of facing adult life are examples of Nick Adams characters. I don't know how, for instance, Sherwood Anderson's "I Want to Know Why" or Isaac Babel's "The Story of My Dovecot" . . . I don't know how those would be Nick Adams stories. The truth is that I called the book *Women with Men,* and somebody said, "I guess you're bouncing a title off Hemingway's wall."

I said, "Why?" And they said that Hemingway wrote a book titled—what is it?—*Men Without Women?* And I said, "Oh, gee, if I knew that I didn't remember it." And they said, "Well, okay, that's fine if you didn't know that, but now you know it; so do you want to run the risk of having people say that you're doing that?" And what I said was, "I don't give a shit. Let them do what they please. I'm not going to sacrifice a good title of my book because of something some guy did seventy or eighty years ago."

HG: I found it interesting that Charley Matthews, the protagonist in *Occidentals,* had written a novel called *The Predicament.* Is writing a process of discovery in that you typically place characters in certain *predicaments* to explore their reactions?

RF: Oh, of course. Absolutely. I think that's what I routinely do. That's why it's important for me to think about a book before I write it, to get in mind a whole series of possible cul-de-sacs or crises that I can anticipate coming to as I write along rather intuitively; because I think that the illumination of character is often accomplished by putting the characters into a situation whose outcome I don't know, and then literally writing out of that tight spot and seeing what happens, seeing what people say and do, how I the writer and you the reader might feel about them once you're on the other side of those predicaments. It's funny, but when I was writing *Occidentals* there was a time when I wanted to call it *The Predicament.* But I didn't want to sacrifice the title *Occidentals,* and it also drew too much ironic and almost tongue-in-cheek attention to that rather subordinated part of Charley's life, his life as a novelist; it kind of made fun of the story all the way to the end by ironizing it, and I didn't want to do that. I wanted it to come out a serious story. I was somewhat shocked when I got to the end at what a dark story it turns out to be. It starts off, as you might agree, in a comic mode and works its way into that darkness, from which it never completely extricates itself.

HG: You have written successfully in all three fictional forms: novel, short story, and novella. Walker Percy said that he chose the novel because he found the short form too limiting. What do you find most appealing about working in the shorter forms?

RF: It gets over in a hurry. Its effects are no more concentrated. I like reading short stories, and I like the thought that I could write one that would make somebody feel the same way that I did when I read all of the thousands of short stories that I have read and loved. But the truth is, I think, I write short stories because they are gratifyingly brief and return a satisfying sense of accomplishment to a rather limited amount of effort.

HG: And the novel? Would you share Percy's view of the novel as being more open to all sorts of possibilities?

RF: Sure, but there is an impulse among many writers to justify what they do. Not that Walker particularly felt this need; I think he felt eminently justified in everything he did in a literary sense, and the books will bear it out. But there is a way in which people say, "Oh, I don't write poems; I would never write poems." Or, "I only write novels. The short story is a lesser form." I just don't like to participate in those kinds of exclusionary logics. The truth of the matter is that I feel that writing essays, memoirs, six-hundred-word "Talk of the Town" pieces for *The New Yorker,* thousand-word op-ed pices for the *New York Times,* short stories, novels, novellas are all the same to me. They are what I do. I'm a writer; that's all I am. So I write, sometimes at this length, sometimes at that. To hang any more notable logic on it wouldn't be faithful to how I feel.

HG: I'd like to know how you regard your role as a writer of fiction and how the reader fits into your conception of that role.

RF: I think to be a novelist, to be a short-story writer—whatever I am—is a high calling, because it's a relationship you establish, through your very best efforts, with a reading public whose welfare you're seeking somehow to ameliorate. I'm sure I came to that role, in part, by thinking about Walker when I first encountered him, back in the seventies, and also from Chekhov. Walker, in a book like *Love in the Ruins,* is particularly interested in having a doctor ministering to a public of some kind. Not that I see that as my role. I don't think that I have that sort of literary/medical value, certainly, but I do think I offer my best efforts, my fondest consolations, and my most important thinking to my readership. And, too, I wouldn't even be a writer had I not been able to imagine finding a readership. Even at the beginning when I gave it precious little thought because it seemed so remote, it was always my intention to write for somebody else to read. Sometimes you hear writers say, "Well, I only do it for myself, or I do it for a very limited audience," or reasons that are basically, it seems to me, exclusive of a wider readership. For me it was always sort of second nature to think that I'd like to have as wide a readership as I could. I don't believe I fully recognized that aspiration until I'd written *The Sportswriter* and was beginning to feel that there were a few people out there whom I didn't personally know who had read books of mine.

HG: *The Sportswriter* has frequently been compared to Percy's *The Moviegoer.* There are some obvious, perhaps superficial, similarities between the two books. Frank Bascombe's narrative voice in *The Sportswriter* reminds many readers of Binx Bolling's voice in *The Moviegoer.* Each character is about to have a birthday . . .
RF: I never thought of that.

HG: Really? In addition, sports seem to function for Frank in the way that movies work for Binx, as a way of avoiding alienation and despair. Twenty years ago you wrote a piece for *The National Review* in which you expressed your admiration for Percy's writing, especially, as you just put it, its "literary/medical value." You also said that you would "rather read a sentence written by Walker Percy than a sentence written by anybody else." Because there are many subtle similarities between the two novels, I can't help but wonder if you were consciously influenced by *The Moviegoer* in writing *The Sportswriter.*

RF: Sure, sure. I hadn't read it in ten years when I started writing *The Sportswriter.* But I would also just say—having said yes, of course, I was quite consciously influenced—there were other books which influenced me as much which are less obvious: *The End of the Road,* by John Barth; *Something Happened,* by Joseph Heller; *A Fan's Notes,* by Frederick Exley. All of them first-person narratives. Wonderful books. They all were as persuasively influencing upon *The Sportswriter* as was *The Moviegoer.*

HG: I would like to explore a few other ways in which your work might be similar to and different from Walker Percy's. Percy's characters often find God by finding one another. This is especially true in *The Moviegoer* and *The Second Coming* where human love becomes a symbol of man's capacity for redemption and reconciliation with a Christian God who both transcends the immanent world and is infused within it. Love, in other words, bridges the gap between immanence and transcendence. In an earlier interview, you talked about your characters being redeemed by affection. Of course, Percy, a Catholic writer, used the word *redemption* in its traditional Christian sense, whereas you seem to have something else in mind. Yet your characters seem to be searching for that same sort of intersubjective relationship, what Frank Bascombe calls "the *silent intimacies* . . . of the fervently understood and sympathized with." In what sense are your characters *redeemed* by love?

RF: This is interesting, I suppose, vis-à-vis Walker, who—I guess he did, he certainly seemed to—believed in an afterlife. It's problematical to me how life on earth, affectionate life on earth, love, can somehow equal the love that God has for us. Maybe it's just in an emblematic way. For me—and I mean for me insofar as I write characters—facing apocalypse, facing the end of life for which there is no redemption about which I feel confident, what we are charged to do as human beings is to make our lives and the lives of others as liveable, as important, as charged as we possibly can. And so what I'd call *secular redemption* aims to make us, through the agency of affection, intimacy, closeness, complicity, feel like our time spent on earth is not wasted.

HG: Percy also belived in the affirmative power of language and in the "aesthetic reversal of alienation" through literature, arising through the reader's alliance with both the alienated character and the author. You have written about the "efficacy of telling" and about the fact that "precious language" has the potential to provide consolation to someone in despair. Am I correct in assuming that you would agree with Percy's view and with Frank Bascombe's assertion that ''words can make most things better''?

RF: I sometimes get painted with a very dark brush for that line, because some people read it to mean a fundamental cynicism about me: that is, you can say anything and make it be true. I suppose the way we cast our dilemmas and affections into language has a lot to do with how we conceive of them, so there is—I don't think of it as cynicism—but there is a way that language colors experience; there's no doubt about that. But I think language is consoling in other ways, is always able to give us pleasure by its sonorities, its poetical qualities, by simply the way it pleasures out ears, and so far as it comes from another, sweetens our view of that other, sweetens our view of the world, a world that can give us literature, that can give us the telling of stories. I think the telling of stories is in and of itself a way of persuading the reader away from whatever is plaguing her or him, and of asking the reader to believe that another and more felicitous order can be put on experience, and that this order has a structure that is, in an almost abstract way, pleasurable, and beautiful to behold. So I don't know how that lines up with what Walker said about those things, but my view, I think, is a great deal more feet-on-the-earth rather than looking on above the horizon line.

HG: Although he believed in the power of language to bring human beings together, Walker Percy often wrote about the exhaustion or devaluation of language in the modern world.

RF: He made a lot of fun of it.

HG: He certainly did. There seems to be evidence in your work that you share Percy's concern about the devaluation of language. I've mentioned what strikes me as an important theme in *Women with Men,* that is, the failure of the characters to connect, the failure of language. There is all of the business about the French translation of Charley's novel. His publisher tells him that "People spend too much time misunderstanding one another." Certainly this is true of Charley and Helen who could use a translator to help them to communicate with one another. Language is a barrier even for two people who speak the same language. When Charley says "I love you," Helen tells him to "Think of some better words." When he can't think of anything better to say, she says they should "Leave words out of it." Would you comment on this notion of the devaluation of language? Is "meaningful language . . . exhausted by routine," as Charley describes his failed marriage to Penny, and as Percy contends?

RF: You sum it up about as well as I could. I don't know that I could improve on that very much.

HG: Well, Percy wrote that "the trick of the novelist, as the Psalmist said, is to sing a new song, use new words." In your *National Review* piece you credit him with doing just that, saying that he does "what great literature would always do if it could: reinvent language moment to moment." In what ways have you tried to reinvent language in your work?

RF: By trying to write sentences the reader does not see through like a clear pane of glass. By trying to imagine language as being a window whose pane and whose surfaces you luxuriate in and, in the process, see beyond. That came to me from all of my reading, much more than from Walker; by the time I wrote that piece on Walker, you know, I'd been to graduate school, been a college professor, done a lot of things. I'd read all of those wonderful people that we now think of as postmodernists in the late sixties and early seventies. I had read a story like Donald Barthelme's "The Indian Uprising," in which a character (referred to only as Miss R) says there is enough satisfaction in "the hard, brown, nutlike word" for "anyone but a damned fool." One idea I came to as a young man was that written language was just a mode of communication to be read in a denotative way. What I came to understand as a more sophisticated reader is that language is a source of pleasure in and of itself—all of its corporeal qualities, its syncopations, moods, sounds, the way things look on the page. So that's what I bring to language that vivifies it, other than simply the use of words out of their usual context in the e. e. cummings sense; but I do it in a novelist's mode, not in the poet's mode, so that my responsibility is, finally, to make a cohesive, linear whole out of something, unlike, say, cummings or Wallace Stevens.

HG: Is your work informed by what Helen Carmichael in *Occidentals* defines as "spirituality"; that is, "a conviction about something good that you can't see"? If so, what would that something good be?

RF: Survival. That you can believe in the efficacy of things you can't predict or see the evidence of, in the faith that if you invent them they will cause you to survive, literally survive. And maybe more: survive with dignity, survive with pleasure, survive with a sense of life's being worthwhile. The scene you mentioned in *Occidentals* when Charley wants to say *love* . . . In *Jealous* there is a very similar scene when Doris sits at the bar talking to Larry and to Barney Bordeaux. She asks Larry about the great themes. She asks, What do you believe in? And she says, you can't say love; you can't say sex. But I believe—meaning me the author here—I believe in the efficacy of love. Those two—at least Charley in *Occidentals*—I set apart from that. I think he is in some ways, because of solipsism, not to be accessed by belief in love. But I believe in that; I believe in the things that draw you sympathetically closer to others, and that the promise of that closeness is a valuable commodity. And other things too—art. For a guy who thinks of himself as almost totally an Aristotelian, I am kind of a Platonist about those things.

HG: *The Sportswriter, Wildlife,* and *Independence Day* are first-person narratives. *A Piece of My Heart* and *The Ultimate Good Luck* are in the limited-omniscient mode. What factors determine your choice of voice? Is it easier for you, as it may be for readers, to identify with Frank Bascombe and with Joe Brinson, the young narrator in *Wildlife*?

RF: I never identify with Frank; I never identify with Joe. I always maintain a rather scrupulous artisan's role toward my narrators. They are always the illusions of characters made up of language, illusions that I myself manufacture, and they are never me, nor do I ever confuse them with being me; thus, while the relationship that the reader shares with the character through the agency of a first-person narrator might seem to be somewhat more streamlined, there is for me, once I establish my hold on that form of narration, no difference between a first-person and a third-person narrative in the actual execution of those novels. Practically speaking, it's all the same when you're writing it; it's just the illusion of address that is different. Finally, once you allow yourself as a writer and can concede on the reader's behalf that the address is working, it doesn't matter which it is. Choosing one over the other is almost a matter of instinctual first principle; which is to say, how I first lay hold of the material. One of the first kinds of decision-making that goes on in my head or in my voice as I'm speaking those lines—and I do always speak lines to myself—however that seems most native to those lines is how I narrate the book. I loved the opening line of *Occidentals* [Ford got up to retrieve a copy of *Women with Men* from a desk on the other side of the room]. There is something about the opening line of *Occidentals* which I had in my head long before I ever really wrote the second line: [reading from story] "Charley Matthews and Helen Carmichael had come to Paris the week before Christmas." Well, that's a line which dictates the point of view, if it is, in effect, going to be about Charley and Helen, which it is. So, it was just a sort of instinctual principle, which became the book's first principle.

HG: Critics often focus on the question of Frank Bascombe's reliability as a narrator in both *The Sportswriter* and *Independence Day.* Do you regard Frank as reliable?

RF: I regard all narrators as works of art. Reliability is for the reader to decide. I mean, I regard him as the thing that all narrators, indeed, all fictional characters, are: they're provocateurs. They say things, and do things, and you as a reader in the sanctity and serenity of your chair can entertain what they say and be moved by or disapprove of or agree with what they say, so that their reliability is actually, really, not much of an ongoing concern because they're not real. They're made up. It matters to me and you, as human beings, whether or not each of us is reliable, but narrators don't have to be. Or maybe another way of saying it is sometimes they are and sometimes they aren't. They don't need to be, or maybe they can't be. There is a great line of Richard Avedon's: "Portraiture never tells the truth." *Characters* don't tell the truth. They hypothesize; they speculate. That's their relationship to their maker, the author; they're speculators about things. They may say things that are useful, and very right, very moving, but their obligation isn't to tell the truth. The *book* may tell a truth by comprising all these other gestures.

HG: You've given your wife, Kristina, a great deal of credit for the creation of Frank Bascombe. She encouraged you to write a novel about a character who is essentially optimistic about life and its possibilities. You've said that you don't identify with Frank, but do you at least share his optimism?

RF: I probably do, because if I don't share it explicitly, I share it implicitly. There's that great line in Sartre which I am always quoting to people which says that "For a writer to write about the darkest possible things is itself an act of optimism, because it proves that those things, whatever they are, can be thought about." To me, no matter how dark the things you're writing about—if you're *Céline,* irrespective—being a writer means making something with language that you give to a readership, which it will entertain into the future; so it is, in a kind of chronological way, optimistic enough to believe that there will be a future in which these books will be read.

HG: Will there be another Frank Bascombe novel in that future, or have we seen the last of Frank? Is there a chance that you will do with Frank what John Updike did with Rabbit Angstrom?

RF: I would write another book about Frank if I could, but it would have to be a book that is at this moment unforeseeable. Which isn't to say that I won't finally foresee it—at the end of *The Sportswriter* I don't think there was any way I could have forecast that I'd write a book in which Frank was a real estate agent. I don't think now that I could forecast what kind of book I would write about Frank, but it would be something more than just what happens next after *Independence Day.* I think a third book about Frank would have to be unique and stand alone and be nonreliant on the other book for its first principle in holding the reader's attention and affection. For me, probably the most difficult part of writing *Independence Day* was not the part to make it a good book, if I can anatomize it in this way; but the most difficult and tiresome and tedious parts were making this book seem like the sequel I wanted it to be. I thought to myself that if I could write this novel and have it be just as good about another character, that's what I was after.

HG: Speaking of Updike, I think of you and Updike as the best observers of life in America writing today . . .

RF: That's a nice compliment, but Joan Didion is awfully good, too.

HG: Indeed, she is. Your novels *The Sportswriter* and *Independence Day* depict life in the middle-class suburbs of America, where you yourself once lived. For the most part Frank delights in his suburban existence, but at the same time there is the ominous sense that all is not as ordered as it appears. Frank says in *Independence Day* that "there is a new sense of the wild world being just beyond our perimeter, an untallied apprehension among our residents, one I believe they'll never get used to, one they'll die before accommodating." What are your greatest concerns for America as we stand on the threshold of a new century?

RF: That it will become ungovernable. That our sense of a whole will deteriorate. And I'm not talking about ourselves as simply a nation-state, but that because of our geographic size, because of the inevitability of greater and greater degrees of multiculturalism, because of immigration, because of economic disparity, because of racial strife, racial inequality, the country will basically balkanize along lines which are not now completely visible, but other than in terms of the states. Whether we know it or not, there is a great deal of strife going on in the country between those forces which are basically what you might call the old states' rights forces (those conservatives who want, in fact, some in good ways, to conserve a sense of America as a histori-cally comprised nation) and those people—and there are a lot of people—for whom that notion of states' rights, federalism, simply has no meaning, and, moreover, who are not served by that particular way of imagining America. There is a lot of strife between those people. The people on the other side are often immigrants who have not been served well by this society's economy, who are on the low end of the socioeconomic scale. Those forces pull hard in a destructive way. If I had to say what one thing was it's that; that we will lose some sense—not that we will lose some sense of the past—lose some sense that it is worthwhile to keep this country whole along some lines yet to be imagined, because federalism, and states' rights, and conservatism, those movements have interesting things to say for themselves, but one of the things that they don't do is that they don't adapt very well, by definition, to new forces, to new demands, to immigration, to multiculturalism, to the rise of the lower classes that have been isolated by race. That makes me afraid that, basically, we will lack the imagination to go on reinventing America in a wholesome way.

HG: You and Kristina moved to New Orleans about seven years ago after living in at least a dozen states over the years. As a native New Orleanean, I have often puzzled over the passage in *The Sportswriter* where Frank says that "a town like New Orleans defeats itself. It longs for a mystery it doesn't have and never will, if it ever did." What exactly does he mean? Do you share that view?

RF: That's an answering knell to one of Walker's characters in *The Last Gentleman,* who says the place where I was living when I read those books— Ann Arbor—was a *nonplace.* That was me, basically, lobbing a salvo back over Walker's wall. But, yeah, I think that even more profoundly today. I mean that New Orleans steeps itself in its history and obfuscates all of its fundamental urbanness and modern problems by turning its head, by letting there be so many variant views of the city. I actually wrote an essay about this very thing for Canadian Broadcasting over the winter. I mean, New Orleans deludes itself more than any city I've ever lived in, and I've lived in most of the major cities in the U.S. It deludes itself that it's "the city that care forgot," it deludes itself into believing that it's "the Big Easy," it deludes itself into sort of somehow living up to all of its sobriquets. The fact is it's a great big urban complex with a theme park in the middle, and everything else about New Orleans is just like every other city in America. Yeah, but I think, currently, the city is as little deluded as it has ever been, with the casino falling flat, with the murder rate up, and with a pretty good, aggressive mayor running things. I think it's probably about as close to facing facts as I've known it to be certainly in the time I've been there. There isn't in New Orleans a past—in a municipal sense—there isn't a past to look back on in which there was a great period of realism, where people saw what they had here and mounted a campaign based on that. Most of the campaigns that have been mounted in the past have been of the pie-in-the-sky variety. Building the casino was like building the Superdome. The city has had a hard time over the years facing facts.

HG: In *Occidentals,* New Orleans is Helen Carmichael's "favorite American city." Is it yours?

RF: [Laughing] I did that as a nicety to my wife. No, it's not my favorite American city, not by a long shot. Chicago is. Probably New Orleans would be second. And maybe if I didn't live here, it would be first.

HG: You gave up writing fiction for a time. As you look back at that period now, would you say that you stopped as a result of frustration brought about by the fact that your first two novels, *A Piece of My Heart* and *The Ultimate Good Luck,* were not commercially successful?

RF: Yeah, using as indices of commercial success whether or not they sold a lot of copies, whether or not they got sold into paperback (and thus kept in print). It was probably generally true that I gave up writing in 1981 because it was a year of extreme personal heartache and stress in my life. My mother was dying, and Kristina and I were somewhat unsettled—not in our married life, but in our geographical life. I was not liking living in the suburbs of New Jersey. There was a lot of upheaval in my life, and one of the things that I thought was, "Well, you've published two books, you've had a good shot at this whole enterprise, and you haven't made much of a go of it, so get on with finding something that you can make a go of." And maybe, in a way, I might have begun to see the anxieties, and the contingencies, and the uncertainties of trying to make a writer out of myself as slightly absurd at that moment because so much else in my life was not settled, and so much else in my life was sorrow.

HG: In 1996, *Independence Day* became the first novel ever to win both the Pulitzer Prize and the PEN/Faulkner Award. What has this recognition meant to your life and career?

RF: I'm sure it's changed some things. I have more readers. Probably, the most significant thing that's changed is that—just on the strength of that book's having a good publishing life and then later on winning the Pulitzer Prize—it caused a lot of people to read that book that hadn't read books of mine before. I'm not—and you can get other people to disagree with this—but I don't think of myself as a very competitive person, and I'm not goal-driven in the sense of looking covetously at prizes and things like that. But, at the same time, when those things, just by happenstance, come to you, there are certain little anxieties in your life—there have been in my life—that I wouldn't have even ever admitted that I felt, and didn't think I did feel, that have to do simply with the recognition of myself as a guy who is trying and to some extent succeeding in making at that point a contribution to the world. Some of those anxieties were not resolved but were simply *demarked* from how they had been before. It was as though the world said to me, "Okay, okay, okay, we admit it; you're a writer." But those moments in your life come, and then you just relinquish them; and other people get those kinds of accolades. I went over to the doctor's today and I was looking at a copy of *Newsweek,* and here's this wonderful book, *Cold Mountain,* by Charles Frazier. And here is somebody else coming along for whom it is said, "If there ever was a great American novel, a novel which could be a masterpiece, this is certainly it." So however I felt a year ago when I got that prize, I felt it at that moment; and then I went back to feeling the way I always feel. And I wrote another book, and I'm well on the way to writing another book, so life had a nice high moment, and then it just resolved itself back to my usual practices and habits.

HG: As an English professor, I wonder about your attitude toward teaching and your feelings about the academic environment. Your characters Frank Bascombe and Charley Matthews express their disillusionment with teaching and with academia. You taught writing earlier in your career but quit, I believe, to devote more time to your own writing and because, as you once said, quoting Eudora Welty, you "lacked the instructing turn of mind." Yet you recently returned to the classroom to teach a creative writing course at Northwestern University. What made you decide to teach again? And what are your feelings about teaching and the academy?

RF: To answer a question that you didn't explicitly ask, on the way to answering one that you did, my experience in universities, as an observer of other people, has been that it's life like everywhere else. It's life like at IBM, it's life like at National Cash Register; it's full of the petty grievances, the backbiting and low-horizon anxieties and agonies of every other life; whereas it poses as something of a higher order, so that the discrepancy between how things are and how things purport to be is always quite vivid to me. Which totally excludes, quite frankly speaking, my own experience, which has been—from the times I've taught in my life—actually quite rewarding and sometimes even—exultant. But I'm not typical because I don't come and stay, and I'm sympathetic to those people who do. It think it's harder for them to keep their sense of mission, their sense of dignity, and their sense of importance alive under the onslaught of years, under the onslaught of students, under the pressures of colleagues who are somehow just putting in their time. I went back to teach at Northwestern at the end of a long project— *Independence Day*—and with that comes the belief that maybe I know something new, that maybe I have a renewed vigor for the vocation of writing that I might have exhausted earlier. I always try to go back into the classroom at times when I feel like I'm most enthusiastic to try to talk to young students on the strength of my own experience as a writer. I couldn't do it year after year after year, because I'm relying so much on the wind filling my own sails from my own work, whereas a person who is a true, trained literary scholar has that great canon of literature always to fill his sails.

HG: I recall a letter that Flannery O'Connor wrote in response to a professor's outlandish interpretation of "A Good Man Is Hard to Find." She said, "Too much interpretation is certainly worse than too little, and where feeling for a story is absent, theory will not supply it." Do academics, especially the "anti-mystery types" that Frank Bascombe encountered in his brief stint at the academy, have a tendency to drain the life out of literature?

RF: I don't know. I don't read the things that are written about my books. I just can't. I've tried to, every once in a while, but I just haven't been able to sustain any but a kind of vain and sometimes antagonistic interest. But the only way I came to read literature with any wider sensation at all—other than just the really palpable sensation of the language—was by reading R. P. Blackmur, by reading Harry Levin, by reading *The Nature of Narrative* [by Robert Scholes and Robert Kellogg], by reading all kinds of critics. So I have never found that, as a rule, the true literary criticism, which is broad-based and humanistic in character, eviscerates or denatures literature at all. It's only small minds that denature and eviscerate literature. Everything else, I think, is perfectly fine. A notion embodied in Blackmur's essay "A Critic's Job of Work," in which he talks about what criticism is for and how its varieties can be applied to the text, what value it can hold for the reader, I think, is a substantiable and corroboratable position to hold. I read great critics when I was young, and I've never been sorry. I read William Gass, Frank Kermode . . .

HG: Cleanth Brooks?

RF: Yes, my God, you can't generalize about the pusillanimous quality of criticism with people like—giants like that.

HG: What about your work habits? I think it was O'Connor who said that she wrote for three hours every morning and spent the rest of the day getting over it. Do you try to write every day?

RF: I've been a writer now—it will be thirty years next year—and during that thirty years I routinely go through periods when I don't work. But when I am working on something, which is to say, when I have a task for myself— I'm writing a story, I'm writing a novella, I'm writing an essay, I'm writing a novel—I work at it every day. And if something comes up, like having to go to the doctor or having to attend to some emergency, I feel grudging when I don't work. So I generally—particularly more effectively in the last ten years—have streamlined my life so that when I'm working on something, nothing gets in my way; and I work on what I work on seven days a week, holidays, Thanksgiving, New Year's, same thing, until it's done.

HG: How many hours a day do you put into writing?

RF: Never fewer than four, usually five or six.

HG: Do you use a word processor?

RF: I do in the stage of writing a story in which I want to get it into type, but I write with a pen. I used to write with a pencil, but finally—much as I like sharpening pencils and niggling around with them—I found that a Bic pen works best; a regular old twenty-nine-cent Bic pen is great.

HG: I believe that you sold the film rights to *A Piece of My Heart.* How did that turn out? Was the film ever produced? Have you sold film rights to other works?

RF: I did do that. I sold the option, anyway, to Paramount, and I went out to Paramount in 1975 and wrote a screenplay for a really wonderful man named Richard Sylbert. My screenplay wasn't any good, and before we could really get worked around to do a revision of it, Sylbert was discharged as the vice-president of production. Dick Sylbert is a three-time Academy Award-winning production designer, and he was the first person in Hollywood history to be brought from what is called below the line, which is to say, from a nondirectional artistic position to become a studio head. And he lasted a year and a half. He's a great guy—he's a friend of mine to this day—and a supremely talented man, but he was let go before that project could ever come around again to have a serious rewrite. So then it languished, and over the years for practically every book I've written there have been options. Only one thing has been made, a movie called *Bright Angel* with Sam Shepard and Dermot Mulroney, which I wrote myself in 1989, and which was not very good either. And now next year, next fall, somebody is going to make a movie out of *The Ultimate Good Luck.*

HG: Has production started yet?
RF: No, but they're in preproduction now. They start filming in November in Mexico.

HG: That's a very cinematic novel.
RF: Yes, it is.

HG: Do you think it's your most cinematic work?
RF: I have to think about that. There are plenty of those stories in *Rock Springs* that are fairly cinematic to me. Probably it [*The Ultimate Good Luck*] is as cinematic as anything I ever wrote, but I don't think much about that as a measurement for a book.

HG: You recently returned from Berlin where *Independence Day* was translated into German. I understand that your popularity in Europe is growing.

RF: I've really had good publishers in Europe; and they have just, in a kind of assiduous, long-term way, been steady in trying to get my books published. And when I go over there—as I do a lot because I like to go—they do as much, seemingly, as they possibly can—and more than I've seen done for almost anybody else—to get my books in front of the public. That translation of *Independence Day* has sold more than fifty thousand copies in hardback, which was quite a lot. But I think one of the things that has made it possible for me to publish books well in Europe is that I didn't go to Europe until I was forty-two, and when I went I still had the kind of wide-eyed awe and enthusiasm of a young man. And so I have been willing to continue going back, and going back, and going back, and I don't know that every American would be as lucky as I have been or would take to it as much as I have. But I have been so romantically enthusiastic about going to Europe that I think the Europeans—the people I've met, the journalists, the booksellers— they sense how glad I am to get to do this, what a privilege it is, and how lucky I feel like I am to get to do it. And, in a way, they cotton to it, which isn't to say that I have always gone out and sold my books, but I do think that my own enthusiasm for it is winning. Generally, though, Americans of our generation who do go to Europe go with our hat in our hand. The generation before ours was the generation that fought World War II, and they went to Europe with a sense of their own inherited or earned worth which our generation, who watched America plunder through Vietnam and finally retreat, never felt. We always felt like we were guests of another country because we had been such poor guests of so many countries. So, I think, most Americans when they go to Europe now are extremely sensitive to the culture that they are visiting and extremely decorous and try to both represent our country well and to offend the host country as little as possible. It doesn't make us any smarter; we're just quite well-behaved.

HG: You mentioned a new project. Have you started a new novel?

RF: No, I probably won't even think about that until the winter. I don't know what it will be. I've got a few stories that have been lingering around in my mind and proving their worth to me. I finished one this week, and I've got another one that I'd like to write when I go back out west in August. I think maybe with some perseverance, in a couple of years or maybe in another year, I might be able to write what I think of as a suite of stories, ten stories. I'll probably by the end of the summer have three, maybe one more in the fall. I'd like to have five stories finished by January; that would be half of the book. But that's all I'm working on. I've got a couple of essays to write. That's about all. I'm supposed to write a book. I have a long-term contract with Knopf, and it does have a schedule which commits me to writing a novel; but nobody really cares if I do or I don't as long as I keep on working. And I don't care either. Novels are easier to sell to readers than short stories, but I feel like if I can write something well, whatever it is, I ought to do that.

HG: Richard, thank you for talking to me.
RF: My pleasure. Thank you for taking such care with this.

An Interview with Richard Ford

Kevin Rabalais and Jennifer Levasseur / 1998

From *The Kenyon Review*—New Series 23.3 (2001). Used by permission.

Richard Ford's novels include *A Piece of My Heart, The Ultimate Good Luck, The Sportswriter, Wildlife* and *Independence Day,* which won the Pulitzer Price and PEN/Faulkner Award in 1996. He has written two collections of stories, *Rock Springs* and *Women with Men.* He has edited *The Granta Book of the American Short Story, The Granta Book of the American Long Story* and *The Essential Tales of Chekhov.* Jennifer Levasseur and Kevin Rabalais interviewed Mr. Ford at his home in New Orleans on June 3, 1998. Kevin Rabalais met with him again on December 4, 1998.

Interviewer: It has been more than twenty years since the publication of your first novel, *A Piece of My Heart.* How do you look back on your body of published work, particularly the early novels.

Richard Ford: I don't think about it unless somebody comes along and makes me think about it. My idea about those books is that I like them, and I feel about them today exactly the way I felt about them the day they were finished. I'm not a person who looks back at something and revises my opinion of it, particularly work I can no longer affect, change, or improve. It goes without saying that if I were to set out to write a book called *A Piece of My Heart* today, I would probably do it differently. But that's not what's going to happen. There's a wonderful story by Jorge Luis Borges called "Pierre Menard, Author of the *Quixote.*" In that book, a man named Pierre Menard decides he is going to write a book. The book he wants to write is *Don Quixote.* He hopes to write, without access to the other book, exactly *Don Quixote.* That, in a way, is Borges saying something about the nature of how we look at time, how we look at the past and past events, how we would like to change them or repeat them. But we can't; that's an absurdity. I'm very happy about all my books. The thought that somebody might read *A Piece of My Heart,* or, as is going to happen this fall, make a movie out of *The Ultimate Good Luck,* thrills me. I'd be neurotic if I constantly picked away at those earlier accomplishments. I'm not neurotic.

Interviewer: *The Sportswriter* and its sequel, *Independence Day,* differ both in sentence structure and in tone. Was the change in Frank Bascombe's life something you wanted to set up through the length and structure of the sentences?

Ford: I wanted, without knowing how it would eventuate, to have *Independence Day* record change in Frank. I didn't know what the change would be because there ain't no Frank. I make Frank. Frank existed in one book; then when I started to write *Independence Day,* he didn't yet exist in that book. I knew a good working conceit for a sequel would be for the book to record a change in Frank's persona. But I didn't know how it would work. The opening sentences in *Independence Day* are as they were when I first wrote them. Virtually unchanged. That was the mood, tone, sentence weight and syncopation that was first available to me in *that* book. I thought when I was writing it that it was the same prose as *The Sportswriter.* It was only after I put the two books up side to side, very late in the process of writing *Independence Day,* that I realized the sentences are much shorter, much less complex, generally more succinct in *The Sportswriter.*

Interviewer: Did you re-read *The Sportswriter* before you started work on *Independence Day?*

Ford: No. I very deliberately did not. Eventually, I had to skim through it to try to be sure the street names were the same. A couple of times, I had to be sure I hadn't simply repeated myself with a certain image. It's a complex and involved clerical process to write long novels. There are so many things you have to remember and keep straight, and when a book is related to another book, that just exaggerates the clerical morass.

Interviewer: *The Womanizer,* the first story in your collection *Women with Men,* was written during a plane trip to the United States from Paris. *Independence Day* was written over a four-year period. How different is the level of intensity you experience when you write a novel from when you write a contained piece in one sitting?

Ford: When I was on that plane coming back from Paris, I was writing, I guess I'd say, feverishly. I had all this stuff bubbling out of my head, and that doesn't happen to me very much because I have the instincts of a novelist. That is to say, even when I'm writing short stories, I pace myself so as to always be fresh and not run myself into the ground. With a novel, I don't want to work myself silly because I'll get frustrated and write beyond my capacities to be good, and the next day I'll have to throw stuff away. I am very measured in how I work. I go at the thing, and then I stop. I do this all during the day, all during the week, all during the year. So it was very different writing that story on the plane. I sat down on the plane and realized there were some things I had to write down. I started writing, then the plane left, and I was still writing and filling up all these notebooks. When I got back, the story wasn't precisely finished, but it was drafted out. That was pretty intense. It was very unusual.

Interviewer: Is it true you wrote many of the stories in *Rock Springs* during the time you were writing *The Sportswriter?*

Ford: At least half of them.

Interviewer: How did you make the transition from novel to stories?

Ford: There isn't really anything difficult about that. You just stop doing one thing and start doing another. First you wash the dishes, and then you dry them. On minute you are doing this kind of work, and another minute you are doing that kind of work. It may seem to be a feat, but it isn't. When I would come to periods in writing *The Sportswriter* when I wanted to stop or I was tired, I would write a story. I can be very diligent. One of the things my mother taught me was to try to make everything seem as normal as you can. Don't let the world dictate to you that there is something more difficult than your experience tells you it is. If somebody says, "I don't know how you can have this tone going in your head all the time and then switch over to something else," tell him, "Well, maybe it isn't really that hard." Earlier, I was talking on the phone, and somebody said, "Has there ever been anything in your life you wanted to do but thought you mustn't do?" I said, "I don't think so." I don't want many things, so it should be possible, given the modest number of things I want, to do them. In a way, writing may create magic in the heart, but it is not performed magically. I wouldn't be able to do it if that were the case.

Interviewer: Gabriel García Márquez has written that stories are more difficult for him than novels because stories force the writer to constantly begin again. What has been your experience with these forms?

Ford: Writing is writing to me. Sometimes you write long; sometimes you write short. Stories are easier, of course. But for me, they each have different pleasures. They each afford different problems. It's just my impulse not raise the profile of the problem.

Interviewer: You've said that you have the instincts of a novelist. Don DeLillo has said, "The novel is a meat-eating form. It devours everything."

Chekhov, however, often wove more texture through his short stories than others fail to achieve within a 300-page novel. In terms of the story's open-ended form, what do you feel are the differences in potential between stories and novels?

Ford: I think about the most obvious ones, that it is the difference between a good big fish and a good little fish. Which would you rather have? To me, novels are a more estimable form because they include more. By including more, they present the possibility of a wider variety of effects, a wider variety of experience, possibly a wider variety of moral insight and challenge. To me, they are a more engrossing narrative form than the short story (if you think engrossing is good). It's not so much that big is better or that small is less good. I just happen to think that short stories, one by one by one, are less important than novels. It is also true that stories like "An Anonymous Story," "The Darling," or "Peasants" could very likely, in all of the categories that I just described, be better than nine out of 10 other 500-page novels, in terms of their felicities, complexities, their sustained analysis and sustained notice in their importance. But I write both, and I am the world's greatest expert about my own experience. For me, one form is more potent and more valuable than the other. But, you know—we don't really have to choose. We're free to read them all.

Interviewer: What kind of relationship do you have with your characters?

Ford: Master to slave. Sometimes I hear them at night singing over in their cabins. And sometimes, I'll wake up at night and write down what I hear and what I think of, what seems to be in their voices. Other than that, they don't have an existence I don't confer on them. I'm kidding, of course. but they don't talk to me. They don't tell me what to do. I make them do whatever I want them to. I'm basically practical, cut-and-dry about characters. They're made of language. They're not people, and I can change them as such. I can change the color of their eyes, their genders, their races. I can do all those things to them. They are totally subservient to me. Which isn't to say that I always plot out their every action. I act on a whim at times, and they have to exist upon that whim. I'm very disdainful of these aesthetes who talk about, "My characters wouldn't do that," or, "I just start writing it and then my characters write the book." Horseshit, is what I say. It's a ruse to get out of taking responsibility for your mistakes. Authorship means I authorize everything.

Interviewer: Many of your stories and novels begin with setting. You've also said you are not necessarily concerned with getting the setting "right."

For instance, if you're writing about Mississippi, it doesn't have to look like Mississippi looks.

Ford: It can't because Mississippi only looks one way. It looks the way you see it when you get there and get out of your car and walk off into the cotton field and look out at the levee. That's how Mississippi looks. It only means one thing. I can try, through the agency of language, to provoke you into that mental picture, but right away, you understand that language never gets anything that accurately—nothing that's physically provable. Anyway, language is more interesting to me in its poetic and non-cognitive qualities than is the mental picture I might betray. So I'm willing to alter the mental picture on behalf of certain pleasures of language. In any case, landscape in my stories is always just background to what the characters do. Plus, even if you could be "accurate," different readers would always envision if differently.

Interviewer: You seem to have a strong interest in the weight of words within a sentence—the sound of one word and its relation to others within the sentence. Where did your interest in language originate?

Ford: I don't know. From reading Faulkner. Maybe from getting immersed in those long, sometimes endless sentences, and sometimes losing my antecedent, losing my pronoun reference, and sometimes losing all sense of where the sentence is going and still liking it. Maybe from being dyslexic and having to pour over sentences so gravely that I became more attached to the physical qualities of the words than to their referents. From being a very slow reader and always weighing the word as I read it just as I do now when I write it. Those things. I grew up in Mississippi and, for reasons I can't begin to tell you—but Eudora Welty is the same way—I grew up making word jokes and puns. We weren't particularly educated, but we were inventive with words. I've always assumed we grew up with a strong sense of irony and absurdity in Jackson because of the basic absurdity of racism: words meaning different things from what they seemed, etc.

Interviewer: Did reading Faulkner at a young age and noting his attention to language allow you to see the possibilities of writing fiction?

Ford: I can't very well say, "No," because you read his sentences and you see what they do, how lush and profuse they are. I never really wanted to do that; I never really wanted to write like Faulkner, although I think for a while I was kind of immured in it because I wanted to write about the South, and that came with it. But I don't think Faulkner was particularly stylistically influential in terms of the types of sentences I wrote or the ones I write now.

I recognized when I read Faulkner that he was one kind of writer, and that he was probably not the kind of writer I was ever going to be if I was moved at times to imitate him. I never thought there was anything to gain by emulating him. There were other writers who were influential to me on the level of the sentence. Ford Madox Ford was a very affective writer for me. Pinter, Borges and other writers, too. My view of what sentences are is a very licentious view. I think sentences are not conceptual formulations the writer sets out to fulfill. They are totally spontaneous, invented things you have to restrain somewhat to make sense.

Interviewer: What type of process do you go through to create dialogue?

Ford: That's a thing I do first by ear. Probably most writers, including letter-writers, do the same. I try to hear the sentence. I write a sentence I like tonally that has the right number of beats in it, that sounds right, and then I see if it is interesting. If it isn't, I start rearranging it. I end up changing its tonal qualities to adapt to what sense it makes or promises to make, and then I develop a new tonal structure for it, a new structure of sounds and relationships, and then sometimes the sense changes. That's one way invention occurs. It's very much like rhyming poems, or poems in metric patterns. The poet starts trying to figure out how he can accommodate sense with the poem's sound structure, and then the poem develops. You start out with a set of understandings you don't finish with, and that's good; you've learned something.

Interviewer: *The Ultimate Good Luck* was originally written in the first person, then changed to a third-person narrative.

Ford: I didn't like it in the first person because it was too short. There really wasn't much of a book there. I showed it to my friend Geoffrey Wolff, and I said, "I wrote this book to the end as I understood it to be, but it's just one hundred and fifty pages long. That just isn't enough. It doesn't feel like enough of a book." He read it and said, "Well, you're right. It's not enough of a book. It's not a story, and it's not a novel." He said, "You may have to try it in the third person." I thought that was an interesting idea, and when I started doing it, there was the book waiting to be imagined, but in another intellectual mode. I was teaching at Princeton then. I was young and ignorant and didn't know how to do it. I certainly had no idea how hard it would be, or how much a different narrative mode using the same focus character would change, or cause me to re-imagine a story. That was a learning process. It made me realize I had to be more scrupulous when I start a book so that I can try to anticipate mistakes.

Interviewer: Much of your work is in the first person. Do you feel more comfortable writing from that point of view?

Ford: No, that's just the way a lot of the stories turned out. I did notice something, and I can't account for it right now, but in stories like "Empire," *Occidentals* and *The Womanizer* (all stories written in the third person), I have a much harder time finding redemptive language for events and characters. Those stories all turn out to be—and I don't know if it's just coincidental—harsher stories. The moral quotient to those stories tends to be of a more negative kind. They tend to be stories that indict their characters more than the first-person stories. Why? I don't know. But I'd like it not to be so.

Interviewer: Do you think you have more flexibility, then, with a first-person narrator?

Ford: I don't know. I don't feel, when I'm writing a story in the first person, any different from how I feel when I write a story in the third-person view. There are no tactile distinctions about those two methods for me. You can almost, in a falsely spatial way, say that from a third person you're above the earth a little more, whereas with the first person you are very close and personally involved with the characters. Maybe the first person enjoins the reader and the writer to be more sympathetic to the character. Maybe to be god-like is naturally harsher. I wrote a long story in Berlin, which *The New Yorker* published, that is in the third-person point of view. with a woman as focus, and it is a much kinder story than any other story I've ever written in the third person. It's a Christmas story. Maybe Christmas helped.

Interviewer: Several of the stories in *Rock Springs* are set up as stories within stories. There are points when the narrator addresses the reader, saying that now he is going to tell a story. Many of the stories also end in hope. Are these themes you wanted to carry throughout the collection?

Ford: You're talking about the deliberate invocation of storyness and the deliberate attempt to find something affirming about the story. Both things are deliberate on my part. I want a reader at the beginning of a story to understand that he or she is reading a story. I'm trying to make a clear, almost contractual arrangement with the reader of the story, which says, "Okay, now quit thinking about this and that. Here's a story. It's made up.

It's a contrivance made of words. It's not your life. It's something else. It's special. I made it as well as I can. Enter into it. Take pleasure." I think that submission and entry are pleasurable for a reader, or can be.

The other is another matter. That's something I kind of stumbled on. The first two books I'd written had a rather dark view of the world. My friend Walter Clemens, who's dead now—he was the wonderful book critic for *Newsweek* magazine—told me once that he thought I had somehow or other short-circuited my sense of humor by writing *The Ultimate Good Luck,* and he wished I hadn't done that. In the process of musing about Walter's remark, I began to realize that in those two books, what I had been looking for, and what I would probably always be looking for, was drama of some kind of high order. And I had begun, out of youthful ignorance and ardor, to associate darkness—emotional, spirtual, moral darkness—with high drama. It's not unheard of. But by the time 1982 rolled around, I realized I could no longer sustain identifying darkness with drama. I just sort of ground to a halt. I needed, and this was at my wife Kristina's suggestion, to write something that was optimistic, or that concerned redemption of a secular kind. And that, with a couple of notable exceptions, has remained my purpose. When you get to the next to last movement of the story and you have one more move-ment you know you are going to write, you have the option of making that last movement anything you want it to be. My impulse is always to say, "Sometimes I'm defeated. How can I contrive this ending to be the proper ending and to give the reader something affirming?" It's just an instinct. I am, basically, an optimist. I think every writer has got to be an optimist. It's in the character of literature.

Interviewer: Throughout your career, you have edited several fiction an-thologies: *The Best American Short Stories 1990, The Granta Book of the American Short Story, The Granta Book of the American Long Story, The Essential Tales of Chekhov* and two volumes of Eudora Welty's stories and novels for The Library of America. Why have you chosen to focus much of your energy on the work of other writers?

Ford: Well, for my colleagues, really, and for readers. And also to keep myself reading. If you write all the time and your life is taken up with trying to find something interesting to write and letting yourself be talked into doing this, or talking yourself into doing that, most of your energy is spent writing. One of the things I don't feel I do enough of is read. I take these projects on so I can read something I haven't read before. The Chekhov project is a case in point because I was reading many of those stories for the first time. I was interested in the *Granta* project of long stories because I wanted to read those stories again. They were stories I wanted to champion. The case of Eudora Welty's work was a matter of doing something I felt compelled to do because of the excellence of her work and because this was such a good opportunity to have all that work consolidated into one place. Ultimately, though, these projects are for others, but also for me, too. I do get paid for it, but not much.

Interviewer: In 1992, you edited the *Granta Book of the American Short Story.* How did you choose those stories?

Ford: I knew a lot of the stories I wanted to put in the book. It was exactly the kind of process you would think: I sat down and made many lists of stories I'd read and remembered liking. The important thing is that, with a project like this, you don't do it all in a day, but that you give yourself a long time. I went back and flipped through the contents pages of a lot of books and looked for stories I remembered liking. I then got together my long list and read the stories to see if they held up to my remembrance. Then, I decided how I would organize the book and how I would represent the different decades in which the book was focused on: 1940s through the beginning of the '90s. I wanted the best stories I could find, really. It was very unscientific. But what isn't?

Interviewer: What are the differences in editing your own work and selecting works for an anthology?

Ford: When I read my own stories that are in progress, I try to read with as critical an eye as I can. I think I take on the role of the reasonable reader who would be stopped by something that didn't make sense, or who would be bored by something that went on too long, or who misses something due to some imprecision. When I read stories for compilation in an anthology, I'm reading stories that are finished and that are already excellent. I don't feel that the way I read my own stories in progress—or the way that I read my own stories in public readings years after they've been published—is at all like how I read a story for possible selection in an anthology. I read those latter stories as an admirer, even as a hungry student. I certainly did find that all of Chekhov's stories were not as excellent as the best of them, but I also found that my affection for his stories did not always cause me to choose the stories I thought everybody would conceive to be most excellent. I had favorites of my own that I realized would probably deviate from the general canon

174 Conversations with Richard Ford

of Chekhov's excellence, which normally champions his work written after
1890.

Interviewer: Because Chekhov is regarded as the master of the short form,
do you think he is a looming presence for many writers? How do you think
he affects writers today?

Ford: Chekhov was a very humane writer, and the kinds of ways he would
be most influential would be through those features in his stories that illumi-
nate our complexity. His formal view of his own stories was quite undoctrinal
and various. He wasn't a writer who, as say Hemingway, would bias young
writers toward a certain way of putting a story on the page or of writing
sentences. Chekhov's writing is so various that he wouldn't affect you very
much as a writer in any one way. He is often said to be the master of irresolute
endings, but that isn't always true. His endings are not open-ended; many are
quite conclusive. I think most of the ways Chekhov would be likely to affect
a writer would be ways he or she would want to be affected. That is to say,
he would encourage a writer to be more searching in his analysis, more humane in his view of people readers might otherwise in a conventional way be
likely to dismiss. He would be encouraging in asking a writer to write about
people who might not ordinarily seem natural subjects. He would encourage
writers to pay attention to landscape. He would teach writers all kinds intensi-
ties: the intensity of notice, of sustained analysis, of the intensity needed to
imagine human motive. He would teach someone that writing is a high calling, but not necessarily sober-sided, which would make him a good influence.
And we are also reading his stories translated into English, so we don't have
them in their original language, only in that buffer zone of English, which
may (if Ms. Garnett was any good) stress larger thematic matters and stress
less matters of surface style and local effect.

Interviewer: In your introduction to *The Essential Tales of Chekhov,* you
say, "His wish is to complicate and compromise our view of characters we
might feel we understand at first." What goals do you feel short fiction should
attempt to achieve?

Ford: Whatever goals the writer wants. That's just what Chekhov did,
which were estimable goals; but that's no reason to think it's what anybody
else should try to do. Anybody else should do what he or she wants to do.
The short story is a form that is certainly open. Henry James wrote that the
terrible whole of art is free selection.

Interviewer: What do you feel is the importance of a community of writers?

Ford: In a way I would probably not be able to specify, it's very important. Some of its particulars are—and I'm fierce about things like this—that we writers not run each other down in print. I know that because I did it once, and I didn't think I was right. It's important that we try to be as much as we can be forces for good in the lives of our colleagues. I was at an American Booksellers Association convention the other day, and I was standing in line, waiting to get a hot dog. Tim O'Brien came into line and grabbed me and said, "God, I haven't seen you in a long time. How are you?" That was important to me. He and I started off together as young writers. I realize how much it meant to me, seeing him. I hadn't seen him in years, but there was that sense, and we both felt this without having to say it, that we've both been through this together. It's probably just a small thing—like Shriners meeting other Shriners. But I liked it. I know we both have the same kinds of aspirations, which is to make a contribution to the world in some way using our best selves. I don't always like my colleagues personally, but I regard them highly as people who are writers. I write them fan letters, and they do the same for me.

Interviewer: You grew up across the street from a house in Jackson, Mississippi, that Eudora Welty once lived in. How do you look back on this coincidence?

Ford: My family came to North Congress Street a good while after she had gone. The house was by that time owned by a Supreme Court justice. But when I was growing up at that place, 736 North Congress Street, I never knew Eudora Welty had lived in the house across the street. It was only in the '80s that I found out from somebody, maybe her, that she had lived there. She always likes to say, "We were neighbors." And I'm happy to think so, too. We did go to the same grammar school, which was next door to my house. We're 35 years apart in age, but we had some of the same teachers. It is a sweet coincidence.

Interviewer: Since then, you and Ms. Welty have become close friends. With Michael Kreyling, you recently co-edited two volumes of her work for The Library of America. How does she feel about your involvement in that project?

Ford: She was glad I was involved for mostly personal reasons. I was sort of the neighborhood boy, and so I think she felt that I would do as good a job as I could, and indeed, I didn't have to do very much. People who were involved in that project did much more than I did, however: Michael Krey-ling, who was my co-editor, and Noel Polk, a Eudora Welty scholar at the University of Southern Mississippi who did very important reconciliations of Ms. Welty's manuscripts. My job, I sometimes think, was largely ceremonial, but I am happy to be associated with the project because, for us Mississippi-ans, her work embodies something indestructible and incontestably good. I care for Eudora and I am her literary advisor and her neighbor.

Interviewer: You have also written recently in *The New Yorker* about your friendship with Raymond Carver. What does a literary friendship involve?

Ford: A literary friendship is one like any other friendship: it offers the faith that someone will act on your behalf, if by acting on your behalf one doesn't have to betray oneself. For writers, I think, specifically, an ongoing interest in the work one does is essential, a willingness (and this is hard) to not always give the most favorable answers to questions when the truth is asked for. That is to say, a willingness to be amiably candid, if value is put on that.

Interviewer: In that essay, "Good Raymond," you describe a time when you and Carver collaborated on a screenplay. What has been your experience with literary collaborations?

Ford: I've worked with other people, but writing screenplays is inevitably a collaborative business. But with Ray and me, that was nearly twenty years ago. Ray was getting to be famous, and I was plugging alone. He had some contacts with movie directors, and I didn't, so I felt fortunate to be working on that project, even though it never came to anything.

Interviewer: How do you feel about the way your career has progressed since then?

Ford: Before any really serious good luck came my way—and good luck is always just temporary, I think—I spent years writing and experiencing the normal vicissitudes of a writer's life in America, which is to say working a long time and not having many readers, having publishers drop you, having your books not picked up for paperback, normal things. I didn't think any of it was exceptional and still don't. When days finally came that I had a bigger readership and things seemed to work out for me better for a while, my habits as a writer, my expectations for what my work would enjoy and what plea-sures I took from being a writer, were already very well established. It would have been hard to have shaken me off the ground I thought I was standing on. Even if the ground grew in elevation, I have always had the certainty that it will re-descend.

Interviewer: The subject of luck runs throughout your work. Have you developed any theories on luck throughout the years?

Ford: I've always been struck by how things happen in your life in an unplanned way: your father dies on a Sunday afternoon; your dog gets run over by a car; you have a child, and the child suddenly dies. You don't want these things to happen. Everything you've done in your life has been designed to prevent these things, at least if not from happening, from happening in a way that totally surprises and defeats you. And yet they do. So much of the world is driven by that randomness, which I sometimes call luck. I've always preferred the old adage turned on its ear: design is the residue of luck. I think everything basically, is subject to unexpected intervention and that our character as human beings, if we can be said to have character, has a lot to do with how well we accommodate, how well we try to invent a vocabulary and a moral scheme that allows us to take responsibility for our actions in a universe that is much affected by randomness. That's how we stay cogent to ourselves. Of course, some things aren't random at all. Some things we or others predictably cause, and we must own up to them.

Interviewer: Luck also seems to reverberate in your life: the chance upbringing near Eudora Welty and being invited to a writers' conference and meeting Raymond Carver when you were both just beginning. How do you look back on these encounters?

Ford: In the aggregate, that is how everything happens. There are courses that cause people to collide. I used to have a friend in New York who wasn't a very good friend. When I would publish something, or when someone would write something in the press about me that was complimentary, he would always come to me, and in a suspicious way, say, "How do you think that happened?" or "Do you know someone there?" He was always slightly impugning any good luck I had. And I always think of it as being just good luck. But the truth is that those kinds of collisions take place one way or another. Sometimes it is just the quality of one's work that wins out, and sometimes you're in the right place at the right time. Sometimes it's a mistake. But I've never had the feeling that in the literary world the fix was in. It isn't profitable enough to want to fix. Consequently, it's just nicely timeless and free. I do still believe that all good writing will eventually find a readership. I mean, so much *bad* writing does. Why shouldn't the good enjoy its small victories?

Interviewer: Much of the attention you are giving colleagues seems to be strengthening the international reach of contemporary American fiction.

Ford: I'm pretty familiar with contemporary Irish, Scottish and English writing. I'm a little familiar with contemporary French and Spanish language literature, but beyond that, everything has to get into translation for me to be admitted to it. But my assumption is that my generation of American writers, not excluding any others—the one after me, or the one before it—but my generation, people who are now in their early '50s, has produced a remarkable number of very fine writers. And I take great pleasure in that because we went through the same periods of life. We didn't follow the same tracks necessarily, but so many of us do try to write about American culture in a humane and considered way, many of the ways I describe that Chekhov would influence writers. It is one of the reasons that I try to promote the work of others in the way I do. It's good for me to do that, and it's natural. But I never want to argue that American literature at this particular moment is better than another culture because it doesn't *have* to be better. It only has to be good. And my work is to find the good and call it so.

Interviewer: *The Sportswriter,* the book that launched a wide readership for you, was a paperback original. Was it your decision to publish the novel this way?

Ford: Yes. It was my choice. The people at Vintage told me, "If we publish this book in Vintage Contemporary format, we will be able to get a lot more books out there. We aren't exactly sure we can get review attention for it, but let's roll the dice. We'll do our best, and we'll put a lot of books out, and we'll really get behind it." Vintage had had great success with *Bright Lights, Big City* a couple years before, so I thought I had nothing to lose and everything to gain. It was just that time when paperback originals were a novelty. I caught that wave and got lucky. Gary Fisketjon, my editor at Knopf, said, "We should try this." The book sold well and continues to sell well. But it was published well.

Interviewer: You've said your working schedule becomes more intense the deeper you become involved in a project. How do you find your rhythm?

Ford: There really isn't much of a rhythm. You quit one day and start the next, and try to catch the way things sounded the day before. There may be something of a rhythm when you work at something many days in a row. I can detect it when I break it. If I write six or eight days steady and the work is going in a fairly harmonious way, if something comes along that causes me to take three days off, then I'm aware that something has been interrupted. So if it's a rhythm, then OK. In an odd way, I don't really like to work that much. But I have found over the years that in the context of my life, it satisfies me to work. It's a little bit like eating spinach. You are not supposed to like spinach when you're a kid, but people make you eat it. After a while, you begin to like the taste.

Interviewer: I've read where you said your choice to become a writer was an arbitrary one you decided on when your mother asked you what you wanted to do. Is that really how it started?

Ford: Yes, but I must've been thinking about it. There's such a long time between now and 1968. But when you are at the beginning and you say you would like to be a writer, you don't really know what you are saying. You're just saying a sentence that seems plausible that nobody can refute and that doesn't cause anybody embarassment. You set about doing it. After many years, it begins to have the appearance of genuine purpose. But at the moment of embarcation, I didn't know what I was saying. I could have easily said I wanted to be a chimneysweep. I guess if I'd said that, I'd have probably gone on to do it.

Interviewer: Were you writing before the time of that decision?

Ford: No. I had been in law school until three days before. I had been at Washington University, and Stanley Elkin was the adviser to the literary magazine then. I remember hauling out one of the stories I had written as an undergraduate and dressing it up, smoothing it out, getting it proofread, and taking it over to that magazine. Of course, it got rejected. But there must have been something percolating in me in 1966 and '67 that made writing stories attractive. What was left after law school were those words about me becoming a writer, totally ridiculous words, baffling to my mother. She didn't say no to the idea, but she just looked at me with a sort of wan despair.

Interviewer: You've written a memoir of your mother's life, and you've said if it weren't for her, you wouldn't be a writer.

Ford: True, but if it weren't for my wife, I wouldn't be a writer, either. If it weren't for a lot of other people, I wouldn't be a writer. My mother, at least I can say, never discouraged me from being a writer. She never thought it was a terrible idea, though I don't think she understood it very well. She told me when I was young, and later when she was dying, "You must make yourself happy. Go toward those things that make you happy. Stay away from those things that make you unhappy." Now, I don't believe that just deciding to be a writer will make you immediately happy. But some inner peace may be conferred upon you by trying to do something you consider inherently good. My mother was very instrumental in that way. All through the years between 1968 and 1981, when she died, I was trying to write books, and she was very respectful of that. It's important that your parents not impede you, that they not castigate you or reproach you for doing something they didn't do or something they must not understand. She was always firm in her conviction that if this is what you want to do, then do it.

Interviewer: The memoir of her, *My Mother in Memory,* was published in *Harper's* and later in a small, fine edition. Have you thought about trying to get that book reprinted for a larger audience?

Ford: If I could, I guess I would like to write a memoir about my father, which I have tried to do—two or three years ago—without any success. But that—those two—might make a book. I'm not, nor have I ever been, dying to put everything I write into print. It just so happens everything I have ever written has made its way into print. That isn't the thing that motivates me. For instance, I was looking at my curriculum vita the other day, and I noticed how much nonfiction I have written. I've probably written three times as much nonfiction in my life than I've written fiction, particularly short stories. Some people over the last ten years have said, "Why don't you collect your nonfiction?" But I just don't want to. I don't care about making a book out of any of those pieces of nonfiction. I just don't feel like it's a worthwhile publishing gesture.

Interviewer: It seems that, for a writer, work and life are one and the same. It is not a nine-to-five job where you leave the house to go to work. How has this affected your relationship with your wife and friends?

Ford: I've never thought about that. I guess, at an early stage in life, it felt a little queer to always be home, but then I got over that. Sometimes, when I was an unknown writer who was staying at home writing books and there wasn't any product and no evidence that I was actually doing anything, people would laugh about it—being a househusband and not doing anything. That ended, though. I don't think it's had a really big effect on my relationship with other people at all. When I started to publish books, the naysayers slipped to the back row. As far as my relationship with Kristina is concerned, we started out in life this way. The year we were married, '68, was the year I started trying to write stories. So we never had a life that didn't involve me staying at home writing stories or that didn't involve her getting in a car and going to work, which she did and does to this very minute. That's the only life we've ever known. She was certainly never reluctant to have me at home. We are pretty conventional people in most ways. We have a house with pictures on the wall; we have dogs running around. I have a motorcycle and a car. But at the same time, we are not much inhibited by convention. We don't let it tell us what's right and wrong. This is the way we've always set out to live. It didn't seem to me to be radically divergent from what other people did. It was never an issue.

Interviewer: The short story doesn't seem to be in as wide demand as it has been in the past. What do you feel is the reason for this?

Ford: Magazines. There aren't many magazines. Writers would write stories if there were more magazines. There are plenty of little magazines, but little magazines don't get read very much. And the reason they don't get read very much is because there are a lot more writers than there are good writers; there are a lot more stories than there are good stories. You have only to edit *The Best American Short Stories* to understand that. But there are still enough good writers and good stories floating around in America to fill the quota of many more good, wide-circulation magazines. What you detect to be a sort of falling off in the popularity of the short story is, I think, accurately detected in these reasons: magazines are under terrible financial pressures; they are going out of business; they are having a harder time finding a niche in the American consciousness, they have a lot of competition.

Interviewer: Aside from the magazine issue of publishing stories, it seems that collections of stories are becoming more difficult to publish.

Ford: That's always been the case. Eudora Welty, all through the late '30s and '40s, didn't want to write any novels. One of the things she warred against in the publishing world then was that you had to write a novel. She didn't want to. She didn't do it for a long time. She preferred stories. We've sold a lot of copies of *Women with Men*. We're already on the third printing of the paperback, and it's been out only three weeks. I think books of stories, probably not commensurate with the number of books of stories that are being published, do OK. I know that Tom (T. C.) Boyle just published an enormous book of stories. He's a moneymaking novelist. But if the publishing industry was not doing fairly well with collections of stories, they wouldn't be publishing them. As a writer, you can't worry much about things like that. You can't fight battles for which you have no armor. You're not, as a writer, in the publishing business. As long as publishers are publishing short stories, then you should be writing them. If they finally hang the shingle on the door and say, "Sorry, no more short stories," then maybe you should no longer write them. But if you think, "Well, people do publish stories, and I know I've written some good ones," then go ahead and do it.

Interviewer: At a signing in New Orleans held just after the publication of *Women with Men,* someone asked you about the cover of the book. You mentioned that when you chose the photograph for the cover, some of the women at Knopf didn't like it because they thought the woman in it was not pretty enough. Some critics have branded you a writer who writes for male readers, but although many of your male characters are decent people, or they are people who are trying to be decent, it is the women who are stronger characters.

Ford: Well, what that means is that you've read the stories. It also means that people who brand me a "male writer" haven't read my stories. I like to hunt, and I like to fish. I used to box. I've got a pretty wife. I just get sort of typecast as a certain kind of guy. Even if the fiction doesn't bear that out, I still get typecast. I rather hate to think, though, that I've been writing books all these years, working this hard, for only half the population. I would never do that. If I really believed I was doing it, I would quit. I would say, "No more of that." Women and men are so much alike as human beings, and they need to be addressed in ways that cause them, by the agencies of that address, to seek out the places they are alike rather than just hide behind the gender distinctions.

Interviewer: How do you and your wife respond to comments like that against you and your writing?

Ford: I've never been surprised by it. I've been surprised by how long it's held on. When you first make your entrance in the world as a writer, there isn't much for the press to hang on you. So they hang whatever they can hang on you, often something superficial or just invented. Maybe living in the West as I have, or being a Southerner as I am, or being the kind of guy I seem to be, maybe that made sense at one moment. But for it to persist so long is silly. I think what Kristina felt when she first saw it was, "Well, you are kind of a male guy. You are not ashamed about being a man, and you do have certain tastes that are traditionally male pleasures." It didn't bother her. I get mad in a sort of flash way when I see somebody dismiss me for being something I'm not. But other than that, please spell my name right. My idea about these things is that you really have to start worrying when they get it too right, when somebody's got you all figured out.

Interviewer: Is there a third Bascombe novel planned?

Ford: I was thinking of having Frank be a Negro. I was thinking of having him become a woman. That's just a way of saying, "Yes, I have." I have to imagine a third book that is so distinct from the other two it's almost not qualified as a sequel. So I'm in the process of accumulating the information about that. I've been doing it for a year, and I'll go on doing it for a couple of years while I do other things. I think probably in a couple of years I'll sit down and see if anything makes sense. As it was, there was an impluse in me when *Independence Day* was published to think, "Well, I've written two. Maybe I could write three." But at that point all I could figure out was what I could write next—what happens the next day after *Independence Day* was over. And to me that's not what a sequel really it. A sequel is a distinct book from its predecessor. I need the intervention of time to cut me off from any of those stylistic conceits or sentence structure so that I can hatch something new, if indeed I can hatch anything at all. I know a lot of things already about how I would like to write that third book: I know where I would like it to take place; I know where I would like it to be set; I know some things I want to have in it. I don't have yet, and I'm kind of sensitive to this, that big conceit that I had in *Independence Day.* But that's OK. I will have to hope to find it.

Interviewer: I see that you have books by Vaclav Havel, essayist, playwright and president of the Czech Republic, on your bookshelf. What do you feel is the role of the writer in American society?

Ford: In America, writers are totally marginal and not taken too seriously, which may be freeing. Here we have become a country of professionals, and writers are not professionals. We are amateurs. We don't have any rules for governing our daily lives or for our quasi– would-be vocational lives. We are inventing new things all the time and working within and outside established modes. We don't fit in, but we're not left out completely, either. A writer is a person who looks at the world from across a frontier, V.S. Pritchett said. That's kind of the way it is in America. Our role as writers is to try to write about the most important things we know and hope that other people will agree about their importance. I don't, however, think the concerns of novels finally formulate the public consciousness very much. In fact, we're always tugging at the coattails of American culture. We're followers, not leaders. We're always writing about things that have already occurred. In that aspect of the arts, we are always slightly retrospective. There's almost no way in which narrative art can be avant-garde. It's always reacting to something in the culture.

Interview with Richard Ford

Meghan O'Rourke / 2000

From *The Saint Ann's Review* 1.1 (2000):89–107. Used by permission.

St. Ann's Review: I thought I would start at the beginning, and ask you what you begin a novel or a story with—a character, a plot, an idea, a sentence?

Richard Ford: Well, even when I was starting out, I started with the idea that I was going to write a *novel.* I took on the form as my ambition. I still do it that way, instead of, I suppose, just noodling around and backing into it. And then once I suspect I'm going to write a novel, the unoccupied form provides a sort of hollow vessel, into which I just chuck in all kinds of stuff. Almost as you might keep a notebook, I begin collecting material, keeping in mind the germinal notion of what the novel might be. I don't have a complete plan for it, just some beginning intuitions about formal features that might be interesting to work with. And with that in mind I kind of assess as I make notes, "Would this work in a novel?" And the stuff can be errant bits of dialogue, or locations—when I wrote *The Sportswriter* I thought that I wanted to have it end in Florida. I don't know why. Or it might be names, or pieces of description, and what are to me actual ideas. I noticed when I was working on *Independence Day* that the word "independence" kept floating around in my notebook.

So I really don't start with any one specific thing. I think that the experience of a novel for a reader should be very much like the experience of life. So I collect and assess the material for a novel in a very random way, very much in the way that a person would try to make sense out of the random experience of waking up and going to work, and indeed that's the way the material gets introduced into the book as I'm writing it. It's random, and then I (or a character) try to make sense of it.

SAR: So would you say that for you the structure of a novel has to do with trying to capture different levels of experience?

RF: Well, a novel's structure for me certainly does develop as a function of the character of the material that's going into the book. Structuring a novel is not something I'm very good at. Maybe I don't really have the patience to imagine very sleek structures; or maybe it's a feature of a narrative that strikes me as particularly contrived. Maybe I'm not smart enough to contrive more interesting structures than I have. But I *am* always more interested in the material than I am in the structure. The structure for me represents how I've been able to link different things together. And I guess my "vision" about structure tends to be always focussing on specific linkages. I'm happy to have a story that involves a trip, or has some arc built into it. I get a structure given to me that way.

SAR: Maybe you have an intuitive sense of structure?

RF: It certainly *feels* intuitive. And who knows, maybe in people who become writers there *is* an intuitive sense of structure. Maybe there's something about a tripartite structure that's native to some people and not to others. I know when I'm writing stories I have a very strong but ill-defined sense that there *is* a structure to what I'm doing. I'm never just writing, writing, writing. I'm aware when I write a *story*—particularly a story—where the climax comes, where the highest point of the action is. I'm very clear in my mind about the ending. Maybe that qualifies me as not hopeless.

SAR: In a recent piece for *The New York Times,* you suggested that it can be a good thing for a writer to reconcile themselves to not writing. After reading it, I was remembering a piece you wrote for *The New Yorker* about Raymond Carver. In that piece, you talked about the need for a writer to be "at their station," so to speak. And I was wondering if there were periods of not writing, especially early on, when it was difficult to—

RF: Know if you were doing the right thing?

SAR: Yes.

RF: There's a wonderful remark of Henry James's, which I think comes from the introduction to *Roderick Hudson.* The line is "The terrible whole of art is free selection." I think he meant something very specific to writing a story, but it's the same free selection that anybody has to exhibit and exert about how his time is allocated. When you're just not doing anything, there's nobody to tell you whether or not you're wasting time. There's nobody to tell you, when you're working really hard, whether or not you've worked past the time you should have stopped. There's just no authority other than yourself. And there is a lot—it's one of the liabilities of being a writer—of gazing at yourself and wondering if you're doing the right thing, with you being both the doctor and the patient.

SAR: Self-diagnosed.

RF: Yes. It's terrible, in a way, because it makes bores out of us. I'm sure there are plenty of other vocations for which this is true. But you have to like it that there's no professional ethic, that there's no institution to give you clues about how you do things. You have to feel that it's good to be completely on your own. And to know, if the anxiety grows particularly unpleasant—or if the pleasure in something gets intoxicating—that this in and of itself is not necessarily indicative of anything important. For instance, you can feel, upon a day's writing, that you are the best writer in the world. And when you look at the work a day later you find that you aren't that at all. There are lots of times when you come to the end of a working day or a working week and you think to yourself, "Well, I just don't know why I'm doing this. It is obviously something I have no skills for at all." And then later you look at the work and it's great. Or at least acceptable.

SAR: What are your writing habits? Do you have a regular schedule?

RF: Well, I do when I do and I don't when I don't. When I'm working on a story, I work every day all day, for as long as I can feel alert. But unlike, say, Ray [Raymond Carver]—and I don't know if he was lying, he lied about his habits as much as he could—but unlike what he said about his own habits, I don't usually write a story in a day. Even a story that's three thousand words takes me a couple of days at least. But Ray used to say that once he got his little boat in the water, he stayed in it until he got to the end of his story—which is to say he would write from six in the morning until nine at night. Or so he said. You have to be careful about what writers say. Sometimes they say things to protect themselves. Sometimes they say things to make what they do seem easier, or sometimes they say things to you to make it seem that you could never do what they do. It's been my goal, though, as a writer to try always to tell the truth about these things because I don't want to say anything that would discourage a young writer from feeling that she or he could do what I do.

SAR: How much revision do you do once you get through a story? Does it depend on the story or novel?

RF: Volitional revision? I do as much as I can [laughs].

SAR: Right. There are two kinds of revision.

RF: There's the kind that *you* make me do, and the kind that *I* make me do. But I write everything out in longhand, and then I type it.

SAR: Which is its own form of revision, I would imagine.

RF: It turns out to be. And then I'll monkey with it for a while, and let it sit a while, come back to it and do what I can, and see what stays intact. But, because I'm meticulous about first drafts, most everything—I'm referring to the order of things—stays intact. That doesn't mean that it doesn't need bettering. But mostly when I put things down in an order those things stay in that order, even though I'll go along and niggle around with sentences. You know, it's funny, I never think about revision. When I was a kid, there was an expression going around that used to annoy me, which was "You need to run that through the typewriter again." It was like sending your shirts to the laundry—it seemed so perfunctory. So, habitually, in my own vocabulary of describing what I do, I just say I work at things until I can't work at them anymore. And sometimes that means concentrating on an ending for a while, and sometimes it means concentrating elsewhere, but I never just send a shirt to the laundry. I work within a story all the time, but never all the way through every time. It just isn't like that. Eventually, of course, I do read it before I hand it over to somebody else to read.

SAR: When did you decide or know that you wanted to be a writer?

RF: I made the decision that I was going to try to be a writer in 1968. And between then and 1976, when I first published a book, I did all of those things that I guess writers do, which is to say I tried this and I tried that and I tried again and I failed and I went to graduate school and I got out of graduate school and I stayed out of work and I did all kinds of things. But never cared much about publishing. I cared about trying to make what I did better, trying to keep out of my consideration all sorts of concerns that I thought were extraneous: I tried to keep my bad work out of print. I tried not to be lured by my friends getting their work published around me all of the time—lured into submitting work that wasn't so good. I mean, I did send a few things to quarterly magazines, but none of it got published, which made me feel like I wasn't any good at writing stories—which was true. That lasted from 1968 until basically 1975 when the book [*A Piece of My Heart*] was published. And then the next book I, well, I thought, you write one book, you should try to write another one. And I actually had a book to write. But it kind of failed. I had a hard time getting it published, and it didn't go into paperback, and then I quit in 1980. I stopped writing, because I thought I wasn't getting anywhere. So I had two juvenesses in a way, because I had one when I was young, and I had one when I started writing again in 1982.

SAR: And when you started again, was that when you were working on *The Sportswriter* and *Rock Springs?*

RF: I was, yes. I was doing that at the same time. For four or five years I was working on one novel [*The Sportswriter*] and on a book of stories [*Rock Springs*]. They were very different in character, too.

SAR: And do those books feel very different to you in terms of the kinds of things you were trying to do with them? I'll ask you a more specific question. *The Sportswriter* has a lot of abstract language, there's a kind of abstract language as if you were trying to represent a kind of experience that is elusive. The stories in *Rock Springs* uses language in a different way, and seem to try to represent experience without abstraction.

RF: That's right.

SAR: I was wondering if you were conscious of the difference at the time.

RF: They seem stylistically very different to me. There's a kind of literary cliché—people sometimes say to me, "I can recognize a sentence of yours anywhere." I think, "Oh, no you can't." Or they say that there's a Raymond Carver story or a Lorrie Moore kind of story. Each of those writers, me included, has a whole variety of stuff that we are able to do, ways our work sounds, length of sentences, attitudes toward experience. On and on. Graham Greene said that being a writer means to impersonate somebody else. And that's really what we're all capable of doing—impersonating all kinds of people. And so to have those two discrete strains of utterance is natural—not only to me writing two books at the same time, but to human beings in general. You know, we all talk to our various friends in different ways. We tell them the truth, but sometimes we tell it using different vocabularies, or with different tones. I can always tell when Kristina is talking to her mother on the phone. She sounds different from when she's talking to me. Our gestures for assuring our reliability are different depending on, among other things, what experience in life we've shared. I don't think this means what someone might take it to mean—that we are evil and speak with forked tongues. We *do* speak with forked tongues, but that doesn't mean we don't tell true.

SAR: I suppose that usually we think of that variation as happening at different times in the writer's career, though.

RF: If you mean that I don't write the same way now as I did when I was thirty, yes.

SAR: Does the writer have to have a reliable relationship with language?

RF: Yes, but the mode or the nature of language can change. Voice is the music of a story's intelligence, which is a variation on something Susan Sontag wrote once. But that voice, that music, can be very different. Each piece can be different music—a different relation by which language expresses its intelligence. Then there are times, obviously, that you see writers writing in a voice they don't control as well as other voices. And what you say is, "Well, he doesn't have a very good grasp on his idiom there."

SAR: Did you ever think of yourself as a regional writer? Or was there ever a fear that you would be called a regional writer?

RF: It was never a fear. It was a determination of mine that I would never be a regional writer. If I had to be a regional writer—which is to say, given that I'm a southerner, that I wrote only about the South, or that my readership was principally in the South, or that anything else was circumscribed by southernness—I would quit. Because I wanted to be not only a great writer, but a writer that anyone in the world could read and feel that he was reading nothing but a guy who was American who writes in English. Anything else was somehow a lessening of my aspirations.

SAR: Do you feel very firmly rooted in America? And in a tradition of writing that is particularly American?

RF: Well, I feel very firmly rooted in America—I'm happy to be in America, I'm happy to be an American writer, I'm happy to be writing for Americans—but I have spent a lot of time in France and a lot of time in Europe, especially in the last few years. I got as educated as I ever got reading American and English and Continental writing. Many Europeans who like my work, who read it in English, say that my stories feel very European. And I think that this is just their way of saying they like the stories, it's their way of making themselves feel comfortable. I don't know whether or not the stories are "European." Europeans are wont to say that Europe itself is a place, that it is alike within itself. But I've never found that to be so. France is very different from Germany in a literary sense. They're both very different from Spain. So I wouldn't know what it means to be European. That's one of those things that you hear back from the world that you can't pay very much attention to. Just take it as a compliment and go on.

SAR: Who are some of the writers that you admire? Has your appreciation for them evolved?

RF: Nobody surprising. It's evolved in the sense that the people I read when I was your age I don't read anymore and can't. I'll start at the beginning: Faulkner, Sherwood Anderson. To a lesser extent, Flannery O'Connor and other southerners. I thought there was a lot to learn from those people. I think that's why the first book I ever wrote was set in the South. After that, the people who really affected me—let me think about this so I say it truly. Cheever. A big influence. Harold Pinter. He had a huge effect on me. Ray [Carver] obviously had a huge effect on me because by dint of our friendship he encouraged me to write stories, which I had never been any good at. And I'm sure that the first stories I wrote when he and I were freshly friends were specifically influenced by him. And then, when I realized that reading him was affecting my stories, I had to quite reading him, too. Which was a loss. I can't go back and read the stories now, even though I know they're wonderful. I don't want those infectious rhythms and tones getting into my stories. And as time goes on, the writers who affect me are in some ways more classically good, like Elizabeth Bowen. She's just one of my huge favorites. And Chekhov. I'm interested now less in bon mots and in some ways even less in felicity, though I work hard at trying to make sentences felicitous. But I'm interested in stories being important. I'm interested in the stories being about something important, which, when I match myself to the subject, or when the subject is finally discovered, I hope I am able to say something smart about. I don't want the story to have to be dependent on some stylistic peculiarities—not that style is separable from substance; only that style can sometimes distract you from realizing that nothing of much importance is going on. I don't want it to be terribly hard to translate a story of mine into another language—and my books have been translated into twenty-one or twenty-two other languages. I want the story to be peculiar for what it's about, for what it says that it's about. When I read *The House in Paris* by Elizabeth Bowen, or when I read all those Chekhov stories two years ago, I think, "Gee, I'm really in the presence of a wonderful mind." They speak to me directly about things I care about.

SAR: And do you think that that presence can be manifested in all different kinds of genres and styles?

RF: Yes. I'm just writing a lecture about this subject. Stories can be smart in many ways. Sometimes you might have a character in a story who is very smart, as in Thomas Mann. Sometimes what makes a story smart is the dramatic situation. *The House in Paris* is a good example—something that is almost extrinsic to the lives of the characters themselves. There's an Argentine movie director whose name I can't remember who said, "Drama is interesting when the villain says something that is true." So that's a way to be smart. Convention would lead one to think that villains are bad, and that all they're going to do is prove how bad they are. But we think things are smart when they contravene expectations and persuade us. That's one reason why Shakespeare's good. Just because you hate somebody, or loathe him, doesn't mean he isn't capable of telling you something you didn't know, of surprising you. Iago, for instance. And stories can be smart in how they are put together structurally. You see a story like "The Indian Uprising" by [Donald] Barthelme, and what comes next and what follows upon that, and what follows upon that—that's where the story is smart. In "Self-Reliance," there is a line in which Emerson says that great drama, great meaning, great intelligence, lies in the transitions between things. When one thing stops and another thing begins. Sometimes in the blunt abutting of pieces of a story, that's where the story's smart—where it provokes us, make us feel something we haven't felt before, think something we haven't thought. When you're reading one part of a story, you think you know what's going to follow—all of your conventional expectations lead you to anticipate this—and then suddenly something else, something shocking maybe happens that seems persuasive. That's really great. It tells you something important about . . . oh, expectation, and about consequence.

SAR: What do you think about the idea of moral vision in fiction? And whether there is moral vision in American fiction today?

RF: It's everything to me. It's everything to me that the stories be about the most important things the writer knows about. And that a writer contracts with his reader, to use all of his power, in those ways that we were just talking about—structurally, directly, rhetorically, tonally—to go on and invent something new and of moment from those important issues.

SAR: Do you think there's much concern with moral vision in American writing today?

RF: If there's not now, there will be. If for some reason or another blind vogue has championed a certain kind of silly work—and I don't mean to say it has—it still won't last because as humans coping with our lives, we have an appetite for being told or being shown, or having suggested to us what's important. I read a lot of novels this year. And when I decide one's not very good, it's because this sense of moral vision is not foremost in the story. I'm not saying that stories have to be simplified, and I'm not implying any stylistic rules or preoccupations. It's just that when all of the features of the story that seem to be load-bearing are paramount, then I become interested in the story. Maybe I'm just an old-fashioned guy.

SAR: Do you ever think of editing as a kind of democracy, as something that takes the edges off?

RF: This is connected to that idea of terrible free selection. I have to decide whether something being suggested to me is something that will homogenize my story, or whether it's smart and good. It's a very imprecise science. It's imprecise for you and it's imprecise for me. I try to keep the whole story in mind. I try to ask, how much does this suggestion, this change—which might in fact make something move a little faster or become more accessible—how much does it take away from what's most good about the story? I think editors are my friends. Not all writers feel that. If you ever edit Jim Harrison, you'll see that he doesn't feel that way. Working with editors, though, is very, very, very complicated and exhausting. I try to take on all that's said to me. And when I take it all on—which is to say I start working with another human being who may be my age, who may not be my same age, who may be older than I am, by which I just mean is obviously different from me—but who has a vision of my story which may improve my vision of my story, which may be less good than my vision—it's just exhausting. And [Gary] Fisketjon [an editor at Alfred A. Knopf] is a prime example of this. He's such a wonderful editor—he's an exhaustive editor. I mean, he comments on about eighty per cent of everything I write. And I have to think that my engagement with his comments, or with your comments, is always good and useful, and is never coercive. But I'm always thinking: Is this story becoming something that I don't want it to become? Is it becoming neutered or homogenized in some way? Because it's *my* responsibility. Your responsibility is to do your best to make suggestions or observations which you think will make what's best about the story more apparent without oversimplifying it, or depriving it of its grace notes—without making it *your* story. I sometimes think, as I get older, that I need less editing, that my stories would not be palpably better with editing. But I'm committed to the procedure in an almost ethical way. Still, most of the editors who work with me find me very difficult. But I don't think I am difficult. I think it's just my job to keep the alembic hot. The thing that won me over with you, and that has won me over with editors in the past, is when I ask, "Why do you want to make that change?" you always have an interesting answer. Even if you have to make the answer up. That's part of what editing is: sensing something and giving it plausible language. I had a friend who was a wonderful writer, and at a certain time he and I came to have the same editor. And the editor commented to me one time, he said, "You know when I give X comments, all he ever says is 'You're right about that. We'll do it.' " [Laughs]

SAR: An editor's dream.

RF: And I thought, Oh boy, I can't do that. Imagine? No. Over the last few years I've been very interested about what are my most native responses to things. Because so much of your response is tinctured by all kinds of foreign forces. I mean, working with an editor is tinctured by his or her personality. And I realize that my most native response to dealing with an editor is that I am going to pursue this work we do in my own scrupulous way. It's always worthwhile to ask yourself all the time, "Is what I'm saying actually what I believe?" Sometimes you say something that isn't what you believe. I'm always worrying about this—not worrying, but worrying at myself—questioning. The work is important. Why should I be less than wholehearted?

SAR: I wanted to go back to ask you a question that is related to moral vision. The idea of accommodation shows up frequently in your novels and stories, and I wanted to hear you talk a little bit more about this idea and what place it has in the moral landscape of your characters.

RF: Accommodation is a much better word than compromise, which is such a loaded word in our culture. One of the things that I've always been interested in, without trying to be interested in it—and this is very Emersonian in its nature—is the distinctness between two human beings, and how that distinctness, the insurmountable separation that exists between two people, can be taken advantage of in a dramatic way—putting two different people into some dynamic setting—but then trying as the writer to invent accommodations between the two in behalf of the story's providing some consolation. I fail at this sometimes, even though the story may still succeed. It's a continuous negotiation. There's a line of Stevens's in which he says, "In a world of disbelief it is for the poet to provide the satisfactions of belief with his measure and with his style." I think that in writing about putative human beings, I am trying to find consolations, or trying to make the story useful for the reader in order that he locate consolations—to provide a substitute for belief or any other abstract thing.

SAR: The guiding light, whatever it might be.

RF: Yes, I think that everything stops and ends with what two people do.

So I'm always interested in how people move away and come back, in how you let someone down, how you disappoint somebody, in how you try to satisfy someone, love someone. Separation is the nature of human life. I'm confident about that. I'm confident that that's a really important fact, and that what we do to take good advantage of that fact, or to minimize its bad effects, is also important. It's necessary for a writer to feel that his subjects are unassailably important. I don't think that this is the kind of subject that will win a Nobel Prize, because it isn't geo-political in nature, or about the clash of civilization and things like that. But I do think that it is truly important; as a subject it makes a small landscape sometimes and at other times a large one.

SAR: So when you say "important" you mean that it is relevant to many kinds of experience, to human life in its various guises?

RF: Yes. When I say, "This is a story about a father and his son," I expect the reader to experience a light going on in his head that says, "This is primary." Or if I say this is a story about a father and his daughter (which is what I'm going to write about next), I want someone to say unqualifiedly, "Yes, this subject is interesting." So when I read stories that are *not* about primary concerns—and goodness knows there are many primary concerns, there's quite a variety of possibilities—those stories are really facing an up-hill climb with me. Of course, they *can* succeed in that uphill climb. But it's harder.

SAR: I'm curious about the fact that *Independence Day* shares its protagonist with *The Sportswriter.* I think Updike is the American writer who returns to a character most frequently, with Rabbit Angstrom and Henry Bech. Why did you return to Frank Bascombe? Did you feel that you had more to say about him?

RF: I realized that I was writing notes in my notebook that sounded like notes from that prior book—that is, Frank's voice. And for a period I thought, well, maybe this is just the detritus of that prior book hanging on. But after I'd accumulated enough, I thought, maybe this is really something that has a continuing resonance in my brain; so maybe this is a given, maybe this is a donnée for me. I actually strived hard *not* to write a book that was connected to the first, because I never thought of myself with that kind of a wide grasp. But that voice and a certain sense of aspiration that came from accumulation of raw evidence made me think maybe I could try this. And it was all done rather incrementally and not with a sense of grand design at first. John Updike may have had a grand design from the first. I'm sure that by the time he wrote the two Rabbit books and was aiming at the third, a sense of design was in place. I've never talked to Updike about this. I've in fact always shied away from talking about this with him. Some things you just have to do on your own. And even though I haven't read all the Rabbit books (I've really only read *Rabbit is Rich* all the way through) I knew about them for a long time, and I have the absolute certainty that if he hadn't written those books, it's highly likely I wouldn't have written a connected book.

SAR: Did you feel that Frank Bascombe's character evolved?

RF: I didn't, but other people did. I wanted him to. I thought it was necessary to distinguish one book from the second. At the time of writing *Independence Day,* I felt like I was writing in the voice of *The Sportswriter.* I wasn't aware that the second book was as distinct from the first as it was, for instance tonally, in terms of the idiom, length of sentences, in all the things that make a book specific. It seemed to me more like the first than not, even though I knew that the subject matter was different, and that the book was longer.

SAR: Do you reread your books and your stories?

RF: No, because when I finish them I've done everything I can do to make them as good as I could make them be. To go back and read them would be to inflict on myself the possibility of grave unhappiness [laughs]. Poets can do it, because they can go back and read one poem and think, "Oh, that wasn't very good, I'll rewrite it." It's a jab. But when you have a book that's 450 pages long—this would be a long, life-rending ache. I do have passages in them that I can read aloud in public, where I've got things so well hammered out that it's O.K. to read from them.

SAR: What do you think of your positive critical reception? Has that ever been a factor at all for you in writing? There are so many writers who don't receive positive feedback.

RF: I've always gotten bad reviews, which is to say that even in a good season for a book, I've never gotten uniformly good reviews.

SAR: Do you think anybody does?

RF: I always think they do [laughs]. I think they get all good reviews, and that I get a mixed bad every time. Although, without having read all the reviews of work by people I admire, like Bob Stone, Tim O'Brien, Ann Beattie, I'd guess that they probably get as mixed a bag as I do. I don't hope they do. I hope they get all wonderful reviews for their excellent work. When

I wrote the first book that I ever wrote, I had the extremely unpleasant experience of having my editor call me up and read to me a very bad *New York Times* Sunday review. And that set the tone for my attitude towards reviews, which is that this kind of stuff is always terrible. And I guess that if I'd had all bad reviews of everything I did, it would have had a daunting effect on me. I didn't, but for a while I got very adept at reading my reviews, trying to find in them cues or clues as to whether or not I should be doing this— writing. Trying to figure out if a review was positive but stupid, or if a review was negative but smart. Fortunately, nobody ever said to me, except for that evil nitwit Yardley, down in Washington, that I shouldn't be writing. He did say that no one would or ever should read what I wrote, and that I was a boob. But when I used to read bad reviews, I would think, "Is somebody telling me that I'm wasting my time, or are they saying that they didn't like this book?" I was able to make that distinction. And then, after 1990, I quit reading them altogether. I just thought the emotional up and down, the roller coaster of reading these reviews, was finally deleterious to my life. And once I quit reading my reviews—good and bad—I became a much happier boy.

SAR: Was it hard to quit reading your reviews?
RF: Absolutely not [laughs].

SAR: No pangs of curiosity?
RF: Not a dram. Once in a while somebody, Kristina, maybe, will say, "Let me read you something." And I hear that. But when a book of mine gets published I assume that there are bad reviews I don't know about. And that doesn't bother me. Mark Kram, who is a very wonderful sportswriter, probably the best sportswriter around, called me up about two years ago and said, "Did you read that review of *Women with Men* in some big-circulation something or other?" "No," I said, "I didn't." "Oh," he said, "It was terrible. It made me so mad." I said, "Don't you ever, ever, call me up and tell me about a bad review." And I haven't talked to him since. There are German words for what he was up to. I don't know German.

SAR: So what about sports? Are sports something that you're particularly interested in?
RF: I don't much read the sports section. I can't read *Sports Illustrated,* anymore—no offense to the magazine. I've just lost a measure of interest. People are forever calling me up wanting me to write about sports, trying to put me on a panel about sports. It's nice to have that little cachet, because I

was a sportswriter once, and it's nice to be thought of as smart about it. Though if I ever was, I'm not any more. I've even lost my enthusiasm for boxing.

SAR: You said something earlier that made me think of the Wallace Stevens line "The hum of thoughts evaded in the mind." This sensation of evasion is one that seems present in *The Sportswriter* and in *Independence Day*—they both are concerned with getting down something elusive about the characters' experience. At one point, Frank's son, Paul, compares his thinking process to a series of concentric rings he can't get to "fit down flush on top of each another." Is this elusiveness—or perhaps you have another word for it—something that resonates with you? Is it something you consider important in writing fiction?

RF: Absolutely. It's what I think art, in general, is for—or can be if it chooses. And not just literary arts, but all kinds of arts. There's a line of Octavio Paz's which says, "Between what I see and what I say, between what I say and what I keep silent, between what I keep silent and what I dream, between what I dream and what I forget [is] poetry." Art expresses, among other things, the stuff which in conventional, ordinary, daily life goes unexpressed, or is expressed in some way we don't take in. Jasper Johns wrote something like "Art is about things that we know so well but we don't always see." It doesn't have to be hidden stuff. It could be right there, apparent. I was reading something recently, it wasn't Stevens, I think it was Virginia Woolf, about this idea of "hum" audible—she felt—in the world before the first World War, and that literature somehow resonated. The idea or the figure of a *hum* gives representation to something that really wasn't there, of course. Or it gives a representation of something that doesn't seem to be there. When a writer is set to deliver something onto the page, you could say that he or she has been "listening" to some such hum. That representation is a way of giving verbal evidence of what a piece of fiction responds to. When Octavio Paz says "between," well, there's no actual "between," right? It's very much in the spirit of what the Romantics thought—that there is a verbal portrait, a poem, say—that is like a mold poured on something extant but invisible in the natural environment. In "Mont Blanc," Shelley's narrator asserts that the mountains and the rills sing, that they have a voice. That's his way of saying, "What I'm writing here really does respond to something out there." And so that idea of a hum is a very nice idea.

SAR: Who are other people who influenced you early on? As teachers?

RF: E. L. Doctorow. He was my teacher in graduate school. And Galway

Kinnell, who I didn't have in a class, but who taught at Irvine when I was there, and was writing *The Book of Nightmares* more or less right in front of us. He was a very affecting presence, and I loved his poems. Still do. And a man who is dead now, Howard S. Babb. You won't recognize his name. And a wonderful poet, James McMichael. Most of my important teachers have been poets. After that, Donald Hall. Maybe it's why I don't do very well structuring novels and care more for the local effects.

SAR: Did you ever think about writing poetry?

RF: Yes. I'd love to be able to write poetry. In fact, I read a poem of Paul Muldoon's last spring, and I sat down and wrote some lines that I thought would make a poem. And I told Paul this, and he said how glad he was, in the way a person might if you'd helped him bring his groceries in from the car. [Laughs] I didn't show him the lines. My favorite poets come out of the Whitman strain of American poetry, through *Paterson,* to Galway and James Wright, Richard Hugo, some Elizabeth Bishop, C. K. Williams. I'd include Louise Glück in this line, but maybe not everybody would agree. I just like her poems.

Poems can seem easy to do when they're so appealing to read. But when you sit down and try to do them, then they aren't easy. I don't think a good story seems as easy to write as a good poem; you're dealing with so many more word choices. But by the time you get to be a reasonably good fiction writer, choices of words are less a problem than writing *sentences* that you know are good sentences, where you're getting words in the right order. If you come to be dissatisfied with some of the words, you change them. But with poems you have so few words that have to be so right. That's harder. There are more good poets that can write novels than there are good novelists who can write good poems. Life isn't fair. Again.

SAR: Poets may have fewer word choices, at least in lyric poems, but there are many more choices about line, and structure.

RF: Oh, yes, yes. And then it just gets to be miasmic. So when Paul didn't seem very excited that I had written a poem inspired by his, I thought, well, this is the world telling me to stay on my side of the street. Paul might disagree with this and claim he was honored and elated.

SAR: Is there anything that you regret publishing?

RF: No. The closest I came to it was that long essay I published last spring in the *New York Times* magazine about race. But I only feel what I feel about it because there was a disproportionate amount of effort that went into a very small amount of bang I personally felt on having it in print. Mostly I'm very clear that the pieces of writing I do are for the reader. Its destination is its principle reason to be. However much I get pleasure out of it, however much I work to make it a good book myself, however much I learn, it's finally not for me. That essay had a lot of purgative value for me. And part of the difficulty in writing and then publishing it lay in first identifying my personal investment in it, and then struggling to getting beyond that value to discern what virtues or values the piece had for its readers. I'm not sure I did that very well, though I surely tried. But the experience weighted the writing of it more than is usual, made me unusually sensitive.

SAR: When you say the "purgative value," are you referring to something you wanted to express about your experience growing up in the South?

RF: Yes. When I write stories, I never have or organize things I want "to express." I'm delighted by the things that I make up, but I never start with things—views, for instance, that I want to express. Ordinarily I create a fictive environment made of things I want to put into play, and then work out or invent what the story eventually makes clear. I tried to make that essay a piece of art, and it was a greater than usual task, because uncharacteristically I *did* have things I wanted to express as a way of putting them into play. And those things were parts of my past. I had, then, to subordinate them to the essay's larger aspirations—whatever I discovered them to be. Anyway, basically, art, any kind of art, fiction—to me—is not a mode of self-expression.

SAR: Eliot said that poetry is not the expression of personality but the escape from it.

RF: Right. You see great writers and painters saying things like this all the time. Duchamp says that taste is the great enemy of art. And there is a line from Berryman that I keep around, in which he talks about what a poem is. And he says it is not so much inventing things as acquiring things. Roughly, he says, poets acquire things from here and acquire things from there, and make them come together with the stuff that you may in fact dream up. But, Berryman also says that it all comes out of your personality. And at this point my heart goes whump, because it's so self-regarding. That is the one part of his little theorem which makes me stop, makes me regard him less favorably. Because, in a purely negative capability way, I don't want my personality to be the publicly authorizing agency in what I write that's any good. Personally, my personality would just be a ball-and-chain around the story's ankle.

Randall Jarrell said it best: "When a poem is good, it *is* good." It certainly doesn't mean *I'm* good.

SAR: But then maybe that's part of what a writer's voice is. That little element of personality in there among all of the things that you acquire. I think Berryman was talking about a very personal relationship to art. I mean, his poems themselves can be quite personal.

RF: Extremely personal. To their detriment, I think. It makes him a more attractive subject for biographers.

SAR: He may not have meant that in writing you need to bring yourself into the poem or the story, which is perhaps different from having an element of personality in there almost accidentally.

RF: I suppose. But I just don't like the notion that the poem's sanction, the authority of the poem, the thing that finally makes it real and persuasive, both emanates from the author and ultimately returns there. I'm always trying to get everything into its own life on the page, and let it achieve excellence that way.

SAR: And what about non-fiction? You write a fair amount of that. Have you ever considered writing a non-fiction book?

RF: No. I wouldn't be any good at it. I'm not a good researcher and I'm not a good reporter. But it's nice because, in spite of myself, I do have a personality and the kinds of non-fiction things I get to write usually ask me to devise a personal opinion about something. Sometimes you write a piece of non-fiction or an opinion page essay, and it is like writing a piece of fiction, because you don't have an opinion at first. You have curiosity, maybe moral curiosity. And by writing you're creating an opinion you're willing to stand by. There is a situation in which the source of the piece's authority really is me, or at least some fairly good representation of me. And I like that. I like being responsible. In any piece of fiction, even if you can't say about the author, "This is about his life," you can say very reliably, "This is about a whole lot of things that this person cares about." And that's an invit- ing idea. Even though it may not be personally inviting.

SAR: Are there things you'd like to write that you haven't written?

RF: Here's what I think along those lines. I wrote two books that I really liked that didn't do very well, and then I wrote *The Sportswriter* and *Rock Springs* at the same time, and at that point my writing objectives seemed to be describable (by me, even, and I'm really loathe to do such things, believe me) as having two main thrusts—I was writing books in two ways. Montana stories, and what became, with *Independence Day,* two New Jersey novels. My little novel *Wildlife* was a Montana story, and so was a novella I wrote called *Jealous.* Then when I wrote the two Paris stories in *Women with Men* I realized I had another way to write.

SAR: Can you characterize that?

RF: The stories in it are in the third person. They're much more morally stringent. In some ways they're less personable stories. Their principal characters, I realize, are not admirable—even to me. But, as stories, I think they're as useful to readers as any other kind of story. So, I have followed that strain in the work I have done over the last three or four years, and maybe I'll get to the end of it this year. But there is another book that I want to write, which I can write, which I haven't had quite the energy to write in the last year or so. I think it is wholly different. A new sort of stylistic tack. For me, writing has always involved exhausting a seam. And sometimes I don't exhaust a seam with one book. Sometimes it takes two or three books or more. But I think I've exhausted the seam in my writing that is roughly describable as those first-person Montana stories. And I hope I will exhaust the seam of the stories I've been writing in the last two or three years—these third person, severe, dark stories. "Crèche," and "Quality Time" and "Privacy," stories *The New Yorker* has published.

SAR: Chill.

RF: They are chill. And I'm sorry for that in a highly personal scene. But as objects, as pieces of literature, they have the highest aspirations. I finish them with the same sense of completeness as anything I've ever finished.

I have a couple of other projects. One of them, at least, is on another rail, which I have never tried before. If I were to say what it was most like, I would say that it is a little like Graham Greene's novel *The End of the Affair,* although it's not about an affair. I read that book years ago, and it made a big impression on me. I was given a story last year that I got interested in, and then lost interest in. But each time I look at it in my notebook I realize this is something I really have to do. It seems entirely different from anything I've ever tried to do. This is what we started off talking about—I really would love it if a person could read my work and not know it was mine. How can I put it? Well, my editor at Knopf, Gary Fisketjon, says to me sometimes, "You know, I read that story, and I wouldn't have known who wrote it." I really like that. It means I've made something that exceeds my mere self. That seems to me a superior accomplishment—even, in an indirect way, for what it says personally about me. It's a complement. I don't care at all if somebody reads a story and knows it's mine. What I want is that when you read a story, it's the story, not the author, that makes an important imprint on you, becomes permanent in your life. That's all.

Index

Actor's Theater of Louisville, 80
Alcorn, James, 13
American Academy and Institute of Arts and
  Letters Award for Literature, 78
American Booksellers Association convention,
  85, 89, 175
Anderson, Sherwood, 85, 148, 191; "I Want to
  Know Why," 148
Ann Arbor, Mich., 16, 37
Arkansas Gazette, 1, 46, 77
Avedon, Richard, 155

Babb, Howard (mentor), 140, 199
Babel, Isaac, 148; "The Story of My Dovecot,"
  148
Barth, John, 135, 151; *The End of the Road*, 135,
  151
Barthelme, Donald, 34, 35, 153, 192; "The In-
  dian Uprising," 153, 192
Beattie, Ann, 6, 12, 196
Bennington, Vt., 25
Berryman, John, 200
Bishop, Elizabeth, 199
Blackmur, R. P., 140, 161; "A Critic's Job of
  Work," 140, 161
Borges, Jorge Luis, 165, 170; "Pierre Menard,
  Author of the *Quixote*," 165
Boston Globe, 67, 76
Bowen, Elizabeth, *The House in Paris*, 191
Boyle, Tom, 181
Bright Angel (film), 77, 83, 91, 162
Bright Lights, Big City (McInerney), 178
Brooks, Cleanth, 161
Bush, Fred, 57

California, University of, at Irvine, 1, 3, 8, 16,
  37, 42, 54, 59, 72, 75, 128, 199
Carver, Raymond, 6, 12, 14, 25, 34, 36, 40, 42,
  68, 85, 97, 101–02, 104, 105, 176, 177, 186,
  187, 189, 191; "Cathedral," 25
Cather, Willa, 85
Céline, Louis-Ferdinand, 156
Cheever, John, 191
Chekhov, Anton Pavlovich, 55, 150, 168, 172,
  173, 174, 178, 191; "An Anonymous Story,"
  168; "The Darling," 168; "Peasants," 168

Clemons, Walter, 115, 172
Conrad, Joseph, 56, 70
Cool Hand Luke, 147
cummings, e. e., 154

Death of a Salesman (Miller), 111
DeLillo, Don, 167
Didion, Joan, 156
Dixie (Brittany Spaniel), 5, 15, 39
Doctorow, E. L., 59, 75, 138, 198
Dostoevsky, Fyodor, 137
Duchamp, Marcel, 200
Duggin, Richard, 6, 8

Editors' Choice Stories, 8
Eliot, T. S., 200
Elkin, Stanley, 36, 55, 179
Ellis, Bret, 62
Emerson, Ralph Waldo, 120, 143, 146, 192, 194;
  "Self-Reliance," 192
Entrekin, Morgan (editor), 76
Ernest Hemingway Award, 11, 16, 41, 76, 98
Esquire, 1, 6, 13, 54, 62, 63, 71, 77, 81, 85; "Lit-
  erary Universe" chart in, 63
Esquire Reader: 1984, 8
Exley, Frederick, 14, 151; *A Fan's Notes*, 151

Faulkner, William, 10, 11, 27, 31, 41, 43, 56, 62,
  72, 76, 77, 105, 134, 138, 144, 169; "Barn
  Burning," 144; "A Rose for Emily," 134; *The
  Sound and the Fury*, 105
Fields, Michael (film director), 77
Fifty Great Years of Esquire Fiction, 8
Fifty Who Made the Difference (anthology of
  short fiction), 8
Fisketjon, Gary (editor), 40, 62, 68, 76, 178,
  193, 202
Fitzgerald, F. Scott, 27, 77, 85
Flaubert, Gustave, 46
Ford, Edna (mother), 1, 3–4, 15, 26, 28–29, 45,
  49, 50, 111, 120, 128, 158, 179–80
Ford, Ford Maddox, 55, 70
Ford Foundation Scholarship, 1, 4, 16
Ford, Kristina Hensley (wife), 2, 4, 5, 7, 8, 10,
  13, 15, 18, 24, 25, 31, 33, 36, 37, 40, 45, 50,
  53, 54, 55, 59, 60, 61, 66, 71, 72, 74, 75, 77,